Introduction to Ecumenism

Jeffrey Gros, F.S.C., Eamon McManus,
Ann Riggs

PAULIST PRESS
New York/Mahwah, N.J.

The Publisher gratefully acknowledges use of the following materials: Selection from the English translation of *The Roman Missal*, copyright © 1973, International Committee on English in the Liturgy, Inc. Selection from the *Book of Common Worship*, © 1993, Westminster/John Knox Press. Selections from *Baptism, Eucharist and Ministry*, "Canberra Statement"; *A Documentary History of the Faith & Order Movement, 1927–1963; A Documentary History of the Faith & Order Movement, 1963–1993; The Ecumenical Movement: An Anthology of Key Texts and Voices;* "Prayer of the Fifth World Conference on Faith and Order"; "Streams" chart of the ecumenical movement from Edinburgh to Harare; © WCC Publications, World Council of Churches, Geneva, Switzerland. "Major Christian Traditions" chart from *Christian Confessions*, © 1996 by Ted A. Campbell, used by permission of Westminster/John Knox Press. Scripture excerpts are taken from the *New American Bible with Revised New Testament*, © 1986, 1970 by the Confraternity of Christian Doctrine, Inc., Washington, D.C. Used with permission. All rights reserved. Selections from *Sisters of the Spirit*, edited by William Andrews, © Indiana University Press.

Cover design by Cindy Dunne

Library of Congress Cataloging-in-Publication Data

Gros, Jeffrey,   1938–
    Introduction to ecumenism / Jeffrey Gros, Eamon McManus, Ann Riggs.
        p.   cm.
    Includes bibliographical references and index.
    ISBN 0-8091-3794-1 (alk. paper)
    1. Christian union—Catholic Church. 2. Ecumenical movement. 3. Catholic Church—Relations. I. McManus, Eamon, 1931–   . II. Riggs, Ann,   1950–   .
III. Title.
BX1784.G76   1998
262′.001′1—dc21   98-11279
                                                                          CIP

Published by Paulist Press
997 Macarthur Boulevard
Mahwah, New Jersey 07430

Printed and bound in the
United States of America

Contents

Preface

As Christians cross the threshold of the third millennium and celebrate the anniversary of the Lord's incarnation among us, we pray with Pope John Paul II that the years ahead may see the Christian churches closer to the unity for which Christ prayed on the night before he died for us.

When the World Council of Churches brought together in common witness, dialogue, and collaboration the major Orthodox and Reformation churches in 1948, the rich harvest of dialogues, common instruments for action together, and the rich spiritual experience of ecumenical prayer and relationships that have developed could only have been a faint hope. When Pope John XXIII announced a Council in 1959 and lifted the hope that this Council might serve the unity of Christians, he fired the imagination and enthusiasm of believers everywhere.

The Lord has richly blessed the churches in the last century as they have begun to move out of their isolation into productive engagement with one another in the modern movement toward visible unity in faith, sacramental life, and witness. The initial leaders of the ecumenical movement, Pope John XXIII among them, could only pray that the Holy Spirit would bless the encounter and guide the pilgrimage of the churches together toward Christian unity.

The early days of the ecumenical movement brought a measure of often unfocused enthusiasm. In the last fifty years, however, relationships have deepened, dialogues have borne theological fruit, prayers have begun to be answered, and we have considerable resources in ecumenical results, which invite our reflection, study, and local action. The steps necessary for unity to be achieved have become clearer. This volume will be a helpful beginning for those initiating their ecumenical pilgrimage, a support for those deepening their ecumenical understanding, and a resource for those in the day-to-day life of the Church.

The ecumenical movement is primarily a movement of the Spirit calling us to conversion, to a deeper penetration of the mystery of Christ in the Church, to a more intense relationship with other Christians with whom we share a common baptism, the Scriptures, and other elements of the faith to which Jesus calls us. We are called by the divine imperative, affirmed as a pastoral priority by the leadership of the Catholic Church in recent years. It is a call to prayer, to a spirituality of dialogue, and to common action to enhance understanding and eventual unity among Christians.

Christians committed to Christian unity bring a profound fidelity to their own tradition, avoiding any hint of relativism and tolerant indifferentism, as they enter into a spirituality of dialogue. Indeed, as this volume will show, commitment to the unity of the Church is a commitment to fidelity to Christ, embodied in the traditions of the churches, subject to the Tradition of the Gospel in history. Neither isolation nor relativism characterizes Christian identity. The ecumenical dialogue is one of love and of truth.

May this introductory volume be useful to those of us who are in leadership in our churches, especially Catholic leaders; to educators, pastors, and other pastoral agents; and to all Christians called to understand more deeply their baptismal commitment to the unity Christ willed for His Church. In the United States we have the greatest variety of ecumenical partners in the world and a challenging pluralism of ecumenical contexts in which the churches pursue their ecumenical journey. May this publication enable Christians who come together in dialogue to deepen the bonds of communion that already bind them, and to reinforce the hopes they share for that day when full visible unity in sacramental life, witness, the apostolic faith, and bonds of communion may emerge, under the leading power of the Holy Spirit.

William Cardinal Keeler
Archbishop of Baltimore

June 25, 1997

Abbreviations

AA	The Decree on the Apostolate of the Laity, *Apostolicam Actuositatem*
AG	The Decree on the Church's Missionary Activity, *Ad Gentes*
ARCIC	Anglican Roman Catholic International Commission
ARCUSA	Anglican Roman Catholic Dialogue in the USA
BEM	*Baptism, Eucharist and Ministry* of the World Council of Churches
BU	*Building Unity*
BWA	Baptist World Alliance
CD	The Decree on the Pastoral Office of Bishops in the Church, *Christus Dominus*
CDF	Congregation for the Doctrine of the Faith
CIC	*The Code of Canon Law* (1983)
COCU	The Consultation on Church Union
CICO	*The Code of Canon Law for the Eastern Churches* (1991)
DC	*Deepening Communion*
Directory	*Directory for the Application of Principles and Norms on Ecumenism* (1993)
DH	The Declaration on Religious Liberty, *Dignitatis Humanae*
DV	The Dogmatic Constitution on Divine Revelation, *Dei Verbum*
ELCA	The Evangelical Lutheran Church in America
GA	*Growth in Agreement*
GC	*Growing Consensus*
GS	The Decree on the Church in the Modern World, *Gaudium et Spes*

IS	Pontifical Council for Promoting Christian Unity, *Information Service*
Kinnamon	*The Ecumenical Movement: An Anthology of Key Texts and Voices*
LA	The Leuenberg Agreement
LCWE	The Laussane Committee on World Evangelization
LG	The Dogmatic Constitution on the Church, *Lumen Gentium*
LWF	Lutheran World Federation
NA	The Declaration on the Church's Relations with non-Christian Religions, *Nostra Aetate*
NADEO	National Association of Diocesan Ecumenical Officers
NAE	National Association of Evangelicals
NCCB	National Conference of Catholic Bishops
NCC	National Council of Churches of Christ in the USA
OE	The Decree on the Catholic Eastern Churches, *Orientalium Ecclesiarum*
OL	Apostolic Letter, *Orientale Lumen*
PCPCU	Pontifical Council for Promoting Christian Unity
PCFNA	Pentecostal Charismatic Fellowship of North America
PO	The Decree on the Life and Ministry of Priests, *Presbyterorum Ordinis*
SC	The Constitution on the Sacred Liturgy, *Sacrosanctum Concilium*
SBC	Southern Baptist Convention
TMA	Apostolic Letter, On the Threshold of the Third Millennium, *Tertio Millennio Adveniente*
UR	The Decree on Ecumenism, *Unitatis Redintegratio*
USCC	United States Catholic Conference
UUS	Encyclical That They All May Be One, *Ut Unum Sint*
WARC	World Alliance of Reformed Churches
WCC	World Council of Churches
WEF	World Evangelical Fellowship

Scripture texts in this work are taken from the New American Bible.

Introduction

Initiation into the Christian faith entails welcome into a particular community and a worldwide Church of believers celebrating the third millennium of the Gospel. Central to the identity of the Christian is identification with the Church, and central to Catholic identity and that of the Orthodox, Anglican, and Protestant churches in the modern ecumenical movement is zeal for Christ's will for the visible unity of the Church:

> "Father, the hour has come. Give glory to your son, so that your son may glorify you, just as you gave him authority over all people, so that he may give eternal life to all you gave him....As you sent me into the world, so I sent them into the world. And I consecrate myself for them, so that they also may be consecrated in truth. I pray not only for them, but also for those who will believe in me through their word, so that they may all be one, as you, Father, are in me and I in you, that they may also be in us, that the world may believe that you sent me. And I have given them the glory you gave me, so that they may be one, as we are one, I in them and you in me, that they may be brought to perfection as one, that the world may know that you sent me, and that you loved them even as you loved me." (Jn 17: 1-2, 18-23)

We know that Christians do not live in that unity for which Christ prayed, though through common faith, baptism, and Scripture, they share a real, if yet imperfect, communion. How is it that these fissures in the Body of Christ have emerged? What are the means by which they can be healed? What are the resources within the churches which can realize this prayer of Christ? The call to Christian unity is a call to conversion, to openness to love of other Christians and their churches, and to a commitment to the Christian orthodoxy on which the dialogue

1

of truth is based. Most of all, the call of Christ to the unity of the Church is a call to spiritual renewal that is realized in prayer, mission, ministry, service, and dialogue.

The Purpose of This Book

For Christians being initiated into the faith, for those preparing for pastoral ministry or educational leadership and for those seeking to enhance the ecumenical dimension of their Christian identity, this volume is meant as an overview of the ecumenical movement. For Catholics and for other Christians in dialogue with them, a considerable amount of history and doctrine must be assimilated. In the last fifty years, the texture of relations with other Christians, the authoritative teaching of the magisterium, and the results of interchurch dialogues have produced a monumental set of resources to deepen the Christian faith and the commitment to unity.

As the authors have worked in Christian initiation; catechetical ministry; formation of deacons, religious, priests, and lay pastoral agents; ecumenical agencies and commissions; ecumenical pastoral apostolates; and university and seminary education, a need has developed for a brief, relatively simple and synthetic approach to the ecumenical movement and the Catholic Church within it.

The rich harvest of magisterial statements by Pope John Paul II and institutions and offices of the Catholic Church, universal and local, and the immense quantity of positive dialogue results make it imperative that educational material about and for Catholics be brought up to date. This work is offered as a resource to help beginners on the journey learn the churches' commitments in fidelity to the call of Christ.

This book, then, provides an introduction into ecumenical life from a Catholic perspective. More in-depth study will be needed in the history of the churches, the theology of church, sacrament, Christology, ethics, and the current situation in specific pastoral contexts, in order to fill out the picture presented here.

This book opens doors, it is hoped, to possibilities in pastoral, historical, and theological study which it cannot pursue for the reader. It presupposes the conversion to Christ and adherence to the Church and the Christian impulse toward unity that are essential to Christian identity and the Catholic understanding of the Church and its mission. This is an understanding that is shared in principle by the Orthodox, Anglican, and Protestant members of the World Council of Churches, though each community will develop its ecumenical commitments from its own history and theological understanding. Other communities, not members of the World Council, are more slowly being drawn into the ecumenical movement.

How to Use This Book

The book is a general survey, sometimes using charts and diagrams to introduce the reader to historical and documentary material that cannot be studied here in depth. The ecumenical vocation of all Christians entails conversion to Christ's will for the Church. This conversion includes openness to faith in Christ, to his revelation of the doctrine of the Church, the particular theology of the church into which one is initiated and belongs, and the vision of that church's involvement in the ecumenical pilgrimage. Ecumenical conversion entails a love for all Christians, a love of one's own church and for the churches through which Christ has come to others, a zeal for the unity of Christians, a receptive spirituality that is welcoming of each step closer to full communion, and a willingness to learn those tools and doctrinal developments that serve this unity.

The ecumenical movement is a complex reality. While this volume will concentrate on the theological dialogues among Christians, it is essential to remember that ecumenism is a reform and renewal movement within the churches that is rooted in a search for a common mission, is nurtured by a common spirituality, is lived in common service, and is developed in the variety of cultural contexts in which the Church of Christ finds itself incarnated. There is one ecumenical movement, with its tensions and common hopes, reflecting both the unity that God wills for his Church on the one hand, and sinful and fragmented human struggles to be faithful to this reconciling call, on the other.

The reader will be well served by reading and studying directly the texts noted, in conjunction with the appropriate chapters. Pursuing the details of history, doctrinal disputes, and present church situations will enrich one's picture of the material covered and will enhance the reader's horizon. The reader will see that this is only an introductory journey through the wide forest of information, persons, and institutions that compose the Christian world and its ecumenical hopes, leaders, and instrumentalities. A survey of ecumenical social teaching, ecumenical spirituality, and ecumenical experiences of common witness would make equally informative reading. The reader will need the long-term view of a pilgrim, and the patience of a traveler, to realize that this volume is really an invitation to join the Church on a journey of discovery, deepening relationships and religious awakening that will bear fruit in the Holy Spirit's good time.

This volume is a textual contribution to what is a sacramental, ritual, dialogical, and spiritual pilgrimage under the impetus of Christ's grace. Therefore, in addition to reading some of the texts noted, one should enter into the spiritual process that has produced them. Dialogue, ecumenical prayer, developing relationships with Christians in other traditions, sharing one's commitment to full unity, worshipping in Orthodox, Protestant, and Anglican contexts, knowing the institutions of ecumenical partners, and working together in community are learning experiences that complement the cognitive material provided for the reader in this volume.

There is a certain ecumenical sensitivity necessary in speaking of one another and of ourselves as churches. A fundamental principle is that in nontechnical ecumenical parlance we designate churches and ecclesial communities by names and categories that they use of themselves. Thus, we use *church* of one another, while we work toward full mutual ecclesial recognition. We do not use *sect* or *cult* of one another unless a group applies this language to itself.

Sensitivity is particularly important when marks of the Church—one, holy, catholic or apostolic—are used in the title, or when attributes of the Church—orthodox, evangelical, reformed, and the like—are used. The Catholic Church is the official title of the worldwide communion, though it is often expanded to the Roman Catholic Church. There are many Eastern Churches in full communion with the bishop of Rome. Because they are not of the Latin tradition, they do not wish to be referred to as Roman.

On the other hand, some churches of the Reformation consider themselves catholic, especially Anglicans and occasionally Lutherans, so Roman Catholic becomes a helpful designation in those contexts. In this volume, for the most part, Roman Catholic will only be used in chapters one and nine, and will be avoided where possible as a general term in chapter eight, where Latin or Western Church is more appropriate when speaking of the Roman part of the Catholic communion of churches.

To stimulate reflection and discussion, each chapter is provided with selected bibliography and study questions. The modern ecumenical movement has produced a rich library of literature by theologians, ecumenical study groups, and the churches themselves. The suggested readings bring those titles to view that are most relevant to the topics under consideration and most clearly related to the formal positions of the churches, especially the Catholic Church, and the officially commissioned dialogues.

What Is in This Book

This volume of twelve chapters is organized around two major dimensions of ecumenical life and commitment. An introductory chapter surveys the history of the churches as they have divided and the impulses that have served their unity. There are five chapters on ecumenical principals and foundations, beginning with Catholic ecumenical documents. The theology of communion, *koinonia,* is sketched out as it informs Catholic self-understanding and ecumenism, and as it has emerged in the common understanding of the churches. Chapter four surveys ecumenical principles for pastoral life in the churches. Chapter five focuses on ecumenical formation and the spiritual basis for ecumenical zeal. Chapter six addresses the goal, principles, and implications of ecumenical dialogue.

The second half of the volume treats the specific relationships among churches and the results of the dialogues. Chapters on the contribution of the World Council of Churches, the Eastern Churches, Anglican and Lutheran Churches, classical Protestants, and Evangelical Protestants, each from the perspective of their relationship with Catholicism, complete this section. The concluding chapter attempts to draw together some of the priorities for the proximate future of the ecumenical movement.

Ecumenism is not a category of Christian theology or a bureaucratic task for the Church as an institution. Rather it is a reconciling way of life for the Christian person. From the very earliest moments of the Church's existence there was a call to reconciliation, as Paul notes:

> I urge you, brothers [and sisters], in the name of our Lord Jesus Christ, that all of you agree in what you say, and that there be no divisions among you, but that you be united in the same mind and in the same purpose.... Consider your own calling, brothers [and sisters]. Not many of you were wise by human standards, not many were powerful, not many were of noble birth. Rather, God chose the foolish of the world to shame the wise, and God chose the weak of the world to shame the strong, and God chose the lowly and despised of the world, those who count for nothing, to reduce to nothing those who are something, so that no human being might boast before God. (1 Cor 1:10, 26–29)

The unity we serve is not the work of our zeal, but the paradox of Christ's cross. We equip ourselves to be responsive to the grace of unity, given in God's good time, as we labor to enhance the reconciling power of the Gospel among Christ's people.

Periodicals

Origins
Pontifical Council for Promoting Christian Unity, *Information Service*
Ecumenical Trends

Centro Pro Unione, *Bulletin*
One In Christ
Mid-Stream
Ecumenical Review
Journal of Ecumenical Studies
L'Osservatore Romano
National Association of Diocesan Ecumenical Officers,
  Newsletter
Pro Ecclesia

1

The History of Ecumenism

Christ is made the sure foundation,
Christ, the head and corner stone;
Chosen of the Lord, and precious,
Binding all the Church in one,
Holy Sion's help forever, and her confidence alone.
        Angularis fundamentum (Seventh Century),
            translated by John M. Neale, 1818–66.

The history of ecumenism, to a large extent, parallels the spread of Christianity throughout the ages. As the Church encountered different cultural, linguistic, and sociopolitical situations, the several emphases within Christianity introduced fissures which, if not grounded in common faith, were capable of producing profound divisions.

In this chapter we wish to look very briefly at the development of Christian divisions from New Testament times and at the impulses toward ecumenical reconciliation over the centuries. In looking at the history of division and reconciliation, four Gospel values should be kept in mind: (1) humble repentance, including taking responsibility for the failings of our Christian ancestors and recognizing the failures on both sides of the division; (2) human mistakes and failings that are being rectified in our own time; (3) respect for the gifts of the Holy Spirit to the churches, even in their years of separation; and (4) the biblical, theological, and liturgical renewal in the Church that can help to heal the wounds of the past. God's call for unity should be at the center of our review of the Christian past.

As Pope John Paul admonishes us: "Christians cannot underestimate the burden of longstanding misgivings inherited from the past and of mutual misunderstandings and prejudices. Complacency, indifference, and insufficient knowledge of one

9

another often make this situation worse" UUS (*Ut Unum Sint/That They May All Be One*), 2.

We provide here only an outline of the Christian story. The Christian seriously interested in the unity of the Church should study the history of the development of doctrine, and the development of the structure and theology of his or her own church and its flexibility over the years.

In regard to the first millennium, the divisions concerning Trinitarian and Christological theology; the roles of councils, synods, patriarchs, and bishops; and contemporary agreements on these issues should be explored in detail. In reference to the second millennium, Scholastic, Reformation, and more recent Pentecostal and Evangelical theology; the variety of understandings of grace, sacraments, ethics, and ecclesiology; and the contemporary dialogues healing the differences should be studied in detail.

This chapter is divided into three sections: (1) divisions in the early church; (2) major divisions in the Western church; and (3) the modern impetus to church unity.

Today's ecumenical movement requires us to survey the glorious and tragic history of the "one Church of Christ" and under the inspiration of the Spirit to trust that God will breathe into these dry bones a profound desire that "they all may be one."

THE EARLY CHURCH

The Gospel as preached by Jesus the Jew and spread by his Jewish disciples was embedded in the faith and culture of his native land and people. Soon after Jesus' death and resurrection the Christian proclamation came to expression in Hellenic culture, principally through the work of Paul. Gradually Christianity found itself embodied in the variety of cultures of the Mediterranean basin and, later, in Armenia, Persia, India, Gaul, Britain, and Ethiopia.

Already the New Testament records a diversity of communities, which gave rise to the four Gospels and the variety of letters to the apostolic churches, some of which appear to have an explicitly ecumenical intent, such as Paul's first letter to the church at Corinth. The Acts of the Apostles mentions how "there arose no little dissension" (15:2) in the community. Already there was a division between Jewish and Greek-Hellenistic Christians in regard to religious observance. The first council, recorded in Acts 15, was held in Jerusalem to resolve differences between the apostles. This council remains a model of the desired unity among divided Christian churches.

Acts also gives us clues in regard to what the apostles saw as the essentials of unity for the communion of churches. The *koinonia* of communities in the diversity of cultures should be maintained: "They devoted themselves to the teaching of the apostles and to the communal life, to the breaking of the bread and to the prayers" (Acts 2: 42). A common faith, common worship life, bonds of communion with the apostles, and charity appear to be the constituents of Christian communion from the beginning.

Throughout the New Testament there are references to humility, charity, and unity, which act as undercurrents and reminders that things were not perfect in this early community. Perhaps the most explicit reference in this regard concerns the abuse concerning the Eucharist (1 Cor 11:17–34). The conclusion emerges that the early church was not an ideal community, but that there was a Gospel urgency about maintaining unity.

First Continuing Divisions

Several spiritual, cultural, and heretical movements, such as those of Marcion, Novatian, Mani, and the Gnostics, assisted the early church in clarifying its unity of faith as it spread into a multiplicity of cultures and nations, and assumed a variety of expressions in theology, worship, and church life.

The first councils called to heal divisions, those of Nicea (325) and Constantinople (381) gave precision to Christian understanding of Christ and the Trinity, and recognized the role of creeds, the canonically recognized books of the Bible, and bishops as leaders. Eventually five of the bishops were recognized as patriarchs: those of Rome, Constantinople, Alexandria, Antioch, and Jerusalem. These patriarchates were important in stabilizing the Church in the ancient world and adapting it to the various cultures of the Empire.

After three centuries of persecution, the church gradually began to become integrated with the Roman Empire, assuming its geography and structure, and the emphases of its two dominant cultures, Byzantine/Greek and Roman/Latin. Eventually the cultural center gravitated toward the new political capital, Constantinople/Byzantium. But the great imperial cultural centers of Antioch and Alexandria also had important Christian schools and traditions.

The councils of the fifth century, called by the emperor to unite the debating churches, focused on the relationship of the divinity and humanity of Christ in the Incarnation. As Greek and Latin Christians became more identified with the imperial leadership, the Syrians of Antioch, Copts of Alexandria in Egypt, Armenian, and Persian Christians experienced other tensions, in addition to theological ones, which distanced them from Constantinople and Rome.

At the Council of Ephesus (431) the churches attempted to resolve their differences in speaking of Mary as the mother of Jesus Christ only, or as mother of God as well. Unwillingness to speak of the "God bearer" *(theotokos)* appeared to some to question the full divinity of Christ, while to others the use of the title appeared to question his full humanity. The Persian Church with its patriarchate at Seleucia-Ctesiphon, called Nestorian by its critics, did not accept the Council and fell out of communion with the five apostolic patriarchates. The Assyrian Church of the East, as it is now called, with centers in Iran, Iraq, and the United States, flourished throughout Asia and the Middle East during the Middle Ages. Today the issue of Ephesus, the nature of Mary as the mother of Jesus and mother of God, is being resolved.

The Council of Chalcedon (451) dealt with emphases in Christology debated by the theological schools of Antioch and Alexandria. In this Council the Church confessed:

> one and the same Son, our Lord Jesus Christ: the same perfect in divinity and perfect in humanity, the same truly God and truly man, of rational soul and body; consubstantial

> with the Father as regards his divinity, and the same consubstantial with us as regards his humanity.

A detailed study of both the Christologies of the time and the intervention of Leo of Rome in the Council will be important to fully understand the details of this debate, the divisions that developed, and the claims of the Roman patriarchate. Following this Council the issues continued to be debated for centuries, and several councils were called by the Byzantine emperors, in collaboration with the patriarchs of Constantinople and Rome to heal the divisions and arrive at common formulations of the Christological faith.

However, as a result of these debates, about half of the Patriarchate of Antioch (now the Syrian Orthodox Church) and most of the Church of Alexandria (now the Coptic Orthodox Church) separated from the Patriarchs of Constantinople, Rome, and Jerusalem. The Armenians were not present for the Council, but followed in rejecting Chalcedon. The Indian Syrian and Ethiopian Churches shared these Christological views, as well. These churches are now called Oriental Orthodox, but in the past were often stigmatized as *Monophysite,* while they in turn characterized the Latin and Byzantine churches *Dyophysite.* In our own time Christological agreements have emerged between these churches and the Byzantine, Roman, and some of the Reformation churches.

The Divisions Between the Latin West and Byzantine East

It is claimed that the first millennium recognized a basic unity between the churches. As we have seen in biblical and patristic times, things were more complex. However, for the mass of European Christians and their heirs throughout the world, this period is of particular importance. The rupture of East and West, often dated at 1054, leaves contemporary Christians with a particularly tragic burden. In this section we will look at contributing factors to this division and efforts toward reunion.

After the seventh century the churches of the Middle East and North Africa were either under the control of Islam or

Divisions of Major Christian Traditions

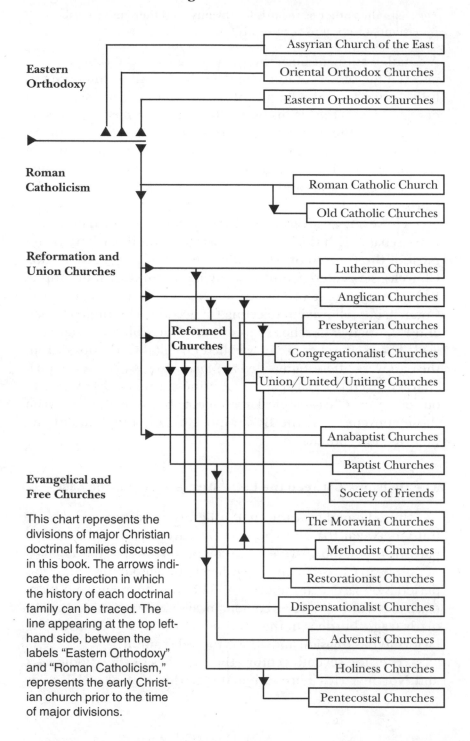

Eastern Orthodoxy

Assyrian Church of the East

Oriental Orthodox Churches

Eastern Orthodox Churches

Roman Catholicism

Roman Catholic Church

Old Catholic Churches

Reformation and Union Churches

Lutheran Churches

Anglican Churches

Reformed Churches

Presbyterian Churches

Congregationalist Churches

Union/United/Uniting Churches

Anabaptist Churches

Baptist Churches

Evangelical and Free Churches

Society of Friends

This chart represents the divisions of major Christian doctrinal families discussed in this book. The arrows indicate the direction in which the history of each doctrinal family can be traced. The line appearing at the top left-hand side, between the labels "Eastern Orthodoxy" and "Roman Catholicism," represents the early Christian church prior to the time of major divisions.

The Moravian Churches

Methodist Churches

Restorationist Churches

Dispensationalist Churches

Adventist Churches

Holiness Churches

Pentecostal Churches

destroyed by it. In the eighth century Muslim rule swept across North Africa and onto the European continent, touching what is today the border of France. In the East, Islam was a pressure on the Christian empire until Constantinople fell in 1453, and the advance continued northwestward until Vienna was under siege in the late seventeenth century. However, during the period after the fifth-century councils through the fifteenth-century defeat of Constantinople, the centers of Christian culture and power were in the Greek East. The western Latin Church was busy about the task of evangelizing the northern European tribes through the vehicles of monasticism and centralization of evangelism from Rome. The papacy eventually worked with these new peoples to establish an empire in the tribal West.

The Alienation

Theological, cultural, political, and ecclesiastical tensions emerged between East and West quite early, crystallizing in different approaches to scholarship, liturgy, spirituality, theology, church order, and relationships to the state. Numerous elements combined to bring about the gradual alienation of East and West, merely symbolized by the dramatic excommunication in 1054 of Patriarch Michael Cerularius in Justinian's great cathedral of Hagia Sophia by Cardinal Humbert, on grounds which all would recognize today as factually inaccurate. Indeed, there was no pope alive in Rome itself when the Cardinal made the dramatic gesture.

It may be helpful to regard the division as analogous to the dissolution of a marriage, where the partners cease to engage in dialogue and gradually fall away from each other. Fortunately, Pope Paul VI and Patriarch Athenagoras were able to put aside the anathemas of a previous day and a dialogue of love has begun to open up the possibility of a dialogue of truth.

In the area of theology, one of the lingering concerns has been the alteration of the *Nicene-Constantinopolitan* Creed, used in both Byzantine and Latin liturgies, to include the phrase "and the Son" (*filioque*), in speaking of the Holy Spirit's procession within the Trinity. The formulation was inserted, probably in

Spain to counteract Arianism. Eventually it came to be used throughout the West despite initial papal objections. The theology behind this addition reflects the psychological images of the Trinity used in Augustine's theology. A different approach in the exposition of the Trinitarian mystery has prevailed in the East. Some Orthodox continue to consider the use of the *filioque* heretical, as Latin Christians once regarded the Orthodox usage. Ecumenical proposals exist that would remove the phrase from the liturgies of various western churches, but such a decision would depend on Orthodox ability to recognize the underlying theology as authentic.

In areas of liturgy, the use of leavened and unleavened bread has been considered to be church-dividing, again because of pneumatological concerns, and rebaptism has on occasion been practiced between the churches. There have been tensions over the evangelization of what is now Eastern Europe and the Balkans in regard to whether Eastern or Western jurisdiction and ecclesiastical and liturgical forms should prevail. The claims of the Patriarchate of Constantinople to be the new Rome and the claims of the Patriarchate of Rome to a universal primacy that was more than one of honor have never been resolved and have often caused tensions.

The rise of a western empire after 800 caused both political and ecclesiastical tensions. Crises in the West during the eleventh century necessitated reforms which entailed papal claims and centralization in both ecclesiastical and civil matters that were not only different from, but in conflict with, the Byzantine understanding of the Church. However, most historians of both East and West now recognize that the fourth crusade of 1204 was the final blow to unity and trust. The Byzantine Orthodox have never forgotten the sacrilegious cruelty of the western "Christian" invaders, who sacked the cities and churches, replaced the canonical bishops with Latin prelates, and desecrated the holiest of sanctuaries.

Attempts at Reunion

Before the founding of the World Council of Churches and the Second Vatican Council of the Catholic Church, there had been attempts towards reunion of East and West. Two councils, Lyons II (1274) and Florence (1439), produced union schemes predicated on understandings of the Church developed only in the West. *Uniatism* attempted to draw Orthodoxy into communion with the church of Rome using Western ecclesiological principles. Both the Catholic Church and the ecumenically oriented churches of the Reformation now take a different approach, espousing a vision of a Conciliar Fellowship/Communion as the common goal of restored unity with the Orthodox.

From the time of the seventh ecumenical council (787), the Latin Church assembled on occasion, calling these Western synods "ecumenical councils." As Turkish pressures mounted on Constantinople and the Eastern empire, and as the Latin Church reached a higher level of culture and security, there were attempts to heal the schism. In 1274 a synod was called by Gregory X, the Second Council of Lyons, with three aims: union with the Greeks, convocation of a crusade, and church reform. In this synod the Greeks acceded to the *filioque* and to claims that in the election of the Roman pontiff the assembled cardinals were electing "the vicar of Jesus Christ, the successor of Peter, the ruler of the universal church." The union of Lyons proved ephemeral despite the political interests of the Byzantine Emperor, which it appeared to serve.

By the time of the Council of Florence (1438–1439) the political situation had changed drastically, when the Turks were at the doors of Constantinople and Emperor John VIII Palaeologus was under political compulsion to seek unity to elicit military aid from the West. In addition to accepting the *filioque* and papal supremacy, agreements were reached on purgatory and the number of the sacraments was resolved as seven. Even in the Council itself, the Greeks were not in full agreement. Upon return the agreements broke down. After the fall of the Byzantine empire in 1453, the role of the Slavic Orthodox churches began to grow. Moscow became a patriarchate in the sixteenth century and claimed the title of the "Third Rome," while the Russian emperor assumed the title of caesar *(czar)*.

The Councils of Lyon and Florence can be seen across the spectrum of two thousand years of ecclesiastical developments as general synods of the West, at which Eastern representatives were invited to submit to positions developed by Rome. These were not the results of a real dialogue of truth. Nor were these Councils equipped with the biblical and historical tools available to the churches today. Nevertheless, they cast a long shadow over the future of East-West relations.

Orthodoxy, under the hegemony of the Ottoman Turkish Empire or in distant Slavic lands, was shielded from the changes occurring in the western society as a consequence of the Renaissance, Reformation, and Enlightenment. Furthermore, the Latin Church became progressively removed from the more communal structure of "sister" churches of the first millennium and developed its institutional, juridical, and triumphalistic ecclesiology in quite different directions. This potent centralizing tendency, which emphasized uniformity and obedience to the pope, began to use the language of "return" and developed the category of "rite" to categorize Eastern churches. It also laid the theological foundation for the practice of sending Catholic missionaries to work among Orthodox Christians, encouraging them to become Catholic, a policy known as *uniatism*. Some groups of separated Eastern Christians petitioned for union with Rome on their own initiative.

Churches that came from Orthodoxy into communion with Rome retained their liturgical tradition, elements of their canon law including a married clergy, and their hierarchy. In 1595 the Union of Brest achieved unity with the Orthodox Metropolitan Province of Kiev, including western Ukraine and Belarus. In 1611 Serbs in Croatia and in 1701 Romanians in Transylvania came into union with Rome. In 1724 a schism within the Byzantine Patriarchate of Antioch brought a Melkite, Arab Byzantine Church into communion with Rome as well.

Through these unions and the movement of small groups leaving Eastern and Oriental Orthodoxy there eventually developed established "rites" in communion with Rome. In most cases there were political and cultural factors as well as religious ones at work, and in no case did the Orthodox churches recognize these developments as legitimate or compatible with the ecclesiology of the early Church and its councils.

These Eastern Catholic churches have often undergone a process of "Latinization," by which they have surrendered elements of their tradition in favor of western practices. In some instances, as in the case of required celibacy among Eastern Catholic clergy in the United States, these alien practices have been imposed by Roman decree, and not by appropriate synodical action of the Eastern church itself. In Eastern Europe, many of the Eastern Catholic churches were suppressed by Marxist regimes and forced to join either Orthodoxy or Latin Catholicism. With the revival of those Eastern Catholic Churches after 1989, tensions with Orthodoxy have increased.

The contemporary Catholic-Orthodox dialogue has urged the setting aside of uniatism in favor of the method of dialogue as the path toward reconciliation, without prejudice to the traditions and rights of these Eastern churches already in communion with Rome. It is only since the 1991 CICO *(Code of Canon Law for the Eastern Churches)* that the language of "rite" has been replaced by that of "autonomous churches," and the Eastern Churches' own traditions of self-governance have, in principle, been approved.

THE DIVISIONS OF THE REFORMATION

Within the Latin Church of the West there were a series of divisions that developed, culminating in the Reformation of the sixteenth century. Some of the pre-Reformation divisions, such as those between rival popes in the fourteenth century, were healed, but not without a burden of distrust and cynicism concerning ecclesiastical institutions. Others, such as those with the Waldensians (excommunicated in 1182 or 3), with Wycliffe (1330–1384), and the followers of the Bohemian reformer Jan Hus (c. 1372–1415) continued into the sixteenth century and eventually were associated with Reformation churches in history, theology, and ecumenism.

The context of the Reformation was set by debates within Scholastic theology among Nominalists, Scotists, and Thomists; by weakened ecclesiastical structures, especially in the papacy, episcopacy, and monasticism; and by the rise of humanism with its return to the biblical and classical sources and languages. The social and political ferment of the time, increased urbanization, commercial developments, emerging concepts of national identity, social dislocation due to plague and crusades, all provided opportunities for new ways of looking at religion, the human person, community, and the Church. There were still sectors in the Latin Church that claimed the council to be superior to the pope, and many states effectively kept papal influence out of their realms. Clerical professionalism and theological clarity were at a low ebb, and calls for reform "in head and members" were common.

Continental Reformation

Martin Luther (1483–1546) began to pose academic questions at the University of Wittenberg out of his pastoral experience with those in confession who felt guilty because they could not afford to buy indulgences to help their relatives in purgatory. Luther's biblical scholarship, especially in Paul, and his theological research, especially in Augustine, led him to a passionate conviction of the importance of preaching God's unmerited justification by grace through faith. This, in turn, led him to question the emphasis placed in the Church of his day on human effort and merit in achieving salvation. He had no intention of creating a schism in the Church, but came to take more confrontational positions as the questions he raised were rejected.

In 1518, at the initiative of his Augustinian superior, he was released from his vows, and after 1521, when he stood up for his convictions before Emperor Charles V at Worms, he became an outlaw in the empire. His emphasis on the authority of Scripture in theology and the Church; the centrality of Christ; and the importance of grace and faith over good works, ecclesial, and sacramental practices brought him into the center of tensions between Germanic forces for reform and the established ecclesiastical and civil authorities of pope and emperor.

The Reformation only hardened into a separation after the Augsburg Confession (1530), which was drafted as an irenic statement of the evangelical princes within the Catholic empire, but became the theological platform for the Protesting leaders against the Catholic Church. In 1580 the theological position of the Augsburg Confession, along with the classical creeds and some subsequent sixteenth-century statements of faith were incorporated into the *Book of Concord*, which became the foundational text for the Evangelical (Lutheran) churches of Germany and Scandinavia.

These churches emphasize the priesthood of all believers, the role of the civil leaders in church life, the centrality of Scripture and proclamation in worship, the real presence of Christ in the Eucharist—simplified and celebrated in the vernacular—and above all the centrality of the Gospel teaching on justification. Many of the Catholic practices—liturgical, spiritual, and artistic—were retained, including, where possible, the episcopal structure of the Church. Eventually the Catholic Church was able to rectify some of the theological and ecclesiastical abuses of the day, and to clarify its positions at the Council of Trent (1545–1563). In our own day common ground has been found in regard to the doctrine of justification and to many other divisive issues of the sixteenth century.

The Swiss Reformation developed from a variety of centers and leaders, the most important of whom were Ulrich Zwingli of Zurich (1484–1531) and John Calvin of Geneva (1509–1564). The churches which emerged from this movement are called Reformed and eventually developed into a variety of confessions and church orders, for example, Dutch Reformed, Scottish Presbyterian, and British Congregational.

Calvin was the great systematic theologian of the Reformation. His *Institutes of the Christian Religion* was completed in 1559. With Luther, he emphasized the doctrine of justification by faith, the centrality of Scripture and grace, the priesthood of all believers, and a simplification and clarification of worship. He differed from Luther particularly in understanding how Christ is received in the Eucharist and in evaluating the importance of law and discipline in church life. The Reformed tradition includes laity in church governance, as did Luther. However, this tradition has put more emphasis on church order than did Luther. The central principle for Calvin's reform was the sovereignty of God.

The Lutheran churches consolidated in northern Europe. Geneva became the center for Reformed leaders, who would develop churches in Eastern Europe, the Low Countries, and

Britain. In Switzerland, Germany, the Netherlands, and other parts of Europe small, separatist groups emerged, which came to be called Anabaptists because they only baptized believing adults. They claimed that the reformers had not gone far enough by not rejecting infant baptism, compromise with the state, and military service. While these groups varied in their emphasis, they were widely persecuted in Catholic, Lutheran, Reformed, and Anglican lands. These are the Mennonites and Brethren of our day.

The English Reformation

In England the Reformation took a very different course. Originally Henry VIII (reigned 1509–1547) was a staunch defender of the traditional faith and a persecutor of reformers. However, following a tradition of English kings' struggles for independence from the influence of Canterbury and Rome, Henry was anxious to establish his autonomy and to provide a successor to the throne. When his Spanish queen, Catherine of Aragon, did not provide him with an heir, he began to seek ways to gain an annulment. It appeared that the only way to free himself to legally remarry in hope of obtaining a male heir was to separate from the authority of papal Rome. This he did in 1529, creating a national church, while retaining the theology and the sacramental and episcopal structure of the Catholic Church.

Under his successor, Edward VI (reigned 1547–1553), Protestant influences were encouraged, and the Anglican version of the liturgy, *The Book of Common Prayer,* and its catechism became the focus of the Church's reform. Thereafter, the English Reformation remained a confluence of Reformation and Catholic elements, with many Anglicans claiming continuity with, and even return to, the situation that prevailed in the medieval period. A short return to the papal obedience under Mary (reigned 1553–1558) was ended under her successor Elizabeth I (reigned 1558–1603). In 1559 the monarch was named supreme governor of the English Church in an ecclesiastical settlement that featured a moderate *Book of Common Prayer,* incorporating Catholic and Reformation elements and an episcopal ecclesiastical order.

A Calvinist minority would have pressed for more radical departure from Catholic traditions. However, it was only with the Puritan revolution in the seventeenth century that a strong Reformed establishment came into power in England. It was this reform that produced the Westminster Confession (1643), which remains central in Presbyterian life today. Eventually the monarchy and episcopal order were restored, but the Anglican Church continues to this day with both significant Catholic and Evangelical tendencies, sometimes in conflict, within its life. Since the Second Vatican Council the Catholic Church has acknowledged a special relationship with the Anglican tradition.

During the seventeenth-century British congregational Calvinism and religious conflicts created the context for the emergence of the Baptist movement and the Religious Society of Friends (Quakers). Like Puritanism, these groups emphasize the sovereignty of God, the priesthood of all believers, and communal authority in the governance of the Church.

Baptists' insistence on the separation of Church and state, on baptizing only believing adults, on understanding baptism and the Lord's Supper as ordinances rather than as sacraments, and on private interpretation of the Scriptures, sets them off from the earlier Reformation traditions. Baptists' emphasis on evangelism and congregational independence has contributed to their becoming the largest Protestant community in the United States today.

American-Born Churches

The eighteenth century produced many revivals within Protestant churches as within Catholicism. In England, John Wesley (1703–1791) spearheaded a revival that spread to the colonies, bringing enthusiasm and a focus on personal conversion and experience to the Anglican people during the industrial revolution and American colonization.

Because of the revolutionary war, the U.S. revival movement evolved into a separate church, called Methodist (1784), a division that also took place in England after Wesley's death. Methodism contains a genius for organization and outreach, which made it most adaptable on the American frontier and in global mission. For many years Methodism was the largest denomination in the United States and is a leading partner in the ecumenical movement.

In the eighteenth and nineteenth centuries numerous divisions emerged among the Baptists and Methodists—over race, slavery, and a variety of doctrinal emphases. There are three large African American Baptist groups (National Baptist Convention of America, Progressive National Baptist Convention, and National Baptist Convention, USA) and three large African American Methodist churches (African Methodist Episcopal, African Methodist Episcopal Zion, and Christian Methodist Episcopal) in the United States. There are, additionally, a cluster of Wesleyan movements which have developed into the Holiness churches, such as the Church of the Nazarene, the Wesleyan Church, the Free Methodists, and Church of God (Anderson, Indiana).

Thomas Campbell (1763–1854) and Barton Stone (1772–1844) attempted to begin an ecumenical movement by developing congregations with open membership, possessing no creed but Christ, and practicing weekly Eucharist and adult baptism. From this movement emerged the Churches of Christ, the Christian Churches, and the Disciples of Christ.

The nineteenth-century urgency about the second coming of Christ at the end of time produced a variety of movements which have developed into churches, the most prominent of these being the Seventh-day Adventists. After the turn of the century, a Pentecostal revival movement usually dated from a 1906 Azuza Street meeting in Los Angeles, California, began. This movement has developed into one of the fastest growing Christian communities in the late twentieth century. Much of the theological impetus for this revival developed out of the Holiness movement and its Wesleyan emphasis on experience, the Holy Spirit, and a second work of grace. Speaking in tongues, faith healing, and baptism of the Holy Spirit are among the characteristics of this revival that eventually gave rise to churches such as the Assemblies of God and Church of God in Christ.

In the United States, the pluralistic context, and the sense of individual initiative characterizing the culture has developed into an environment where a host of independent churches of a variety of types exist, from the storefront preacher of the urban neighborhood to the suburban megachurches.

In the meantime, the Catholic Church was going through its own renewal, with the Council of Trent, increased centralization, and educational and spiritual developments. The First Vatican Council (1870) clarified the role of the papacy in the context of the infallibility of the Church. Catholic canon law was codified in 1917. The definition of two dogmas concerning the Virgin Mary, the Immaculate Conception (1854), and the Bodily Assumption (1950), created new ecumenical challenges to reconciliation with the Orthodox and Reformation churches. However, the renewal of biblical, liturgical, and historical scholarship and the loss of the papacy's political burden in the Italian papal states created a new basis upon which ecumenical developments could eventually be built.

THE IMPETUS TO CHURCH UNITY

In the eighteenth century, the Enlightenment had precipitated a rationalism which sought to reduce Christianity to the postulates of reason. The renewal movement of Pietism, which had begun in the previous century in Germany as a reaction against a Lutheranism that was perceived as dry and cerebral, bore new fruit in the eighteenth and nineteenth centuries in movements such as the efforts of John Wesley and the Awakenings in the United States.

The colonization fever which gripped many European nations in the nineteenth and twentieth centuries, particularly towards Africa and Asia, finally demonstrated the folly of Christian disunity, as Vatican II (1962–1965) would note: "Such division openly contradicts the will of Christ, scandalizes the world, and damages that most holy cause, the preaching of the Gospel to every creature" (UR [*Unitatis Redintegratio*/Decree on Ecumenism], 1). In the following section we will look at the emergence from this context of the modern ecumenical movement, the World Council of Churches, and the entry of the Catholic Church into the ecumenical movement.

Early Ecumenical Initiatives

From the beginnings of each of the divisions recounted above there have been initiatives toward unity: under the Emperor Justinian (reigned 526–565) among the Oriental Orthodox and Greek and Latin Churches; at Lyons and Florence in 1274 and 1439, and in the nineteenth century with Vatican I between the Catholic Church and the Byzantine Churches; and among Protestants in the sixteenth and eighteenth centuries.

In the nineteenth century in the United States, the Evangelical Alliance and related movements in social justice and ministry developed an early ecumenical model of churches with varying theological views working together toward common goals. The U.S. Episcopal Church and the Anglican Lambeth Conference put out a call to unity in 1888 in the context of four points: (1) the Scriptures, both Old and New Testaments, (2) the Apostles' and Nicene Creeds, (3) the sacraments of baptism and Eucharist; and (4) the historic episcopate, locally adapted to meet the varying needs of "the nations and peoples called by God into the Unity of His Church." At the end of the century Philip Schaff, a classical Protestant historian, called for a reassessment of relations between the churches, especially in the study of the history of the Church.

The event credited with giving rise to the twentieth-century ecumenical movement is the World Missionary Conference at Edinburgh in 1910. In the wake of the passing of colonialism and in the context of mission, a number of Protestant churches assembled to discuss their different and mutual problems in witnessing to Christ within a divided Christianity. The membership of the Conference was composed of Protestants and was dominated by North Atlantic concerns. There were no Orthodox or Catholics present. The goal of the assembly was to inspire Christians from the various churches to cooperate in preaching the Gospel to the world, particularly in Africa and Asia. Anglican speakers urged that the omission of Catholic and Orthodox members should be rectified in future conferences.

Bishop Charles Brent (1862–1929), an American Episcopal missionary to the Philippines, reminded the members that practical cooperation among the churches was not sufficient to heal the divisions. He addressed the General Convention of the Episcopal Church and advocated the establishment of a joint commission to study questions of faith and order. He, with others, took his proposal to Rome, Constantinople, and the variety of Protestant leadership centers around the world. In 1927 the first World Conference on Faith and Order met in Lausanne, Switzerland, with representatives of the major Christian traditions of the time, except the Catholic.

Protestant national missionary councils and councils of churches from Africa, Asia, and Latin America joined together in the International Missionary Council in 1921, as the first fruits of Edinburgh. In the area of joint social action, the first Conference on Life and Work met in Stockholm, Sweden, inspired especially by Archbishop Nathan Söderblom (1866–1931) of the Lutheran Church of Sweden. It sought to formulate programs and devise means for the churches' common service in the world.

In many countries national entities called "councils of churches" were established for the purpose of bringing the churches together in common action. By the mid-twentieth century four major international streams had emerged: Life and Work to promote joint social service and action; Faith and Order to seek the theological basis for church unity; the International Missionary Council for common proclamation; and the World Council of Christian Education.

The World Council of Churches

The World Council had been in formation since a 1920 encyclical of the Ecumenical Patriarch of Constantinople, "Unto the Churches of Christ Everywhere," urging the establishment of a permanent "fellowship of Churches" (Koinonia to Ekklesion), and the decision of the churches before World War II to combine their efforts. In 1948, after the struggles and collaboration during World War II and the reconstruction thereafter, Faith and Order came together with Life and Work in the founding of the World Council of Churches. In 1961, the International Missionary Council came into the World Council at the New Delhi Assembly, at the same time as the Orthodox Churches of Eastern

Europe and the first Pentecostal churches. Catholic observers were present at that Assembly for the first time. The World Council of Christian Education entered in 1971. The contribution of the WCC is explored in more detail in chapter seven.

The original constitution of the WCC stated that "The World Council of Churches is a fellowship *[koinonia]* of churches which accept Our Lord Jesus Christ as God and Savior." In 1961 this constitution was elaborated to read: "The WCC is a fellowship of churches which confess the Lord Jesus Christ as God and Savior according to the scriptures and therefore seek to fulfill together their common calling to the glory of the one God, Father, Son and Holy Spirit," thus adding Trinitarian, doxological, and scriptural emphases.

The World Council has had seven Assemblies: Amsterdam, 1948; Evanston, 1954; New Delhi, 1961; Uppsala, 1968; Nairobi, 1975; Vancouver, 1983; and Canberra, 1991. The 1998 jubilee Assembly will bear the theme: "Return to God, Rejoice in Hope." Over three hundred churches belong to the Council, including the Anglican and all of the Oriental Orthodox Churches and the Eastern Orthodox Churches except the Georgian Orthodox Church. The Catholic Church has been a member of the Faith and Order Commission since 1968, provides staff for the mission section of the Council, and collaborates in almost every program of World Council work.

There are significant numbers of conservative Evangelical churches, Pentecostal, Holiness, and some Lutheran, Reformed, Baptist, and Anabaptist churches that do not belong. The Evangelical movement worldwide has organized national and regional evangelical associations, which in turn meet in the World Evangelical Fellowship.

Catholic Ecumenism

On May 16, 1919, Pope Benedict XV received Bishop Charles Brent, then Bishop of Western New York in the Protestant Episcopal Church, as preparations were being made for the first World Conference on Faith and Order. The pope showed interest, and praised the movement, but felt obliged to decline the invitation to participate because he was convinced that Catholic ecclesiology would not allow it. The Catholic understanding of Christian unity remained "return" to the one true Church.

In 1928 Pius XI, in his encyclical *Mortalium animos* (On the Promotion of True Religious Unity), criticized the ecumenical movement and forbade Catholics to participate in it as it was founded on error and illusion. He accused it of seeking to reach unity by too easy compromise and by focusing too exclusively on service. Leo XIII had expressed similar sentiments in *Satis Cognitum* (On the Unity of the Church) in 1896.

Several other statements emerged around the time of the WCC foundation, a warning on June 5, 1948, and an instruction, *Ecclesia Catholica* (The Catholic Church), in 1949. The common assumption in them was that the ecumenical movement was a Protestant affair. Catholics had no need to search for Christian unity as this comes with unity to the Chair of Peter in Rome in the Mystical Body of Christ. The Catholic Church was cautious, fearing indifferentism *(Mortalium Animos)* and false irenicism (*Humani Generis*/Concerning Some False Opinions Which Tend to Undermine the Teaching Authority of the Church, 1951). Furthermore, the ecumenical movement could threaten the doctrine of the identity and nature of the Church and could lead to proselytism where the Church was not securely established.

Suggestions of change can be noted in the 1939 encyclical of Pius XII, *Summi Pontificatus* (Function of the State in the Modern World), which showed friendliness toward Protestants, acknowledging their good will. "Return," however, remained the aim of dialogue. The Holy Office acknowledged in its 1949 *Ecclesia Sua* (His Church) that the ecumenical movement "derives from the inspiration of the Holy Spirit," and is "a source of holy joy in the Lord." Within the strict conditions of Catholic ecclesiology, experts could participate in discussions of faith and morals with other Christians. The pursuit of "spiritual ecumenism" and the Week of Prayer for Christian Unity were encouraged.

Pioneering work of individuals, such as Abbé Ferdinand Portal, C.M. (1855–1926), Dominican Yves Congar, O.P. (1904–1995), Father Paul Couturier (1881–1953), and Dom Lambert Beauduin, O.S.B. (1873–1960), began to lay the groundwork that bore fruit with the Second Vatican Council.

Under the informal patronage of Cardinal Désiré Joseph Mercier of Malines, the Malines Conversations between Anglicans and Roman Catholics (1921–1925) demonstrated that dialogue could be conducted without compromise and with mutual respect and openness. The Swiss Trappist monastery of Les Dombes has hosted an ongoing conversation which first met in 1937 and continues to make contributions to ecumenical theological formulation under the title of the Groupe des Dombes. The Society for the Study of Ecumenical Questions, in Europe, became an important forum on the eve of the Council. A number of persons, such as Monsignor Johannes Willebrands and Father Augustin Bea, S.J., would participate and eventually make their contribution to Catholic ecumenical life.

SOME KEY EVENTS IN THE ECUMENICAL LIFE OF THE CHURCH IN THE LAST FIFTY YEARS

1948	Founding of the WCC (World Council of Churches), Amsterdam.
1954	Father George Tavard attends the Second Assembly of the WCC.
1957	Fathers John Courtney Murray and Gustav Weigel attend Oberlin Conference on Faith and Order with official approval.
1960	Archbishop of Canterbury Geoffrey Fisher visits Pope John XXIII in Rome.
1961	Vatican sends official observers to Third Assembly of the WCC in New Delhi.
1962	Second Vatican Council receives ecumenical observers.
1963	Catholics participate in WCC Faith and Order meeting that produces *Scripture, Tradition and the Traditions*.
1964	Pope Paul VI and Patriarch Athenagoras meet in Jerusalem.
1965	Conciliar Decrees: Decree on Ecumenism, NA (*Nostra Aetate*/Declaration on the Church's Relations with non-Christian Religions), and DH (*Dignitatis Humanae*/Declaration on Religious Liberty).

1965	Pope Paul and Patriarch Athenagoras lift condemnations of 1054.
1966	First Common Declaration of a Pope, in this case with Archbishop Michael Ramsey of Canterbury, beginning the Anglican Roman Catholic Dialogue. Catholic dialogues beginning with many churches: Lutheran, Methodist, Reformed.
1967	Pope Paul visits the Patriarch in Istanbul.
1968	Catholic Church joins WCC Faith and Order Commission and NCCB (National Conference of Catholic Bishops) joins NCC (National Council of Churches of Christ in the USA) Faith and Order Commission.
1969	Pope Paul VI visits the offices of the World Council of Churches, Geneva.
1975	The World Council of Churches Assembly at Nairobi publishes its *Conciliar Fellowship* description of the unity of the Church.
1982	The Anglican Roman Catholic International Commission publishes a *Final Report*. Pope John Paul II visits Canterbury Cathedral with Archbishop Robert Runcie.
1987	Holy See responds to the World Council of Churches' *BEM (Baptism, Eucharist and Ministry)*.
1991	Holy See responds to the Anglican Roman Catholic *Final Report*.
1993	Papacy introduced into the WCC Faith and Order discussions. Holy See publishes its *Directory (Directory for the Application of Principles and Norms on Ecumenism)*.
1995	Pope John Paul places the unity of the churches high on the agenda in preparing for the Jubilee 2000 in his encyclical, *Ut Unum Sint* (UUS/That All May Be One) and in his letter *Tertio Millennio Adveniente* (TMA/On the Threshold of the Third Millennium).

The shifts in ecclesiology embodied in the Dogmatic Constitution on the Church and the Decree on Ecumenism, and the formulations of the Declaration on Religious Liberty and the Dogmatic Constitution on Divine Revelation, which are the essential foundations for what was to become the Catholic ecumenical basis, will be discussed in the next chapter. This can only be considered a preliminary overview, briefly recounting the story up to the 1960s, after which a common history begins to emerge.

Conclusion

Any person who engages in ecumenism comes to realize that the work of unity is the task of the Spirit and not a human project. In this chapter, the several cultural, linguistic, socioeconomic, and theological factors that impact the human character of these divisions disclose, as well, the challenging nature of the work for unity.

Nevertheless, as all of the ecumenical pioneers, Catholic, Protestant, and Orthodox realized so well, the work of ecumenism is a renewal movement that can only be accomplished when believers are prepared to humble themselves, and by prayer and penitence, reform themselves, entering deeply into the mystery of the Lord's death and resurrection. Calling Christians to a renewed sense of holiness was the purpose of the Reformers as it is of the ecumenical movement in the churches. Only in so far as individuals in the Church become a holy people can the unity and mission of the Church be realized. The founders of the World Council of Churches and the fathers of Vatican II enshrined this vision in their foundational documents.

As Pope John Paul reminds us in his encyclical *Ut Unum Sint,* ecumenism is essential to the very identity of the Christian and cannot be seen as a peripheral part of church life. The call to be Christian is the call to Trinitarian life: the *koinonia* of the people of God symbolizes the mystery of the Blessed Trinity.

Study Questions

1. Describe the ecumenical perspectives necessary to approach the study of the history of Christianity.

2. What were the impulses and instruments in the New Testament apostolic Church for promoting Christian unity?

3. Name the churches that separated from one another in the first millennium as a result of the great Christological controversies.

4. How did the separation of the Eastern and Western Churches take place? In what way was it similar to the dissolution of a marriage?

5. Describe the attempts at reunion of Eastern and Western Churches, and assess why they failed.

6. What were some of the forces that led to the Reformation? What were the compelling theological issues that led to the separation of the churches?

7. Trace the development of the English-speaking Reform movements of the eighteenth to the twentieth century. What areas of history will you need to study in more detail to effectively understand the ecumenical mission of the Church?

8. What are the key factors that have contributed to the modern ecumenical movement and the entry of the Catholic Church into it? What are the elements of this story that are most important for the Christian community today? How does this story become part of our common ecumenical memory? What are the contributions of some of the early ecumenical pioneers?

Selected Readings

Borelli, John, and John Erickson. *The Quest for Unity: Orthodox and Catholics in Dialogue; Documents of the Joint International Commission and Official Dialogues in the United States 1965–1995*. Crestwood: St. Vladimir Seminary Press/Washington D.C.: U.S. Catholic Conference, 1996, pp. 5–24.

Brown, Raymond E. *The Churches the Apostles Left Behind*. New York/ Mahwah: Paulist Press, 1984.

Brown, Raymond E., and John P. Meier. *Antioch and Rome*. New York/
Mahwah: Paulist Press, 1983.

Cwiekowski, Frederick J. *The Beginnings of the Church*. New York/Mah-
wah: Paulist Press, 1988.

González, Justo L. *Church History: An Essential Guide*. Nashville: Abingdon Press, 1996.

Kinnamon, Michael, and Brian E. Cope, eds. *The Ecumenical Movement:
An Anthology of Basic Texts and Voices*. Grand Rapids: Eerdmans, 1997,
pp. 1–78, 526–35.

Lossky, Nicholas, et al., eds. *Dictionary of the Ecumenical Movement*.
Grand Rapids: Eerdmans, 1991.

Meyendorff, John. *Imperial Unity and Christian Divisions: The Church,
450–680 A.D.* Crestwood: St. Vladimir's Seminary Press, 1989.

Pelikan, Jaroslav. *The Christian Tradition: A History of the Development of
Doctrine: Vols. I–V.* Chicago: University of Chicago Press, 1971–1989.

Roberson, Ronald G. *The Eastern Christian Churches: A Brief Survey*.
Rome: University Press of the Pontifical Oriental Institute, 1995.

——, ed. *Oriental Orthodox-Roman Catholic Interchurch Marriages and
Other Pastoral Relationships*. Washington, D.C.: U.S. Catholic Conference, 1995.

Rouse, Ruth, Stephen Neill, and Harold Fey, eds. *A History of the Ecumenical Movement 1517–1948*. Ruth Rouse, Stephen Neill, eds. *A History
of the Ecumenical Movement 1948–1968*. Harold Fey, ed., second edition.
Philadelphia: Westminster Press, 1967–1970.

Visser't Hooft, W.A. *The Genesis and Formation of the World Council of
Churches*. Geneva: World Council of Churches, 1982.

2

Catholic Ecumenical Documentation

O Lord Jesus Christ, you said to your apostles,
I leave you peace, my peace I give you.
Look not on our sins, but the faith of your Church,
and grant us the peace and unity of your kingdom
where you live for ever and ever.

Introduction

Each of the churches must provide a firm foundation from within its own understanding of the Christian tradition as it moves from estrangement into dialogue and conversion and toward the goal of full visible unity. The member churches of the World Council began to do this in the late nineteenth and early twentieth centuries. The Catholic Church initiated such a process in the Second Vatican Council, among the major goals of which, according to Pope John XXIII, was the promotion of the visible unity of the Church and the movement of the Catholic Church into the modern ecumenical movement.

The years since the Council's publication of the Decree on Ecumenism have yielded a vast treasury of ecumenical documentation. Pope Paul VI and John Paul II, as well as various offices of the Roman curia, especially the Pontifical Council for Promoting Christian Unity (Secretariat for Promoting Christian Unity from 1960 to 1989), have provided a constant commentary on, and encouragement of, the growing movement.

The present chapter delineates some of this literature from the magisterium of the Catholic Church. Three moments in this development will be reviewed: (1) the promulgation of The

35

Decree on Ecumenicism (1964); (2) the publication of the *Directory for the Application of Principles and Norms on Ecumenism* (1993); (3) recent magisterial documents on ecumenism. The chapter is best read in connection with the documents themselves and in conjunction with similar documents from other churches.

The Decree on Ecumenism

The Decree on Ecumenism is the charter document of ecumenism on the part of the Catholic magisterium. In this section we will note the background to the Council text, the structure of the document, and a review of its contents. As noted in the previous chapter, the attitude of the Catholic Church since the inception of the ecumenical movement had been one of reserve and distance, articulated in terms of "return."

A. Prelude to The Decree on Ecumenism

A more positive evaluation of the ecumenical movement began in the 1950s. In 1960 John XXIII established the Secretariat for Promoting Christian Unity and authorized it to prepare a document on Christian unity. Subsequent history has shown that the decision to invite ecumenical observers to the Council, to found this Secretariat, and to give the Secretariat responsibilities in the formulation of drafts on Religious Liberty and Divine Revelation as well as ecumenism and interfaith relations laid the foundation for a fresh approach to the self-understanding of the Catholic Church.

To understand the Catholic Church's ecumenical program, the debates on the Church, on Religious Liberty, on the Church in the Modern World *(Gaudium et Spes),* and on Divine Revelation must be studied as well as those under consideration in this chapter. Pope Paul VI's first encyclical, *Ecclesiam Suam* of 1964 is another important articulation of the Catholic vision of dialogue.

During the first session of the Council, three separate documents dealing with the unity of the Church were extant: (1) a chapter *On the Church* by the Theological Commission; (2) a document *On the Unity of the Church: That They May Be One* by the Commission of the Eastern Churches; and (3) a draft document prepared by the Secretariat. The Council voted for a single document that would incorporate salient features of each. The Secretariat composed the document and it was unanimously approved on November 21, 1964.

B. The Decree Itself

The Decree consists of three chapters: (1) Catholic Principles on Ecumenism; (2) The Practice of Ecumenism; and (3) Separated Churches and Ecclesial Communities. From its very introduction, the Decree anchors the commitment to unity in the prayer of Christ, in the Trinitarian unity that has never been completely lost among divided Christians, and in the fact that it is communities of believers, and not just individuals, that hear the Word of God and follow his calling to be the Church.

The title of the first chapter is significant, referring to Catholic principles, rather than Catholic ecumenism. There is one ecumenical movement and one call of Christ, which Catholics share equally with other Christians. The chapter goes on to ground the unity of the Church in Christ's saving mystery and the continuity of the Church from the apostles, and makes a significant shift in Catholic emphasis to acknowledge that both sides of a division share blame and responsibility. It affirms our common Christian faith and baptism, which is never lost however deep the obstacles to unity. "For those who believe in Christ and have been properly baptized are put in some, though imperfect, communion with the Catholic Church."

Here the important affirmation from the Constitution on the Church is repeated that the "one true Church subsists in the Catholic Church." This affirmation moves away from the simple identification of the true Church with the Catholic Church as it is presently constituted and acknowledges important elements of the Church in other communities. These ecclesial communities and churches are seen as effective means of grace for their members.

In this chapter dialogue, collaboration in ministry and common prayer are encouraged. The failings of members of the

Catholic Church often obscure its truth. However, the unity of the Church entails unity with the apostolic college of bishops including the successor of Peter. The goal of ecumenical dialogue is set out clearly: "...little by little, as the obstacles to perfect ecclesiastical communion are overcome, all Christians will be gathered, in a common celebration of the Eucharist, into the unity of the one and only Church, which Christ bestowed on his Church from the beginning" (UR 4).

The second chapter delineates principles for the practice of ecumenism. Conversion and renewal are essential in developing the ecumenical spirituality articulated as central to Catholic identity. "The concern for restoring unity involves the whole Church, faithful and clergy alike....Every renewal of the Church essentially consists in an increase of fidelity to her own calling" (UR 5–6).

In addition to prayer, resolve to live in unity and charity; the Decree emphasizes that understanding, study, dialogue, a common search for the Word of God, and common witness, particularly in social matters, will aid Christians in their efforts to serve their common Lord and each other. Growth in holiness, in closeness to Christ, should bring us closer to one another.

Shared worship is both a means and a goal of ecumenical movement. The Eucharist is a potent sign of unity in faith and sacramental life and a means of building communion. Therefore, sharing in worship must be treated with great care, as we will see in the development of the postconciliar Catholic directives. In these matters, the Council notes the role of diversity as well as the authority of episcopal conferences and of local bishops. Ecumenical formation is emphasized, both in getting to know our "separated brethren," our fellow Christians, and in taking the ecumenical point of view into account in theology, history, and other branches of knowledge, especially for future priests. In this chapter the call to social collaboration is promoted and the hierarchy of truths is introduced. In so doing the Council fathers remind the Church that the call to Christian cooperation, both in action and dialogue, is rooted in and illuminated by the central mystery of faith—the Holy Trinity.

The third chapter describes the principal historical divisions in Christianity. In regard to the Eastern Churches, the decree "solemnly declares that the Churches of the East, while keeping in mind the necessary unity of the whole Church, have power to govern themselves according to their own disciplines" (UR 16). Eastern liturgical and monastic traditions, as well as spiritualities, ecclesiastical disciplines, and theological formulations are often complementary rather than conflicting with different usages and formulations found in the Latin Church (UR 17).

There is implicit rejection of uniatism, "return" theology, and Latinization, which characterized an earlier Catholic practice. There is no hesitation to use the words *Church* or *apostolic* when speaking of the Oriental or Eastern Orthodox. The suffering of the Eastern Churches is noted. Quoting Acts 15:28, the Decree emphasizes that one must "impose no burden beyond what is indispensable."

Speaking of the separated churches and communities in the West, the Decree proposes a program of dialogue whereby commitment to Christ as Lord and Savior, loving reverence for sacred Scripture, baptism, and the Holy Supper, and apostolic witness to the Gospel in social action provide areas of agreement as well as areas of present disagreement among Catholics and these Christians. Different approaches to moral matters are noted among the important areas for dialogue. The Decree acknowledges the complexity and variety of Protestant developments and the seriousness of the divisions in faith and culture. The importance of our common Scripture and baptism is developed.

The Decree ends with a plea for God's blessing upon the ecumenical movement, which is animated by the Holy Spirit and is continually inspired by the Spirit's guidance and hope.

C. The Impact of the Decree

The Decree affirms that the Catholic Church, in fidelity to its faith commitment, has entered into the ecumenical movement begun in the World Council of Churches, whose aim is the establishment of the one Church of the *Oikoumene*, in loyalty to the mystery of the Church of Christ. Other non-Catholic Christian communities are termed churches or ecclesial communities and are no longer called "sects" or "heretical" bodies. The criterion of the comparison among the Catholic Church and other churches and ecclesial communities, relates to the apostolic fullness of the messianic promise which, although veiled, is never absent from the Catholic Church, and is always capable of further purification.

The Decree began a new tradition, and the theological, pastoral, and missionary tasks which it entailed were challenging and without precedent. The Catholic Church, since the Council, has entered a series of bilateral and multilateral dialogues with Eastern Christians, Anglicans, Old Catholics (including the Polish National Catholic Church in the United States), and Protestants. In none of these has the Catholic Church discontinued dialogue or departed from the religious principles to which it is committed.

Since the Council, a different sense of the future for the Church has emerged. The majority of Catholics will be in Africa and Latin America during the twenty-first century. Questions of inculturation and globalization are central to the ecumenical agenda in ways that could not have been foreseen in the Decree. In some areas of the world, for example Spain, the task of assimilating the religious liberty teaching of the Church was necessary before the churches could dialogue on an equal footing.

As will be noted later in this chapter and throughout the book, the Decree has born rich fruit in the vision of the *Code of Canon Law;* the institutionalization of the commitment to unity in parishes, dioceses, and national episcopal conferences; and in the official formulations of every area of Catholic life. The reception of this Decree and its implementation in the expanded ecumenical program of the Catholic Church has been received in different ways and to different degrees among the people and structures of the Church in different places.

The solidity and success of the Council's decision ought not to leave one naive as to the challenge before all in bringing the ecumenical agenda and common achievements to all of the people of God. Prejudice, ignorance, and closed-mindedness remain among the catalogue of sins which the Christian people continually confess. Zeal for the unity of the Church is central to Christian identity, including that of the Catholic, but it has yet to mature into a fully conscious spirituality in every individual and community.

The Church is a mystery and depends for its life and unity upon the prayer of Christ, the love of the Father, and the action of the Holy Spirit. Christ remains the principal agent of ecumenical and ecclesial activity. The human promoters of Christian unity are merely his instruments. It is in this purview of hope that the Church and its members must pursue the ecumenical task.

DIRECTORY FOR THE APPLICATION OF THE PRINCIPLES AND NORMS OF ECUMENISM

A. Catholic documents from *The Decree on Ecumenism* to 1993

The present-day institutional commitment of the churches, the Catholic Church among them, could not have been imagined when they each entered into the ecumenical movement, came out of their isolation into dialogue with other Christians, and began the internal renewal called for by faithfulness to Christ's call to reconciliation. In this section the developments between 1964 and 1993, when the Pontifical Council for Promoting Christian Unity published the *Directory for the Application of Principles and Norms on Ecumenism,* will be recounted. *The Directory* became possible after the new *Codes of Canon Law* published for the Western and Eastern churches in 1983 and 1991 respectively.

The development of relations among the churches and in Catholic theology during this same period will be recounted in later chapters. This is an exciting and dramatic story, hardly imaginable during the months of debate surrounding the drafting of the Decree by the Council Fathers. In this section documents from the Secretariat, from the bishops' synods, and several apostolic letters will be surveyed briefly. This overview will be useful as a guide to the texts themselves, or as an introduction to the 1993 *Directory* which synthesizes them.

Under the leadership of the Secretariat for Promoting Christian Unity the Holy See produced a series of important documents, the core of which are directories. In 1967, Pope Paul VI approved the publication of the *Directory Concerning Ecumenical Matters: Part One.* The document advocated: (1) the establishment of local and national ecumenical commissions; (2) the validity of baptism conferred by other churches and ecclesial communities; (3) the fostering of spiritual ecumenism in the Catholic Church; and (4) sharing in prayer, worship, and resources with other Christians. In 1970, *Part Two* of the *Directory* was published, under the title *Ecumenism in Higher Education*. It dealt with the application of ecumenism to higher education and especially to theological faculties and college education.

Reflections and Suggestions Concerning Ecumenical Dialogue was published by the Secretariat in 1970. As a supplement to the Directories, this document discussed the nature, aim, bases, conditions, methods, subjects, and forms of dialogue. It enumerates four objectives of dialogue: (1) Christians enter more deeply into the mystery of Christ and the Church and are enabled to discern commonalities in their differing ways of translating their approach to the revealed mystery into thought, life, and witness. (2) Christians learn to give a united witness to the world in regard to their common faith. (3) The churches learn together the response which the Spirit urges of them in facing the needs of the world, particularly in areas where the Gospel has not been preached. (4) In their internal lives many Christian communities face the same questions and each may be helped by joint approach to these concerns under the guidance of the Holy Spirit. Chapter six on dialogue and chapter seven on the World Council will provide more discussion of these themes.

Another supplement to the *Directories* was published in 1975, *Ecumenical Collaboration at the Regional, National and Local Levels*. This document offers a presentation of the local church (diocese) in the context of *koinonia* and proceeds to enumerate how it can engage in various forms of collaboration with other Christians, for example, sharing in prayer and worship; common biblical study and teaching; joint pastoral care; buildings; collaboration in education and meeting health care, social, and emergency needs; use of communication media; and participation in councils of churches. *Koinonia*, the sharing of the Christian life, its faith, worship, charity, and mission, understood as a reflection of the Trinitarian sharing of the three divine persons, will be discussed more fully in chapter three.

During these early days of ecumenical development, several documents were produced to clarify a Catholic position on sacramental sharing, a phenomenon hardly foreseen by the Fathers of

Vatican II. Catholics have always recognized Orthodox priests and sacramental understanding from a theological point of view, and therefore the Council in the Decree on the Catholic Eastern Churches opened limited sacramental sharing. The Council decided, without Orthodox concurrence, that the Eucharist, anointing, and reconciliation could be shared with the Orthodox in particular circumstances. The Orthodox not only did not reciprocate but were offended by the unilateral Catholic action.

On the other hand, Reformation-era polemic on Catholic sacramental practice would lead one to expect that sacramental sharing would not have been desired by Protestants. In fact, the opposite was the case. Liturgical reforms, both within the Catholic Church and among some of the churches of the Reformation, began to make eucharistic theology and practice much less exclusive than at the time of the divisions. The Wesleyan and Disciples traditions, in fact, had come to a practice of open communion, and other classical Protestant churches had arrived at a more open position in this regard. The Catholic Church had to be clear that its position was distinct from both the absolute prohibition of the Orthodox on the one hand, and from the open table of some Protestants on the other. Later chapters will deal with the present position of the churches on sacramental sharing.

In 1968 the Secretariat published its *Notes on the Application of the Directory*, in 1970 *The Declaration on the Position of the Catholic Church on the Eucharist in Common by Christians of Different Confessions* and, in 1972, *On Admitting Other Christians to Eucharistic Communion in the Catholic Church.* Already different experiences and needs were emerging in different episcopal conferences and dioceses, so that in 1973 a *Note Interpreting the "Instruction on Admitting Other Christians to Eucharistic Communion in the Catholic Church Under Certain Circumstances"* was published.

In these statements openness toward the East is clear. Criteria are outlined for the reception, under certain circumstances and with the oversight of the local Catholic bishop, of Protestants and Anglicans to Catholic Eucharist, penance, and anointing. There is a recognition that differences over the authority of the ordained ministry in Reformation Churches makes this sacramental sharing nonreciprocal. Western churches, such as the Old Catholic and the Polish National Catholic churches, have been judged to be in the same situation as the Orthodox churches relative to sacramental sharing.

The 1967 Synod of Bishops considered interchurch families, and several texts on interchurch families emerged in the same period:

- Congregation of the Doctrine of the Faith, *Instruction on Mixed Marriages,* 1966
- Congregation for the Eastern Churches, *Marriage Between Roman Catholics and Orthodox,* 1967
- Paul VI's apostolic letter, *Matrimonia Mixta,* 1970

The last of these contained a less admonitory tone than prior magisterial documents and presented a more positive approach to the subject. Nonetheless, marriages of *mixed religion,* as interchurch families were called, were still regarded as fundamentally difficult unions. A positive evaluation of such unions would have to await the apostolic exhortation of John Paul II, *Familiaris Consortio,* in 1980.

A number of documents emphasize common witness. In the apostolic exhortation *Evangelii Nuntiandi,* 1975, Paul VI proclaimed dialogue as the essential form of evangelization and related it to human advancement so that the anthropological good of the person evangelized is of primary importance. He further related evangelization to charity, justice, and peace, thus recalling the intrinsic relationship of creation to redemption. In this document we begin to see the link between ecumenism and the New Evangelization. In conjunction with *Evangelii Nuntiandi,* the apostolic exhortation *Catechesi Tradendae* of 1979 continues to interpret the conciliar Decree on Mission in terms of a communion of culturally diverse particular churches that enrich one another and give new expression to the Gospel through "inculturation."

Special guidelines were issued by the Secretariat on translating the Bible, which were revised in 1989, and on ecumenical and interreligious cooperation in communications, also in 1989. In education, the apostolic constitutions *Sapientia Christiana* (1979) and *Ex Corde Ecclesiae* (1990) addressed higher education. Seminary education was addressed in a new edition of the *Ratio*

Fundamentalis Institutionis Sacerdotalis, issued by the Congregation for Catholic Education in 1985.

Of particular significance are the extraordinary Synod (1985), the *Catechism of the Catholic Church* (1992), *The General Catechetical Directory* (1997) and the promulgations of the *Codes of Canon Law* for the Western (1983) and the Eastern (1990) churches. They show a remarkable level of reception, not only of the ecumenical intent of the conciliar decrees, but of the ecumenical developments in the decades following the Council. The Eastern *Code* in particular demonstrates the developments in Catholic ecclesiology and the gradual return to the earlier, common tradition of the East.

B. The *Directory for the Application of Principles and Norms on Ecumenism* (1993)

In 1985, Pope John Paul II, in an address to the Roman Curia on the Feast of Sts. Peter and Paul, expressed the desire for a new ecumenical *Directory* to promote the ecumenical movement and to update its development. The authors of the *Directory* were particularly conscious that it would have to take into account the diversity of the local churches in the Catholic *koinonia* as well as the churches and ecclesial communities in dialogue with the Catholic church.

Such a document would require the qualities of sobriety, clarity, restraint, and exactness. Furthermore, the authors of the *Directory* were also very conscious of the widespread "reception" of ecumenism that had taken place in the past thirty years, particularly in the context of ecumenical dialogues.

During the 1993 Week of Prayer for Christian unity, Pope John Paul II expressed his commitment in regard to the forthcoming *Directory* thus:

> With all my heart I hope that, when it is published, the *Directory* will strengthen the spirit of fraternal love and mutual respect among Christians on the arduous but exhilarating path which they are called to travel together towards full communion in truth and charity (IS no. 85 [1994], 5).

On March 25, 1993, Pope John Paul II approved and ordered the publication of the *Directory,* and it was published the following June 8 by the Pontifical Council. The outline of the *Directory* is as follows:

PREFACE (1–8)
  Reasons for this Revision (2–3)
  To Whom Is the Directory Addressed? (4–5)
  Aims of the Directory (6)
  Outline of the Directory (7)
  I. THE SEARCH FOR CHRISTIAN UNITY (9–36)
    The Church and Its Unity in the Plan of God (11–12)
    The Church as Communion (13–17)
    Divisions Among Christians and the Reestablishing of Unity (18–21)
    Ecumenism in the Life of Christians (22–25)
    The Different Levels of Ecumenical Activity (26–29)
    Complexity and Diversity of the Ecumenical Situation (30–34)
    Sects and New Religious Movements (35–36)
  II. THE ORGANIZATION IN THE CATHOLIC CHURCH OF THE SERVICE OF CHRISTIAN UNITY (37–54)
    Introduction (37–40)
    The Diocesan Ecumenical Officer (41)
    The Diocesan Ecumenical Commission or Secretariat (42–45)
    The Ecumenical Commission of Eastern Synods and Episcopal Conferences (46–47)
    Ecumenical Structures Within Other Ecclesial Contexts (48–49)
    Institutes of Consecrated Life and Societies of Apostolic Life (50–51)
    Organizations of Faithful (52)
    The Pontifical Council for Promoting Christian Unity (53–54)
  III. ECUMENICAL FORMATION IN THE CATHOLIC CHURCH (55–91)
    The Necessity and Purpose of Ecumenical Formation (55)

C. Reflections on the *Directory*

In contrast to the original *Directories,* the 1993 *Directory* was
not composed in an atmosphere of excitement and enthusiasm.
The ecclesiology of *koinonia* was central at the Council, in subsequent Catholic development, and in most of the ecumenical dialogues. Therefore the *Directory* includes a theological section on
communion and its implications for ecumenism. It could take for
granted, however, considerations which the pioneering directories had to address as they moved into uncharted waters. Many elements had developed in the thirty years since the Council. This

document gives a coherent view of the institutional and theological commitment of the Church to the ecumenical movement.

There is a notable insistence upon spiritual formation at all levels (55–91). Ecumenical formation is integrated into spiritual and doctrinal formation, and the *Directory* summons the entire Catholic Church—seminarians, priests, religious, students, and laity—to undertake this mission. The hearing and study of the Word of God is prominently accented (59).

In the ecumenical process, priority is given to conversion of heart, spiritual life, and renewal (63). The hierarchy of truths should be respected (75). The urgency of studying social and ethical questions in common is accentuated, particularly in light of the ethical dilemmas that have arisen from the growing permissiveness of society in regard to sexual morality and developments in the biological sciences and medicine (211–16).

Prayer in common and sharing in nonsacramental worship are highly recommended (102–107). Ties between the search for Christian unity and liturgy are clearly indicated (108–60). A degree of sacramental sharing in baptism and marriage is acknowledged (92–100, 143–60). Some participation in the Eucharist, penance, and anointing of the sick is permitted and even commended. A distinction is made between Eastern churches (122–28) and other churches (129–34).

There is a new interest in approaching dialogue with world religions ecumenically (210). There is a concern in regard to sects and new religious movements (35–36). As will be discussed below, these concerns were unforeseen in the Council and are perceived in different ways in different cultural contexts.

Commitment to ecumenical dialogue as principle and motivation is frequently evoked by the magisterium of the Catholic Church, and its commitment to the ecumenical process is irreversible. The *Directory* also commends the spiritual values and resources present in other Christian traditions as "sources of spiritual life...which belong to the one church of Christ." In addition to the Scriptures and the sacraments, the gifts of the Spirit are found "in the mystical tradition of the Christian East and the spiritual treasures of the monastic life, in the worship and piety of Anglicans, in the evangelical prayer and the diverse forms of

Protestant spirituality." It urges "practical knowledge of other traditions of spirituality" (63).

On the Threshold of the Third Millennium, 1994

In his apostolic letter announcing the Great Jubilee in the year 2000, Pope John Paul II situates the anniversary of the Incarnation in the context of history, which possesses a beginning, middle, and end. It is *kairos,* the "fullness of time," in the context of *kronos,* ongoing time. He proceeds to state how preparation for the jubilee has become a hermeneutical key to his pontificate. Pope John Paul II summons the community to repentance, and among the subjects for repentance in preparation for the jubilee the sin of disunity looms large.

In this Advent of preparation, the Pope advocates an examination of conscience. The entire Church should make a profound act of repentance and conversion in regard to the sins of disunity. This examination of conscience should prompt earnest prayers for a speedy end to disunion.

In examining the role of martyrs as witnesses to Christ and martyrologies as the common heritage of Catholics, Orthodox, Anglicans, and Protestants, Pope John Paul II emphasizes that the communion of saints is a powerful impetus to ecumenism.

Each of the years: 1997 focusing on Christ, 1998 focusing on the Spirit, and 1999 focusing on the Father, possesses its special ecumenical or interreligious component. Finally, the pope proposes a meeting of all Christians in the jubilee year, 2000:

> The ecumenical and universal character of the Sacred Jubilee can be fittingly reflected by a meeting of all Christians. This would be an event of great significance, and so, in order to avoid misunderstandings, it should be properly presented and carefully prepared, in an attitude of fraternal cooperation with Christians of other denominations and traditions, as well as of grateful openness to those religions whose representatives might wish to acknowledge the joy shared by all the disciples of Christ. (55)

The tradition of the Roman jubilee year was begun by Boniface VIII in 1300 in an attempt to focus European attention on

Rome, the centrality of the papal office, indulgences, and pilgrimage. With John Paul's emphasis on the biblical jubilee of Leviticus and Deuteronomy and its social justice themes, and on the role of jubilee preparation and celebration in restoring the unity among the churches, he has radically redirected the attention of the Church toward Christ and the unity for which he prayed.

Orientale Lumen, Light from the East, 1995

In Pope John Paul's apostolic letter he offers a glowing tribute to the Eastern Churches, both Catholic and Orthodox, and extols their liturgies and Eucharistic celebrations, devotion to the Trinity, affirmation of the "divinization" of humankind in grace-filled life, Mariology, sense of tradition, monasticism, and Gospel inculturation. He wishes to advance from knowledge to encounter and encourages the churches to get to know one another, to work together, and to experience unity in a greater measure on the common path to the encounter with the Light from the East.

Ut Unum Sint, 1995

In the twelfth encyclical of his prolific pontificate, *Ut Unum Sint,* Pope John Paul has given vigor and specificity to the ecumenical commitment, to complement the more institutional tone of the *Directory.* Here we briefly outline the letter and provide a few comments.

INTRODUCTION (1–4)
  I. THE CATHOLIC CHURCH'S COMMITMENT TO
     ECUMENISM (5–40)
     God's Plan and Communion (5–6)
     Ways of Ecumenism: Way of the Church (7–14)
     Renewal and Conversion (15–17)
     Fundamental Importance of Doctrine (18–20)
     Primacy of Prayer (21–27)
     Ecumenical Dialogue (28–30)
     Local Structures of Dialogue (31–32)
     Dialogue as an Examination of Conscience (33–35)

The encyclical reaffirms the irrevocable commitment of the
Catholic Church to the cause of ecumenism. Christian unity "is
not just some sort of 'appendix' which is added to the Church's
traditional activity. Rather, ecumenism is an organic part of her
life and work, and consequently must pervade all that she is and
does" (20). Unity and legitimate diversity in the Church are
affirmed. Much of the encyclical is an enthusiastic, passionate

reiteration of the commitments and convictions of the Council, of the Church's subsequent leadership, and of the relations and dialogues developed since then, especially those which the Holy Father has experienced through his own visits and personal encounters.

The real but imperfect communion that already exists between the Catholic Church and other churches and ecclesial communities itself leads toward ecumenical dialogue, a privileged medium of furthering communion (32).

Each partner must examine its conscience not only in regard to personal sins but also in reference to social sin. The encyclical recognizes the infidelity of Catholics in the integral assimilation of the apostolic witness. Ecumenical dialogue thus becomes a "dialogue of conversion" in the interior dimension of conscience and in the pursuit of truth. The ministry of the Church "is completely at the service of God's merciful plan" (92) of unity, which the entirety of the Church is to receive:

> To believe in Christ means to desire unity; to desire unity means to desire the Church; to desire the Church means to desire the communion of grace which corresponds to the Father's plan from all eternity. Such is the meaning of Christ's prayer: "Ut unum sint." (9)

John Paul lauds the World Council of Churches (43) and its Faith and Order Commission (17) for their efforts in regard to ecumenism. He holds up in approval fraternal charity in relations of Christians to one another where formerly suspicion and enmity marred these relationships (42). This solidarity has also spread to the service of humanity in common efforts for peace and justice (43), to the study of the Word of God (44), liturgy (45), and in some cases sacramental sharing, all of which accords with the present real but imperfect communion of the churches.

> In this context, it is a source of joy to note that Catholic ministers are able in certain cases, to administer the sacraments of the Eucharist, Penance and Anointing of the Sick to Christians who are not in full communion with the Catholic Church but who greatly desire to receive these sacraments, freely request them and manifest the faith which the

Catholic Church professes with regard to these sacraments. Conversely in specific cases and in particular circumstances, Catholics too can request these same sacraments from ministers of Churches in which these sacraments are valid. The conditions for such reciprocal reception have been laid down in specific norms; for the sake of the furthering ecumenism these norms must be respected. (46)

Ecumenism Remains the Gift of the Spirit

The Holy Father recalls the specific agenda before the churches in their theological dialogue: (1) Scripture and Tradition, (2) the Eucharist, (3) Ordination, (4) Teaching office including the papacy, and (5) Mary (79). As will be noted below, tremendous progress has been made on this precise agenda. Later in the encyclical he opens his own papal office for renewal and reform in dialogue with other Christians, that it may provide a better service to the unity of the Church, even before full theological agreement is reached (95–97).

The richness of the gifts received from one another, the importance of the healing of memories and of developing common appreciation of our martyrs, the joy in the journey toward full visible unity, and the importance of the reception of the results of the progress made so far in the dialogues are all restated with vigor, with confidence in the Holy Spirit, and with solid determination to follow the course opened up by the Council.

Conclusion

As one surveys the doctrinal development that has occurred in the Catholic Church in regard to ecumenism, one can only marvel at the magnitude of this conversion. Hardly more than a generation ago the model of "return" reigned in Catholic ecclesiology, while at present the model of *koinonia* is taking hold, so that separated Churches and ecclesial communities are no longer regarded as separated brethren according to Pope John Paul, but as fellow "Christians of other communities" (42).

The present quest of the ecumenical movement seeks to

attain the full communion of the separated churches and ecclesial communities. The documents of the magisterium, examined in this chapter, show clearly that the ecclesiology of the Second Vatican Council has been "received" and is being implemented at the highest levels of authority in the Catholic Church.

Study Questions

1. Describe the major shifts in the Catholic understanding of the Church that occurred at the Second Vatican Council.

2. What are the principles and priorities enunciated by the Decree on Ecumenism that govern the Catholic approach to ecumenism?

3. Delineate the developments of the thirty years since the Council that have been most influential in Catholic ecumenism.

4. What are the four major ecumenical documents that emerged from the Catholic Church in the 1990s and what is the significance of each?

5. What are the key provisions of the 1993 *Directory for the Application of Principles and Norms on Ecumenism* and where do they challenge ecumenical life in the U.S.? What are the provisions for sacramental sharing? For interchurch marriage? How have these developed since the Council?

6. In your experience, what has been the most dramatic shift in the ecumenical posture of the Catholic Church since the Council? What exhortations does Pope John Paul place before the churches in *On the Threshold of the Third Millennium*?

7. What elements of the Catholic Church teaching on ecumenism are most challenging for its people today? What are those which are noted in the encyclical *Ut Unum Sint*?

8. What understanding of dialogue does the Catholic Church bring to ecumenical conversation?

Selected Readings

Alberigo, Giuseppe, and Joseph Komonchak, eds. *The History of Vatican II, Volume I: Announcing and Preparing Vatican Council II*. Maryknoll: Orbis Books, 1995.

Dulles, Avery. "John Paul II and the Advent of the New Millennium." *America* (December 9, 1995): 9–15.

Hotchkin, John. "The Wonderful, Sometimes Curious Progress of Ecumenism." *Origins* 24:3 (June 2, 1994): 43–48.

John Paul II. Homily for the Close of the Week of Prayer (January 25, 1993). Pontifical Council for Promoting Christian Unity, *Information Service*, no. 85 (1994): 3–5.

——. Apostolic Letter, *Tertio Millennio Adveniente* (November 10, 1994). *Origins* 24:24 (November 24, 1994): 404–16.

——. Apostolic Letter, *Orientale Lumen* (May 2, 1995). *Origins* 25:1 (May 18, 1995): 1–13.

——. Encyclical Letter, *Ut Unum Sint* (May 25, 1995). *Origins* 25:4 (June 8, 1995): 49–72.

Pontifical Council for Promoting Christian Unity. *Directory for the Application of Principles and Norms on Ecumenism* (March 25, 1993). *Origins* 23:9 (July 29, 1993): 131–60.

Rusch, William G., ed. *A Commentary on "The Ecumenical Vision of the ELCA."* Minneapolis: Augsburg Press, 1990.

Stransky, Thomas F., and John B. Sheerin, eds. *Doing The Truth In Charity: Statements of Pope Paul VI, Popes John Paul I, John Paul II and the Secretariat for Promoting Christian Unity, 1964–1980. Ecumenical Documents I.* New York/Mahwah: Paulist Press; 1982.

Tillard, Jean-Marie R. "The Quest for Truth and Unity: The Road from Vatican II." *Catholic International* 7, no. 2 (February 1996): 76–80.

Unitatis Redintegratio (November 21, 1964). In Thomas F. Stransky and John B. Sheerin, eds., *Doing The Truth In Charity. Ecumenical Documents I.* New York/Mahwah: Paulist Press, 1982, pp. 18–33.

Vorgrimler, Herbert, ed. *Commentary on the Documents of Vatican II.* Vol. II. New York: Herder and Herder, 1968.

Wright, J. Robert, ed. *A Communion of Communions: One Eucharistic Fellowship: The Detroit Report and Papers of the Triennial Ecumenical Study of the Epsicopal Church, 1976–1979.* New York: Seabury Press, 1979.

3

The Theology of Ecumenism

That this evening may be holy, good and peaceful:
We pray to you, O Lord.

That your holy angels may lead us in the paths of peace and goodwill:
We pray to you, O Lord.

That we may be pardoned and forgiven our sins and offenses:
We pray to you, O Lord.

That there may be peace in your Church and for the whole world:
We pray to you, O Lord.

That we may be bound together by your Holy Spirit, in communion
with all your saints, entrusting one another and all our life to Christ:
We pray to you, O Lord.

Orthodox Litany for the Evening

Introduction

Commitment to the unity of the Church comes from the very center of Christian identity, as Pope John Paul II reminds us. Central to the ecumenical movement and to Christian faithfulness to God's will is a firm grounding in the biblical doctrine of the Church and the understanding of Church in the Christian tradition. In this chapter the doctrine of the Church, especially the ecclesiology of the Catholic Church, will be explored as the basis for ecumenical engagement.

The chapter will not attempt to provide a fully elaborated ecclesiology either from the Catholic perspective or from ecumenical perspectives. It will presume that the historical, biblical, and systematic foundations will be explored in other contexts. For those exploring Catholic ecclesiology in more depth, study of the conciliar constitutions and declarations on the Church, the Church in the modern world, bishops, priests, and laity will be of particular importance. For example, the differences between the theology of ministry of some of the Reformation churches and the Catholic Church was intensified by the decision of the Council to recognize a deeper distinction between the priest and the bishop.

However, here the theology of the Church will be surveyed: (1) as it serves as the basis for Catholic self-understanding; (2) as it is emerging in the ecumenical dialogues, especially the World Council of Churches' Canberra statement (1991); and (3) as it provides Catholic ecumenical foundations.

In the period prior to the Second Vatican Council the Catholic Church stood in a polemic inherited from the period of the Counter Reformation, when the emphasis in ecclesiology was on the Church as a "perfect society." The First Vatican Council (1870) began to clarify the limits of papal authority in the context of an understanding of the Church, though its work was disrupted by Italian politics. In understandings of the Church characteristic of the pre-Vatican II period the institutional elements tended to be more emphasized than were the spiritual, sacramental, and mystical dimensions.

The nineteenth-century influences of the Tübingen school, biblical and liturgical scholarship, and of Cardinal John Henry Newman introduced a more organic and developmental ecclesiology into Catholic thinking. Likewise, Protestant historical, biblical, and liturgical studies, bringing attention to the historical and visible components of Church, began to act as a balance to the strong emphasis on spiritual ecclesiology characteristic of Protestant thought. Pius XII's *Divino Afflante Spiritu* (1943) opened the way for critical biblical scholarship. *Mystici Corporis* (1943), while reaffirming Catholic exclusivism, began to open the way toward a more organic and biblical ecclesiology, an opening reinforced by the Vatican's cautious engagement in liturgical renewal and social teaching.

Images of the Church and *Koinonia*

There are many images of the Christian community in the Scriptures or that may be adduced from Scripture: the pilgrim people of God, the Body of Christ, the Kingdom of God, the community of disciples, the missionary band of apostles of the Word, the sacrament (mystery) or instrumental sign of unity with God, the covenant community as champion of justice in service to the world. All of these images are utilized to clarify the human and divine character of the Church within the ecumenical movement.

However, both the World Council, founded in 1948 as a *fellowship (koinonia)* of churches, and the Catholic Church since the Second Vatican Council, employ *koinonia* (communion, fellowship) as focus of theological reflection about the Church:

> The purpose of God according to holy scripture is to gather the whole of creation under the Lordship of Christ Jesus in whom, by the power of the Holy Spirit, all are brought into communion with God (Eph. 1). The church is the foretaste of this communion with God and with one another. The grace of our Lord Jesus Christ, the love of God, and the communion of the Holy Spirit enable the one church to live as sign of the reign of God and servant of reconciliation with God, promised and provided for the whole creation. The purpose of the church is to unite people with Christ in the power of the Spirit, to manifest communion in prayer and action and thus to point to the fullness of communion with God, humanity and the whole creation in the glory of the kingdom. (WCC, Canberra, 1.1)

Koinonia theology of the Church provides the Catholic Church foundation for its ecumenical commitment and for developing the pastoral and theological steps toward unity:

> Thus united in the threefold bond of faith, sacramental life and hierarchical ministry, the whole People of God comes to be what the tradition of faith from the New Testament onwards has always called koinonia/communion. This is a key concept which inspired the ecclesiology of the Second Vatican Council, and to which recent teaching of the magisterium has given great importance.

> The communion in which Christians believe and for which they hope is, in its deepest reality, their unity with the Father through Christ in the Spirit. Since Pentecost, it has been given and received in the Church, the communion of saints.

It is accomplished fully in the glory of heaven, but is already realized in the Church on earth as it journeys towards that fullness. Those who live united in faith, hope and love, in mutual service, in common teaching and sacraments, under the guidance of their pastors are part of that communion which constitutes the Church of God. This communion is realized concretely in the particular Churches, each of which is gathered together around its Bishop. In each of these "the one, holy, catholic and apostolic Church of Christ is truly present and alive." This communion is, by its very nature, universal. (*Directory*, 12, 13)

The Catholic profession of *koinonia* ecclesiology, of course, is more detailed and specific than the World Council statement, as would be that of any other church. A common agreement on the goal of theological dialogue and the nature of full communion is a necessary prelude to achieving it. However, the Catholic affirmation that we are in real, if imperfect, *koinonia* with all who confess Jesus Christ and are baptized means that we already stand within communion in Christ. This communion we perfect by theological dialogue and deeper spiritual communion with churches from whom we are separated, and by renewal of our own practice and understanding of the communion that Christ desires for the Church.

The theology of *koinonia* or communion emphasizes both the divine and human, the vertical and horizontal dimension of the Church, as Cardinal Joseph Ratzinger notes in *Called to Communion* (76):

The Church is communion; she is the communion of the Word and the Body of Christ and is thus communion among men, who by means of this communion that brings them together from above and from within are made one people, indeed, one Body.

Catholic Theological Foundation

The theology of ecumenism of Vatican II is grounded in the ecclesiology of the Council articulated primarily in the

Constitution on the Church and the Decree on Ecumenism *(Lumen Gentium* and *Unitatis Redintegratio),* but was further expressed in The Church in the Modern World *(Gaudium et Spes),* and in the decrees and declarations on Bishops, Priests, the Laity, Mission, and Religious Liberty *(Christus Dominus; Presbyterorum Ordinis; Apostolicam Actuositatem; Ad Gentes; Dignitatis Humanae).* As noted in the previous chapter, this theology is focused and summarized in the *Directory for the Application of Principles and Norms on Ecumenism* (1993).

Prior to the dogmatic constitution, *Pastor Aeternus* (1870) of Vatican I, no church council had attempted to explain the nature and structure of the Catholic Church. The study of contemporary Catholic theology of the Church will be helped by studying the history that contributed to the development promulgated in 1964.

The Ecclesiology of *Koinonia* of Vatican II

The local church, that is, the local bishop surrounded by presbytery, deacons, and laity, is a focal point of the ecclesiology of communion. The Eucharist, especially the Eucharist at which the bishop personally presides, expresses the *koinonia* of the local church and of all the local churches in relationship to one another in both vertical and horizontal dimensions.

A. Vertical Communion with God in the Holy Spirit

The Decree on Ecumenism situates the Church in the mystery of the Trinitarian communion of God and of the "mission" of the Son to the world, to "draw all things" to God. The communion of the faithful, in faith, hope, and charity, with the Body of Christ is a *koinonia* with the risen humanity of the Lord Jesus. In Jesus, God communes with humankind in his own body. By virtue of the resurrection, Jesus joins the *koinonia* of the incarnation to the *koinonia* of glorification.

Participating in this *koinonia* in baptism, oriented toward the Eucharist, the human person enters into communion with

God in the one Body of Christ, and partakes in the *mystery* of God's *koinonia* with humankind and in the divine mission. Such a *koinonia* unites each in solidarity with the other members of the Body of Christ.

Since the Eucharistic mystery signifies *koinonia* with both the glorified and the incarnate Christ, it signifies likewise communion with God and communion with brothers and sisters in the faith. The Church is the community of salvation, a *koinonia* of salvation.

The Church, as the vehicle of communion with God, should be characterized by theological holiness, that is, a sharing in God's glory, to which the contemplative life testifies in a special manner and family life and active apostolates testify in other ways.

The Church can be understood as a sacrament, a sacrament in which every member, in virtue of the charisms received from the Spirit, is fully responsible in cooperation with all the other members, to build up the Body of Christ. The right and obligation on the part of all the faithful derives from the very essence of *koinonia* celebrated in baptism.

Baptism, then, links all Christians to Christ and one another in a fundamental sacramental communion. The institutional elements of the Catholic Church and the ordering of bishops, presbyters, and deacons, including the bishop of Rome as servant of unity within the college of bishops, serve and promote *koinonia* among Catholics in the first place, and among all the baptized. The differentiated character of Christian *koinonia* is what Catholics mean by *hierarchical communion.*

B. The Horizontal Communion of Believers Among Themselves

The Church, built up by the Eucharist, is a *koinonia* of brothers and sisters, which exists on three levels:

1. A *koinonia* of grace animated as faith and charity participates in the mission of God's universal care for humankind. This aspect of *koinonia* is more fully realized in the Church's Eucharistic action, where a *koinonia* of charisms reconciles races, sexes, cultures, and human histories in a *koinonia* of hope.

2. The second level of *koinonia* concerns the bonds which

unite Christians with the apostolic community, that is, the apostolicity of the local church. Apostolicity consists in continuity, within the context of the faith, with the apostles and the ministry derived from them. Each ecclesial community must be founded upon Scripture. Each local community must not only adhere to tradition, but also participate in the communion of all generations and environments in the one faith. Apostolicity secures the "catholic" witness of the apostolic faith in the one Body of Christ through the witness of the Holy Spirit in all places, times, conditions of history, geography, and culture. The *koinonia* of reconciliation integrates the dispersed and separated factions of life in a universal communion.

3. To ensure and guarantee the preceding levels of *koinonia,* the Spirit provides the charism of *episcopé* and ministry, constituted in the sacrament of Orders, in the service of *koinonia.*

The concept of *koinonia,* therefore, has many dimensions. Essentially it refers to the plan of God to reconcile all people and earthly reality in the divine communion of Trinitarian life.

The Constitution on the Church relates the Church to the divine design of the triune God. It explains this *koinonia* in terms of mystery and sacrament; grace and eschatology; people of God and pilgrim people. It is not reduced to human social, political or material concepts such as "perfect society." This allows a more transcendent perception of the Church as a *koinonia* of brothers and sisters, equal in regard to God's grace, but differentiated in a variety of roles where the charisms of teaching, sanctifying, and pastoring that belong to all are exercised in a special manner for the good of all. This theology was reaffirmed in the extraordinary Roman Synod of Bishops (1985), has been fruitful in the bilateral and World Council dialogues, and provides the basis for ecumenical practice outlined in the *Directory.*

C. Collegiality and the Ecumenical Project of the Church

Collegiality is a fundamental principle of *koinonia* in the Council's teaching. Since the Council the theological articulation of collegiality represents one of the major accomplishments of *koinonia* ecclesiology.

The communion of the bishops throughout the world, with the pope as center of the college, is perceived in sacramental terms. The local (or particular) church, where the mystery of sacramental grace becomes operative, the *koinonia* of the local bishop and the Eucharistic community, represents sacramental *koinonia* in an explicit manner.

The *koinonia* of the local Church represents the mystery of sacramental grace. However, it does not exhaust the mystery in its plenitude. The relationship of the local Church to the universal Catholic Church occurs in the context of a communion of communions, of which the pope as the servant of the servants of God, acts as the sacramental representative of the entire communion in relation to one another and to the Church of Rome. The proper balance between the local and universal is under discussion within the Catholic Church in the context of assessing the future role of episcopal conferences and synods of bishops, and in the ecumenical dialogues in which the Catholic Church is involved.

The oversight *(episcopé)* of the bishop is a service to the community. In this community the *episcopé* of bishop, priest, and deacon serve the communion of all. The bishop presides within the community, not in sociological terms, but as the one who is the sign (sacrament, ikon) of Christ, and who effects the unity of the Body of Christ in and on behalf of the community, whereby the mystery/sacrament is realized in the office of pastor, teacher, and sanctifier. As a member of the college, each bishop shares in the universal responsibility for evangelization and unity.

The office and task of the bishop of Rome belongs to his position in relationship to the "college" of bishops. It is not all-encompassing. Neither is it the source of the jurisdiction of the "college," which is constituted by the sacramentality of episcopacy in the local church. It exists as a power and charism of the bishop of Rome in the service of unity and communion of all the churches, and as a link to the apostolic community. Hence, if the bishop of Rome were to speak on behalf of all his brother bishops, his proclamation must be in accord with the faith of his brothers, even if they have not been consulted methodically. The obedience that the faithful owe to the pope does not undercut the authority of the other bishops, since their voices come to expression in the formal proclamations of the Holy Father.

The primacy of the bishop of Rome within the "college" of bishops is a primacy of service to the others. The bishops as a body are not the delegates of the pope, but are joined in this common ministry, to secure *koinonia* among themselves on behalf of the entire Church. It is in this context that the charisms of primacy and infallibility are to be understood. Indeed, primacy must be carefully differentiated, in terms of the bishop of Rome's mulitple roles as bishop of the Apostolic See, patriarch of the West, and as bearer of primacy among the patriarchs of East and West within the patriarchical college—a primacy that has yet to be crystallized in the ecumenical dialogue.

From the Catholic point of view bishops and the pope among them are essential to the church. They exist by divine right and form one communion and are referred to by the title "hierarchy." One must be careful, in English, to note that "hierarchy" does not mean structures of domination or control, but denotes rather a "sacred order" among the people of God. In Christian communities without bishops, where there are constitutional checks and balances, or full participation of all the baptized in decision making, this sense of "sacred order," of "hierarchy" in the biblical sense, and of sacred responsibilities of oversight, *episcopé,* can be as vivid and as profoundly respected as in churches with bishops.

Pope John Paul has emphasized the importance of the role of the papal office in promoting the unity of the churches within the *koinonia* of the still divided Christian community. He opens the exercise of his ministry to reform, even before full doctrinal agreement is reached:

> that we may seek—together, of course—the forms in which this ministry [primacy] may accomplish a service of love recognized by all concerned....This is an immense task, which we cannot refuse and which I cannot carry out by myself. Could not the real but imperfect communion existing between us persuade church leaders and their theologians to engage with me in a patient and fraternal dialogue on this subject, a dialogue in which, leaving useless controversies behind, we could listen to one another, keeping before us only the will of Christ for his Church? (UUS, 95, 96)

Koinonia in Ecumenical Understanding

The churches, together in their pilgrimage toward full visible unity, have articulated in church union proposals, bilateral dialogues, and Faith and Order studies levels of agreement on the biblical doctrine of the Church and its development in the Christian tradition unimaginable when the ecumenical movement began in the nineteenth century. A common Biblical, liturgical, and historical renaissance provided a scholarly base for an emerging convergence in understanding the Church as communion, with elements that can be mutually identified as necessary for a united Church. The process of research and recognition of the common faith and the reception of proposals for stages toward unity move forward gradually in the Spirit's time. From early in the century, with the 1920 encyclical of the Ecumenical Patriarch, *koinonia* language from the Scripture and patristic sources has been used in ecumenical ecclesiological discussions. It has gained richness and precision in common statements of the churches over the intervening years of research and dialogue.

In a series of World Council texts, to be discussed in more detail in chapter seven, a comprehensive and concise articulation of ecclesiological development takes place, beginning with Toronto (1950), highlighted in New Delhi (1961), focused on the united Church as a Conciliar Fellowship (Communion/*Koinonia*) in Nairobi (1975), and most recently explicated in Canberra (1991). The Canberra text, *The Unity of the Church as Koinonia: Gift and Calling,* states:

> The calling of the church is to proclaim reconciliation and provide healing, to overcome divisions based on race, gender, age, culture, color, and to bring all people into communion with God. Because of sin and the misunderstanding of the diverse gifts of the Spirit, the churches are painfully divided within themselves and among each other. The scandalous divisions damage the credibility of their witness to the world in worship and service. Moreover they contradict not only the church's witness but also its very nature.
>
> We acknowledge with gratitude to God that in the ecumenical movement the churches walk together in mutual under-

standing, theological convergence, common suffering, and common prayer, shared witness and service as they draw close to one another. This has allowed them to recognize a certain degree of communion already existing between them. This is indeed the fruit of the active presence of the Holy Spirit in the midst of all who believe in Christ Jesus and who struggle for visible unity now. Nevertheless churches have failed to draw the consequences for their life from the degree of communion they have already experienced and the agreements already achieved. They have remained satisfied to coexist in division. (Canberra, 1.2, 3)

This theological vision of the united Church has consequences for all the churches as they move toward the goal of full visible unity. Since New Delhi, in 1961, the Catholic Church has participated fully in these conversations and formulations, and since 1968 has been a member of the Faith and Order Commission, which drafted the Canberra statement on the Church.

The vision of the Church outlined here is not only a theoretical spiritual vision or a call to action in the light of the *koinonia* that already exists among us. It also enumerates those elements which must be reconciled if full visible unity is to be realized:

The unity of the church to which we are called is a *koinonia* given and expressed in the common confession of the apostolic faith; a common sacramental life entered by the one baptism and celebrated together in one eucharistic fellowship; a common life in which members and ministries are mutually recognized and reconciled; and a common mission witnessing to the gospel of God's grace to all people and serving the whole of creation. The goal of the search for full communion is realized when all the churches are able to recognize in one another the one, holy, catholic and apostolic church in its fullness. This full communion will be expressed on the local level and the universal levels through conciliar forms of life and action. In such communion churches are bound in all aspects of life together at all levels in confessing the one faith and engaging in worship and witness, deliberation and action. (Canberra 2.1)

This enumeration of the marks of a united Church in full communion is both an outline of the steps already taken among some of the churches and an agenda of what is necessary for full Orthodox, Anglican, Catholic, and Protestant visible unity.

However, such a detailed ecclesiology by no means suggests a uniformity that would mute the cultural diversity envisioned in the Scripture and realized in the multisplendored human community that God has called into the Church in space and time:

> Diversities which are rooted in theological traditions, various cultural, ethnic or historical contacts are integral to the nature of communion; yet there are limits to diversity. Diversity is illegitimate when, for instance, it makes impossible the common confession of Jesus Christ as God and Savior the same yesterday, today and forever (Heb 13:8); and salvation and final destiny of humanity as pro claimed in holy scripture and preached by the apostolic community. In communion diversities are brought together in harmony as gifts of the Holy Spirit, contribut ing to the richness and fullness of the church of God. (Canberra 2.2)

This text goes on to outline further challenges, which will be addressed in subsequent chapters. It shows how far the ecumenical pilgrimage has taken us and demonstrates the common theological basis of this ecumenical work, along with developments within the churches, including the Catholic Church. It is becoming clear in the ecumenical movement that the polarization between seeing the Church as spiritual reality and as visible reality, a polarization which has divided Christians since the Reformation, is moving toward reconciliation. However, the details of sacramental, confessional, and authority differences are only gradually coming to resolution through dialogue, reception, and action in the churches.

Ecumenical Implications of *Koinonia* for the Catholic Church

The *koinonia* of the Church is based in the Trinitarian life of God, which cannot be divided. Communion among Christians is meant to mirror the unity of the triune God, but the experience of Christians today is that of alienation. There are separations of human making between and among the present churches and ecclesial communities.

Baptism is the external sign and invisible bond of *koinonia* incorporating each into Christ, in bonds of common faith and love of God, and in a desire to remain faithful to the Gospel. Other communal bonds, of holiness, mission, ministry, and worship continue to exist, sometimes tenuously, despite doctrinal and ministerial differences. But, communion in time and space is weakened, and separate Eucharistic tables prevail. Irrespective of the causes and responsibilities involved, separation of the churches has marred the universal visible Eucharistic communion of the one Church of Christ.

The task of Christian renewal consists in the effort to become the Church which God wants, where every local church lives out the Gospel in all its fullness and seeks to attain its perfection in a *koinonia* of repentance.

Vatican II attempted to depict this diminished but still united *koinonia* of the one Church of Christ. Before the Council, the Catholic Church identified itself with the *one true* Church, with other Christians being *outside* the Church. The Fathers of the Council, relying on a theology of *koinonia*, used the term *subsists in* rather than *is* to explain the relationship of the true Church to the Catholic Church. The term occurs in both the Constitution on the Church, no. 8 and the Decree on Ecumenism, no. 4.

The intent of this understanding of the Church is to avoid the sociological identification of the Church with the present structures and formulations of the Roman Catholic institutions, or to somehow imply that the Eastern Churches not in communion with Rome were in any way "not church." The Decree on Ecumenism goes on further to note that other churches and ecclesial communities contain significant elements of the true Church, and members of these communities come to salvation through the mediation of their communities, and not in spite of them.

The Catholic Church recognizes that there may be elements of the Church better realized in communities of fellow Christians separated from it. For this reason Pope John Paul reminds

Catholics in his 1995 encyclical of the great gifts the Catholic Church has received from other communities. However, the Catholic Church affirms of its history that there is nothing lacking in the Catholic Church of what God wills for the salvation of His people in the Church. Finally, the fullness of the Church will only occur in the final day, when we are transformed in glory, when sacraments and institutional forms fall away before the fullness of communion in God's own presence.

The Fathers of the Council had affirmed the depths of the mystery of grace in regard to the Church and moved beyond a juridical and institutional ecclesiology to a profound consideration of the Christological and pneumatological dimensions of belonging to Christ. The change in language from *est* to *subsistit in* has made it more possible to express the reality of the Church as transcendent, and not reducible to the sociological form of the present institution. The introduction of the concept of "elements" of the Church has enabled an articulation of the spiritual and mystical reality of the Church present in other Christian communities.

The Council did not disavow that ecclesial "fullness" is preserved in the Church that is "governed by the successor of Peter and by the bishops in union with that successor" (UR 4). Rather, affirmation of such fullness is couched, not in institutional terms deriving from judicial and canonical communion, but in the renewed spiritual and sacramental understanding of the Council, where communion with the See of Rome is essential, but ecclesial reality is not presented as reducible to a material understanding of such communion.

"Fullness" of ecclesial reality, then, refers to the life of the Spirit, which is continually celebrated in the spiritual tradition of the Church in its many guises of prayer, liturgy, doctrine, profession, and which the Lord Jesus has bequeathed to the Church from Pentecost until the end of time. The Council did not attempt to make an inventory of such ecclesial plenitude or to comment upon the subjective fidelity of its "members." It spoke of a Church that includes sinners in its midst and needs purification. Neither is there any attempt to declare the Catholic Church self-sufficient or morally superior to other churches. The Council was satisfied to affirm that the Spirit of God resides in the Church and enables the Church to be all that it is called to be.

This theological development, representing a transition from the institutional to the mystical, theological, Christological, pneumatological, sacramental ecclesiology of Vatican II, is of the highest importance as the Catholic Church turns to consider the break with Eastern Christianity in a fresh, reconciling light. The dialogues themselves show the deeper realization of the ecclesial character of the churches of both East and West and the elements of renewal necessary for the Catholic Church to come into closer conformity to Christ's will for the Church.

Conclusion

The theology of *koinonia* is just beginning its process of reception in the churches in the fifty years since the founding of the World Council and in the Catholic Church in the thirty years since the Vatican Council. However in the Catholic Church collegiality, the increased role of the laity, and ecumenical engagement have begun to take their irrevocable place in Christian history.

Development of the role of all the baptized in the theology of communion is particularly important for several reasons: the seriousness with which the laity are engaged in the governance of some of the Reformation churches, based on the doctrine of the priesthood of all believers; the role of the laity in ecumenical leadership as the proportion of ordained decline and some lay persons have more training and calling to this ministry; and the realization of the gifts of the laity in the world as outlined by the Council.

Yet, progress in the reception of church teaching is usually a tedious and protracted affair. An example of this would be the decrees of the Council of Trent in regard to the establishment of seminaries, which reached their golden age in the middle part of this century. Perhaps the assimilation of the *koinonia* ecclesiology of Vatican II may not take so long, but it would be better to be prepared for a longer rather than a shorter journey.

However, the vision of the future is finally the work of the Spirit:

> The Holy Spirit as promoter of *koinonia* (2 Cor 13:13) gives to those who are still divided the thirst and hunger for full communion. We remain restless until we grow together according to the wish and prayer of Christ that those who believe in him may be one (John 17:21). In the process of praying, working and struggling for unity, the Holy Spirit comforts us in pain, disturbs us when we are satisfied to remain in our division, leads us to repentance, and grants us joy when our communion flourishes. (Canberra 4.1)

Study Questions

1. How do the theologies of the Church as perfect society and the Church as *koinonia* differ and what elements do they share?

2. What is the biblical basis for the doctrine of the Church enunciated in the ecumenical movement and in Catholicism since the Council? How are the vertical and horizontal dimensions of *koinonia* related in this theology?

3. What are the elements of *koinonia* ecclesiology that are central to Catholic development? What are the roles of baptism, Eucharist, and collegiality in the theology of *koinonia*? What does the Catholic Church mean when it says the "Church subsists in the Catholic Church"?

4. What are the elements necessary for full communion as articulated in the World Council statements?

5. Where do the ecclesial understanding of the Catholic Church and the proposals of the World Council overlap and complement one another?

6. What are the foundational elements of *koinonia* on which the real, if imperfect, communion among the churches is based? What is the relationship among the bishop, the local church, and the bishop of Rome in the Catholic understanding of *koinonia*?

7. Describe the pastoral implications of living in the *koinonia* that already exists as the churches move toward full communion.

8. What is the implication of a common baptism for ecumenical leadership and development of the laity in the Church? For the churches' relationships with one another?

Selected Readings

Vatican I. Dogmatic Constitution, *Pastor Aeternus.* 1870.

Pius XII. Encyclical Letter, *Mystici Corporis.* 1943.

Best, Thomas, and Gunther Gassmann, eds. *On the Way to Fuller Koinonia: Official Report of the Fifth World Conference on Faith and Order.* Geneva: World Council of Churches, 1994.

Dulles, Avery. *Models of the Church.* Reprint edition, Garden City: Doubleday, 1991.

Gerrish, B. A. *Grace and Gratitude: The Eucharistic Theology of John Calvin.* Minneapolis: Fortress Press, 1993.

Granfield, Patrick. *The Limits of the Papacy: Authority and Autonomy in the Church.* Reprint edition, New York: Crossroads; 1990.

Hastings, Adrian, ed. *Modern Catholicism: Vatican II and After.* London: SPCK/ New York: Oxford, 1990.

Henn, William, O.F.M. Cap. *One Faith: Biblical and Patristic Contributions Toward Understanding Unity in Faith.* New York/Mahwah: Paulist Press, 1995.

Kinnamon, Michael, and Brian E. Cope, eds. *The Ecumenical Movement: An Anthology of Basic Texts and Voices.* Grand Rapids: Eerdmans, 1997, pp. 79–128.

Lawler, Michael G., and Thomas J. Shanahan. *Church: A Spirited Communion.* Collegeville: Liturgical Press; 1995.

Ratzinger, Joseph. *Called To Communion: Understanding the Church Today.* Adrian Walker, trans. San Francisco: Ignatius Press, 1996.

Schatz, Klaus. *Papal Primacy: Its Story from the Beginning to the Present.* Collegeville: Liturgical Press, 1996.

Sullivan, Francis A., S.J. *The Church We Believe In: One, Holy, Catholic and Apostolic.* New York/Mahwah: Paulist Press, 1989.

——. *Creative Fidelity: Weighing and Interpreting Documents of the Magisterium.* New York/Mahwah: Paulist Press, 1996.

Tillard, Jean-Marie. *The Bishop of Rome.* Wilmington: Michael Glazier, 1983.

——. *A Church of Churches: The Ecclesiology of Communion.* Collegeville: Liturgical Press, 1992.

Willebrands, Johannes Cardinal. "Vatican II's Ecclesiology of Communion," *One In Christ* 23 (1987) 179–191; *Origins* 17:2 (May 28, 1987): 27–33.

Zizioulas, John. *Being as Communion: Studies in Personhood and the Church.* Crestwood: St. Vladimir's Seminary Press, 1985.

4

Ecumenical Principles

Separation can never be more than provisional. Cultural or ethnic identity can never be an absolute. Only Christ can be the Absolute, and separation can only be for the sake of a more authentic sharing of diverse gifts in a Christ-given unity.

Lesslie Newbigin

Introduction

The effort to unite in full communion all Christians in the one Church of Christ from their state of division requires the churches, the Catholic Church included, to state the principles which guide their ecumenical aspirations, the priorities before them in both pastoral action and dialogue, and the requirements that are necessary to attain this realization of *koinonia*. In this chapter we will outline three of the fundamental bases for ecumenical commitment as they are formulated in the Catholic Church: (1) religious liberty, (2) spiritual ecumenism, and (3) collaboration in mission.

It will be useful to accompany the study of this chapter with reference to the Council's Declaration on Religious Liberty and subsequent developments in the Catholic Church's relationship to society around the world. It will be particularly important to note the differences of history and developments around this dimension of Catholic life in Latin America and southern Europe, in Eastern Europe, and in Africa and Asia. These histories are in a variety of ways quite different from the experiences of North Atlantic countries and from each other. *The Directory for the Application of Principles and Norms on Ecumenism* will be important in the study of the latter section of the chapter, as will any diocesan incentives and programs that may be available to the reader for consultation. Likewise, the Joint Working Group of the Catholic Church and the World Council has produced texts on proselytism, common witness, and ecumenical formation that expand on the principles embodied in the Council and the *Directory*.

The reader seeking a richer understanding of these topics may wish to parallel the study of the themes here with a detailed study of developments in the ecumenical dialogues, in councils of churches, in missiological writing, and in Orthodox and Protestant bodies on these matters.

Religious Liberty, Foundation for Ecumenical Engagement

First of all, the communion of the Christian Church pertains to the transcendent, vertical *koinonia* of Trinitarian life, animated by the theological virtues of faith, hope, and charity, so that the life of grace characterizes this most profound communion of the Church with God. As is articulated in the Council's Declaration on Religious Liberty, the act of faith by which human persons and human communities respond to God's offer of communion must be a radically free assent to this invitation from God. This assent is not enforced or impeded, but is directed by divine grace to the dignity of the human person, and should be accorded a civil and human right by the civil authorities.

In the realm of horizontal *koinonia*, religious freedom interacts with and impacts other communal and personal human needs. As a recent Vatican-World Council text notes: "The promotion of religious freedom contributes also to the harmonious relations between religious communities and is therefore an essential contribution to social harmony and peace" (Joint Working Group, *The Challenge of Proselytism and the Calling to Common Witness*, 1995).

The Second Vatican Council came to this consciousness in its Declaration on Religious Liberty. In it the Catholic Church acknowledged the essential dignity of the human person related in transcendent *koinonia* with God. While this principle is often taken for granted in the United States and some other North

Atlantic cultures, it was a significant departure from the Catholic past and was debated with some heat at the Council.

It is in the context of this Declaration that the Catholic Church disavows proselytism, that is, coercive or unfair evangelism, as an insult to the dignity of the human person. Faith represents an encounter with the Divine, and should not be the subject of spurious claims or inflated and devious rhetoric. Unjust and threatening measures should not be employed to defame other Christian confessions and prey upon the weaknesses of the uneducated.

The act of faith as the free gift of God must be accepted by the human person. This section will concentrate upon two ecumenical principles that are fundamental for Catholic ecumenical relations: (A) The Declaration on Religious Liberty; (B) Aversion to all forms of proselytism.

A. The Declaration on Religious Liberty

The Declaration on Religious Liberty stands at the forefront of the Church's approach to ecumenical relationships. It dictates the manner in which ecumenical dialogue should proceed; recognizes the inherent dignity of the human person and the necessity to form one's conscience in accord with one's sacred duty; and addresses the delicate question of the relationship of Church and State, which had been an ongoing problem for the Church since the days of Constantine and the subsequent position of the emperor in relationship to the Church

In the eighteenth century, Enlightenment liberals advocated religious freedom as a private and individual right, since they accorded religion no standing or value in the social order. The religious individual was free to believe anything because private faith was a personal matter that impinged on no one else. In this context, the Roman Catholic Church and some other churches developed a history of distrust for religious liberty formulations. Experience of religious life in the United States, where the Church had prospered and deepened its own spiritual life, was not sufficient to convince all of the theological importance of religious liberty.

At the time of the Council, careful debates were necessary to develop a consensus as to the theological basis for religious liberty and its extent and implications. A full understanding of Catholic ecumenism is only possible when it is viewed in the context of Catholic social ethics and its development and the different styles of reception of the Declaration. Likewise, the attitudes of partner churches, both Orthodox and Reformation, are shaped by the behavior and witness of the Catholic Church to religious liberty in society. Dialogue agreements with the Orthodox, Baptist, and Methodist churches have made significant contributions to mutual understandings on this theme. World Council and Reformed-Catholics texts will be noted later in this chapter.

The Declaration is composed of a preface, two chapters, and a final article, number 15. Chapter one deals with the general principles of religious freedom: (a) The right to freedom in religious matters is addressed: freedom from psychological and external coercion, freedom to seek truth, embrace it, adhere to it, and act upon it. Such freedom inheres in every person by reason of the dignity of personhood, which is endowed with reason and free will, conscience, and responsibility. (b) All persons are impelled by nature and are morally obliged to seek the truth and to adhere to it. (c) While Catholics believe that God has offered the true religion to humanity in the Church, nonetheless, such a truth can only impose itself on the human mind in virtue of its own authenticity and veracity. (d) The Council seeks to develop the teaching of recent popes in regard to the rights of the human person.

Chapter two deals with religious freedom in the light of revelation. In revelation the freedom of the person from coercion in religious matters is affirmed. The Council cites the Gospel accounts of Jesus' own actions as displaying the dignity of the human person in grace and the necessity of a human response that is genuinely free. The Council apologizes for past failures on the part of the Church in regard to its fidelity to religious freedom. It is only in a truly free society that the Church can fulfill its mission. Freedom of religion does not absolve one from one's obligations to Christ. The profession of Catholic faith is in no way at variance with the profession of religious freedom.

Finally, the Declaration supports the free profession of religion in private and public, deplores societies where religious freedom is hindered, and advocates constitutional protection of these rights. For many within and without the Catholic Church there is a presumption that separation of church and state is implied in the Declaration. However, where traditional relationships exist, the Declaration does not condemn them. At the present time all of the major states in Europe in which the Catholic Church was formerly established have changed their constitutions so that only Orthodox and Reformation churches remain established there. In Latin America the relationship of the Catholic Church to the states varies widely, in a spectrum from a history of persecution to establishment.

Of itself a doctrine of religious liberty does not necessarily guarantee a culture of tolerance or a spirituality of dialogue. Placing religious liberty at the center of Catholic values was a dramatic Gospel conversion at the Council. The reception of religious liberty is a slow and diverse process in the churches.

B. Proselytism

Some of the basic principles of religious freedom are enumerated in the recent Joint Working Group Between the Roman Catholic Church and the World Council of Churches noted above:

> Religious freedom involves the right to freely adopt or change one's religion and to "manifest it in teaching, practice, worship and observance" without any coercion which would impair such freedom. We reject all violations of religious freedom and all forms of religious intolerance as well as every attempt to impose belief and practices on others or to manipulate or coerce others in the name of religion. (15)

> Freedom of religion touches on "one of the fundamental elements of the conception of life of the person"....For these reasons, international instruments and the constitutions and laws of almost all nations recognize the right to religious freedom. Proselytism can violate or manipulate the right of the individual and can exacerbate tense and delicate relations between communities and thus destabilize societies. (16)

The responsibility of fostering religious freedom and the harmonious relations between religious communities is a primary concern of the churches. Where principles of religious freedom are not being respected and lived in church relations, we need, through dialogue in mutual respect, to encourage deeper considerations and appreciation of these principles and of their practical application for the churches. (17)

It is important, in ecumenical relations, to have a clear definition of *proselytism,* a term used with certain imprecision, even in texts of the churches. The international Baptist-Catholic dialogue document *Summons to Witness to Christ in Today's World* describes characteristics of proselytism and notes: "It is contrary to the message of Christ, to the ways of God's grace, and to the personal character of faith that any means be used which would reduce or impede the freedom of a person to make a basic Christian commitment" (Gros and Rusch, *Deepening Communion,* 9). Practices which the dialogue characterized as proselytism were: (a) employing physical violence, moral compulsion, and psychological pressure; (b) extending offers of education, health care, material inducements, or financial resources with the intent of making converts; (c) manipulative attitudes and practices that exploit people's needs, weaknesses, or lack of education; (d) using political, social, and economic power as a means of winning new members; (e) making unjust or uncharitable references; (f) comparing two Christian communities by emphasizing the achievements of one and the weaknesses of the other.

Proselytism is not the honest hospitality, the welcoming, or even the assertive invitations in which all of our churches practice in the willingness, in a free society, to share the Good News with friends and neighbors. Likewise, history shows that all of the churches—Orthodox, Catholic, Anglican, and Protestant—have past experiences for which we are called to repent. The Catholic Church has published an important document outlining its approach to groups that it considers to be proselytizing its people in certain parts of the world: *Sects or New Religious Movements: Pastoral Challenge* (1985). On the other hand it has published with the Orthodox: *Uniatism, Method of Union of the Past, and the Present Search for Full Communion* (1993), which deals with allegations of proselytism by Catholics. These texts and responses of ecumenical partners to them must be studied if the full range of concerns on this issue is to be understood.

Pope John Paul admonishes all churches seeking unity to look to their painful memories and seek to heal them. The Reformed-Roman Catholic International Dialogue recommends the reconciliation of memories as a priority in healing past experiences of denial of religious liberty and proselytism:

> We see more clearly how our respective self-understandings have been so largely formed by confessional historiographies of the sixteenth and seventeenth centuries. These differing self-interpretations have, in turn, fostered the establishment of whole sets of different values, symbols, assumptions and institutions—in a word, different religious and ecclesial cultures....The very recognition that this is the case marks important progress in our attempt to rid our memories of significant resentments and misconceptions. We need to set ourselves more diligently, however, to the task of reconciling these memories. (IS no. 74 [1990], 102)

This dialogue proposes to the two communities writing together the story of their past differences in regard to areas of conviction and to issues of daily life. Such a common, reconciled history can point the way to future ecumenical efforts.

Spiritual Ecumenism

For all Catholics the pilgrimage toward full communion is a Gospel value. More specificity is given to the Roman Catholic imperative for spiritual ecumenism in chapter four of the *Directory for the Application of Principles and Norms on Ecumenism*. Shared prayer, Bible study, retreats, covenants of mutual support and prayer among congregations and dioceses, and hospitality are all elements of ecumenical life at every level of Catholic life. The Week of Prayer for Christian Unity, sponsored in the United States by the Graymoor Friars in collaboration with the National Council of Churches and the National Conference of Catholic

Bishops, provides a privileged moment during each year for prayer, reflection, and study together.

Conversion to Christ's will for the unity of the Church entails not only the determination and spiritual zeal to seek unity, but also requires attention to the ecumenical content of the dialogues and the priorities of the churches. The ecumenical disciplines of the churches are meant not only to protect fidelity to the Gospel as understood in our still divided churches, but also to contribute to the fullness of Gospel truth to be celebrated in the pilgrimage toward full communion. We dare not lose any of the gifts the churches have received from the Spirit in their separation as they move toward that union to which they are called in Christ. As will be noted below, knowledge, love of one another, and deepened spiritual bonds will precede the visible and institutional communion that serve that *koinonia.*

For the Catholic, sacramental concerns are central to the spiritual sharing and goals of the churches in the ecumenical movement. The *Directory* outlines and encourages the broad range of sharing that is part of common prayer and nonsacramental worship.

Baptism and Eucharist are affirmed as sacraments by most of the churches in the ecumenical movement, but practice and theology vary widely, especially among the churches of the Reformation, and therefore there is an essential ecumenical component in the preparation for and catechesis related to these sacraments. The *Directory* recognizes that interchurch marriages are themselves a form of sacramental sharing and, therefore, deserve special theological, pastoral, and ecumenical consideration. The *Directory* provides special guidance in regard to ecumenical sharing of penance (reconciliation), anointing, and the Eucharist.

The *Directory* notes that concerns are too detailed and the pastoral importance of sacramental sharing too important to be exhausted by its survey. This chapter can only draw attention to some issues that need to be studied in more depth for Catholic sacramental practice to be nurtured in the context of its ecumenical spirituality. In this section we will survey: (a) the principles of sacramental sharing; (b) the central role of baptism; (c) guidelines applied to sharing of Eucharist, penance, and anointing; and (d) significant concerns in interchurch marriages. More in-depth study will be necessary on each of these themes to equip those preparing for pastoral ministry or ecumenical engagement.

Catholics see the Church as a sacrament of Christ's presence in the world, recognizing that the individual sacraments take place "in a concrete community [as] the sign of the reality of its unity in faith, worship and community life. As well as being signs, sacraments—most specially the Eucharist—are sources of the unity of the Christian community" (129). Therefore there are two principles. Access to Eucharist, penance, and anointing are appropriate to "those who share its oneness in faith, worship and ecclesial life," but the Church also recognizes that these sacraments build the unity of the Church and nourish the baptized Christian, so "access to these sacraments may be permitted, or even commended, for Christians of other Churches and ecclesial communities."

These principles must be part of the sacramental preparation of all Catholics, along with a recognition that their emphases—while in some tension—vary from time and place in the Catholic Church and from one communion to another among our ecumenical partners. Catholic guidelines will appropriately differ from bishops' conference to bishops' conference and, in some geographical areas, from diocese to diocese. The sacramental approaches of ecumenical partners differ as well. Generally, one will find the Orthodox, Lutheran Church—Missouri Synod, and some Baptists emphasizing the first principle, often characterized as *closed* communion, while Methodists, Disciples, Presbyterians, and other of the Reformation churches often emphasize the second principle, often spoken of as *open* communion. Further, theological positions may vary even within these emphases depending on the theology of the Church and its relationship to the sacraments.

By baptism "a person is truly incorporated into Christ and into his Church and is reborn to a sharing of the divine life" (92). For many living in a pluralistic Christian context, common baptism and a real if yet incomplete level of church communion is taken for granted. This understanding of common baptism has been reinforced by some of the dialogue results and the production in some parts of the world of common baptismal certificates. From a Catholic point of view, any hint of rebaptism is to be strictly avoided. With certain groups not considered to be fully Trinitarian Christian, conditional baptism is necessary, as with Mormons or "oneness" Pentecostals who become Roman Catholic.

However, this common understanding and recognition of baptism does not dampen the urgency to perfect the full communion to which the churches are called, or lessen the obstacles which we are called to overcome. It is important, even in inter-church families, to recall that baptism is into a particular community, and registration is into a particular church. Ecumenically planned baptisms must take account of the ecumenical challenge while they recognize the common ground the baptism celebrates.

It is important to avoid the abuse of placing baptized Christians who wish to come into full communion with the Roman Catholic Church into programs of Christian Initiation for Adults directed toward the celebration and ritualization of "new" Christians. Baptized Christians are never to be confused with catechumens, who have not yet received Christian initiation. More detailed exploration of Catholic and other initiating practices and theology are necessary for the real implications of our common baptism to come alive in parish life.

In the question of sacramental sharing of penance, anointing, and the Eucharist, Catholics make a careful distinction between the Assyrian Church of the East, the Oriental and Eastern Orthodox Churches, and the Polish National and other Old Catholic Churches whose orders and sacraments are not questioned, and the churches of the Reformation, whose sacraments of order and Eucharist are not yet fully recognized. It is this distinction which makes Catholic sacramental practice seem complicated and juridical, but it is in fact a theological and pastoral approach based on the two principles enunciated above.

For the Eastern Churches and Polish National Catholic Church, the Roman Catholic Church is "allowing and even encouraging some sharing...given suitable circumstances and the approval of church authorities" (122). However, this openness also requires respecting the Eastern disciplines as much as possible. For all of the Eastern Orthodox and most of the Oriental Orthodox Churches, there is neither reciprocity nor encouragement for their members to receive from Catholic ministers.

Therefore care is necessary to let the Roman Catholic position be known while not encouraging violation of the discipline of the other church. This is a particularly sensitive area in situations, such as in Catholic schools and hospitals, where the pastoral needs are most apparent. On the other hand, agreements with the Assyrian and Polish National Churches and a Common Declaration between Pope John Paul and the Syrian [Oriental] Orthodox Patriarch of Antioch make sacramental sharing with these communities more possible.

The situation with the Reformation churches is even more complex, both because of the diversity of theologies of the sacraments and the lack of reciprocity. The levels of agreements in the dialogues, especially in the case of Lutherans and Anglicans, need to be taken into account in catechesis and application of the norms of the Church. The conditions for administering these three sacraments are quite clear, and should be made known to both Catholic and fellow Christians. The prospective recipient must: (1) ask for the sacrament on her or his own initiative; (2) manifest the catholic faith in the sacrament; (3) be properly disposed; and (4) be unable to have recourse for the sacrament desired to a minister of his or her own church.

The *Directory* and the *Code of Canon Law* specify that "a Catholic minister may administer" these three sacraments, but it also specifies that bishops and episcopal conferences may establish further guidelines, including reserving the pastoral discernment to diocesan leadership under the bishop. Since this is a pastoral decision made in common between the prospective communicant and the Catholic minister, it will be important that pastoral leadership be carefully prepared for this task. This involves knowing the results of past and ongoing dialogues, the spiritualities of our ecumenical partners, and the practices of partner churches.

For Catholics, it can be amazing that there is even an interest in Reformation churches in communicating, on occasion, at a Catholic mass, given the polemics of the sixteenth century. It is a tribute to the ecumenical liturgical renewal in all of our churches that this now becomes again an open question, and an imperative to careful common catechesis. Our people need to understand together where we are on the pilgrimage toward full sacramental unity, where we have been, and what are our common hopes. What often presents itself as a pastoral moment of tension is an invitation to ecumenical formation and deepening of mutual understanding.

Finally, interchurch marriages are one of the most intimate instances of sacramental sharing among divided Christians and one of the most challenging pastoral opportunities before the churches. Thorough study of marriage theology, practice, and law are important for anyone who wishes to serve these unions in the Church. However, all church members need to have as part of their catechesis the ecumenical implications of interchurch marriage, especially before occasions emerge where decisions are already being made, sometimes without reflection on the divided character of our churches and the implications for the wedding, the upbringing of the children, or the Christian nature of the family.

The Catholic Bishops of the United States have published national materials for its members assisting them with Catholic/Eastern and Oriental Orthodox marriages. Many Catholic diocese have guidelines for interchurch marriages with particular partner churches, often worked out collaboratively. Two international dialogues have taken up this issue, and Anglican and Catholic bishops in Canada have developed guidelines. Most churches discourage, in principle, interchurch and interfaith marriages because of the strain they place on the family. However, as the *Directory* notes: "In all marriages, the primary concern of the Church is to uphold the strength and stability of the indissoluble marital union and the family life that flows from it" (144). Therefore, careful provisions are made for the pastoral care of interchurch couples and families, for maximum ecumenical attention to the weddings and for appropriate follow-up nurture.

Pope John Paul's *Familiaris Consortio* (1980) provides the basis for this more positive attitude toward mixed Christian marriages. After reviewing the difficulties, the Pope suggested that such marriages can also have a beneficial effect on the effort to restore unity among Christians. His words are an encouragement for both parties to be faithful to their religious duties. He noted especially their common baptism, the grace alive in them and through them, their pursuit of common moral and spiritual values, and the religious celebration of what they share as Christians.

The Catholic party makes a promise to do all in his or her power to raise the couple's children in the Catholic faith, a promise that many other Christians make regarding their own traditions as well. There are no canonical penalties for the Catholic party should the children not be raised Catholic. The couple may need to be helped to see the importance for the unity of the family of the positive religious upbringing of the children and the ecumenical tenor of the home.

Ideally, the couple would be able to raise children to be comfortable in the traditions of both parents while they have an ecclesial identity in one church. The family can be a sign of the unity that the two churches can enjoy as well as their hopes for the restoration between the yet divided churches. There is a special opportunity and challenge to provide the children with an appreciation of the traditions and practices of the parents' churches and with a zeal to overcome the remaining divisions that keep them separate.

The married couple will assume new roles in the church community. Just as marriage partners have a responsibility for the building up of the Church, so too the church community has a responsibility to help each Christian family foster its life of faith. Pastors in particular are called to provide spiritual assistance to couples in mixed marriages and to help them foster the unity of their families.

The wedding preparations themselves are a major ecumenical experience for an interchurch couple and their families. The ease, seriousness, and intentionality of the undertaking need to be maximized with pastoral care. The fact that weddings with an Orthodox partner, for the most part, still must take place in an Orthodox church can be an element of tension and must be dealt with delicately. Among the churches of the Reformation, Anglican, classical Protestant, and evangelical Protestant weddings will have each their own challenges and require attention to the sensitivities of both families, the couple, and the ecclesial communities. Usually the Eucharist is not recommended. With some Catholic families considerable ecumenical formation will be necessary if the Eucharist is not planned, while it may be equally necessary on the part of the non-Catholic Christian community if celebration of the Eucharist is indicated.

Ecumenical Collaboration in Mission

Every Christian, in each dimension of life, has an opportunity for prayer, charity, and ecumenical collaboration, according to one's vocation.

> Thus, the entire life of Christians is marked by a concern for ecumenism; and they are called to let themselves be shaped, as it were, by that concern (UUS 15)....there is a clear connection between renewal, conversion and reform....No Christian community can exempt itself from this call (16).

> Cooperation based on our common faith is not only filled with fraternal communion, but is a manifestation of Christ himself. Moreover, ecumenical cooperation is a true school of ecumenism, a dynamic road to unity. Unity of action leads to the full unity of faith....In the eyes of the world, cooperation among Christians becomes a form of common Christian witness and a means of evangelization which benefits all involved. (40)

The Catholic Church, like all of the churches in the ecumenical movement, not only encourages and forms its members for ecumenical collaboration, but also provides supports for such collaboration on the various levels of its life. There is a Pontifical Council for Promoting Christian Unity in the Holy See, a Bishops' Committee for Ecumenical and Interreligious Affairs in the National Conference of Catholic Bishops, an ecumenical commission and ecumenical officer proposed for each Catholic diocese, and a chapter (V) in the *Directory* devoted to cooperation and common witness. At national and international levels, collaboration in Bible translation, development of liturgical texts, relief, social witness, education, and missionary activity are well developed, and need to be more widely known.

In local communities there are ministerial associations and ecumenical organizations. Some dioceses have mandated a parish ecumenical representative to work with each parish council and neighboring congregations of ecumenical partners to promote collaboration. In over forty countries of the world and in regions such as the Caribbean and the Pacific, the Catholic Church, through its episcopal conferences, is a full member of councils of churches. In over half of the dioceses of the United States there is membership in state and city councils or conferences of churches. These councils enable regular dialogue, prayer, Christian service in the community, projects of common evangelism and education, and common witness to concerns in the society.

While the Catholic Church has no theological reasons that would inhibit it from membership in the World Council of Churches, questions of size and the diversity of relationships between the over three hundred WCC member churches and Catholic communities around the world make collaboration rather than membership a preferred means of communal participation at this international level. The Catholic Church is a full member of the WCC Faith and Order Commission, provides staff to the mission unit of the Council, has been a major partner in projects for peace, justice, and environmental concerns, and has had observers at all of the Assemblies since 1961. A regular Joint Working Group provides studies and communication that enhances unity around the world. Pope John Paul has recognized the centrality of this ecumenical community in his encyclical:

> It happens more and more often that leaders of Christian communities join together in taking a stand in the name of Christ on important problems concerning man's calling and on freedom, justice, peace and the future of the world....It is clear, as experience shows, that in some circumstances the united voice of Christians has more impact than any one isolated voice. (43)

The missionary movement has been one of the earliest stimuli for collaboration in the history of ecumenism. Catholics tend to come at the ecumenical movement from theological, historical, and institutional perspectives, and understand the importance of cooperation in spreading the word of God from other means. However, missionary outreach is one of the central dimensions of the pilgrimage toward unity:

The destiny of evangelization is certainly bound up with the witness of unity given by the church....At this point we wish to emphasize the sign of unity among all Christians as the way and instrument of evangelization. The division among Christians is a serious reality which impedes the very work of Christ. (Quoting *Evangelii Nuntiandi,* UUS 98)

Pope John Paul has spoken repeatedly of the New Evangelization especially in the context of secularized Europe and the inculturation and catechetical needs of Latin America. For him, the ecumenical dimension is an essential element of this "newness" in Catholic evangelization:

The new evangelization is therefore the order of the day. This does not mean the "restoration" of a past age. Rather it is necessary to risk taking new steps. Together we must again proclaim the joyful and liberating message of the Gospel to the people of Europe....The task of evangelization involves moving toward each other and moving together as Christians, and it must begin from within; evangelization and unity, evangelization and ecumenism are indissolubly linked with each other....Because the question of the new evangelization is very close to my heart, as bishop of Rome I consider overcoming the divisions of Christianity "one of the pastoral priorities." (*L'Osservatore Romano,* English ed., 27/5 [3 July 1996] nos. 3, 5)

Local collaboration in evangelism entails careful planning. Catholic styles of evangelization often differ from those of Evangelical Protestants. However, there has been collaboration with the Billy Graham Crusade, for example, from the 1950s, well before the Council. With such mass evangelism, care needs to be taken to see that there is adequate Catholic participation in the planning, that there is no direct conflict with Catholic teaching, and that those advising the "converted" or newly rededicated direct Catholics back to their churches. Special sensitivity needs to be maintained in work with immigrants and with crusades that target groups like the Hispanic community.

Groups of churches in a neighborhood may provide welcoming teams and brochures attempting to situate newcomers in active churches of their own background. Others may organize door-to-door groups to invite people who are not currently adherents of any faith tradition to a congregation where they have had roots or might now be nurtured into the Christian faith. In such evangelism care needs to be taken so that preparation can be truly ecumenical, and that sensitivity to Jewish, Muslim, and other believers can be maintained. Programs of public common witness in a community are an important testimony to the levels of communion already experienced.

For those preparing for international or home mission away from their own communities, cross cultural, and ecumenical training is essential in the contemporary Catholic understanding of mission. There are national collaborative programs between the U.S. Catholic Mission Association and the National Council of Churches serving such collaborative mission training needs and other areas of cooperation in the mission of the Church.

While there are many avenues of formal and institutional collaboration among the churches, creativity, initiative, and openness among the laity, clergy, schools, and parishes create the bases from which institutional and sacramental communion emerge as the logical outcome of the impulse of the Holy Spirit in the communities of faith.

Conclusion

In looking closely at the principles for ecumenism, even as we emphasize the evangelical mission of the Catholic Church, it becomes increasingly clear that even in our separation we can no longer operate alone. A common commitment to religious liberty is foundational to our approach to society, to recognizing the dignity of one another, to sharing a common struggle for the Gospel in society, and to respecting one another's members in our common task of evangelism. Pope John Paul has repeatedly spoken of the New Evangelization, especially in Europe and Latin America. Restoration of the unity of the Church, reception of the religious liberty vision of the Council, and a common witness with our ecumenical partners to the unchurched and secular world are integral to this New Evangelization.

Resolution of outstanding difficulties on sacraments and

authority is central to the quest for visible unity. However, in the daily spiritual life of the Christian churches together, administering the sacraments, living out the implications of our common baptism, and providing support for and receiving testimony from interchurch families are at the same time integral to the pilgrimage itself. Collaboration in councils of churches, clusters of parishes and congregations, and in the host of missionary activities in which individuals and communities are involved are the incarnation of our ecumenical conversion, faith, and charity.

The continuation of the ecumenical movement demands responsiveness to the Holy Spirit, spiritual conversion, and zeal for unity. Yet, for a Christian of the Incarnation, there is no spiritual ecumenism unless prayer and love find embodiment in visible structures of charity and pastoral care. The journey toward the unity for which Christ prayed is complex and sometimes tension filled, but the very challenge to come closer in Christ has its rewards in spiritual appreciation, nurture, and growth.

Study Questions

1. What is the importance of the common affirmation of religious liberty to ecumenical relationships? What is its impact on the consciousness of Catholics?

2. How might understandings of religious liberty vary in different cultures and different political contexts? What is meant by *proselytism*?

3. How might the ecumenical element in Christian identity be seen as integral to the spiritual life? What is the role of conversion in ecumenical spirituality and its importance in the quest for Christian unity?

4. What are the Catholic principles of sacramental sharing and their implications for practice? How do these compare and contrast with these principles in other churches?

5. What are some of the opportunities for collaboration, common witness, and ecumenical evangelism among the churches? To what concerns, dangers, and principles do the churches need to be attentive in following these avenues?

6. What are the promises and challenges of interchurch marriages as seen from the point of view of the couple? from the point of view of the local parish community? from the point of view of the wider Christian community?

7. What are the challenges in the experience of the Catholic Church in bringing the priorities of religious liberty, ecumenical spirituality, and common witness into parochial and national life?

8. How do the different situations in which the Church lives influence the different priorities in ecumenical common witness and spiritual ecumenism?

Selected Readings

Gros, Jeffrey, and William G. Rusch, eds. *Deepening Communion*. Washington D.C.: U.S. Catholic Conference, 1998.

John Paul II. "Linking Evangelization and Ecumenism," (June 22, 1996). *Origins* 26:9 (August 1, 1996): 139–41.

Joint Working Group Between the Roman Catholic Church and the World Council of Churches. *The Challenge of Proselytism and the Calling to Common Witness* (September 25, 1995). In Jeffrey Gros and William G. Rusch, eds., *Deepening Communion*. Washington D.C.: U.S. Catholic Conference, 1998.

———. *Common Witness: A Study Document of the Joint Working Group of the Roman Catholic and the World Council of Churches*. Geneva: World Council of Churches, 1980.

Kilcourse, George. *Double Belonging: Interchurch Families and Christian Unity*. New York/Mahwah: Paulist Press, 1992.

Kinnamon, Michael, and Brian E. Cope, eds. *The Ecumenical Movement: An Anthology of Basic Texts and Voices*. Grand Rapids: Eerdmans, 1997, pp. 263–324, 461–95.

Lawler, Michael. *Ecumenical Marriage and Remarriage: Gifts and Challenges to the Churches*. Mystic: Twenty-Third Publications, 1990.

Meyer, Harding, and Lukas Vischer, eds. *Growth in Agreement: Reports and Agreed Statements of Ecumenical Conversations on a World Level*. Ecu-

menical Documents II. New York/Mahwah: Paulist Press, 1984, pp. 277–306.

Murray, John Courtney. *The Problem of Religious Freedom.* Westminster: Newman, 1965.

——, ed. *Religious Liberty: An End and a Beginning; The Declaration on Religious Freedom, an Ecumenical Discussion.* New York: Macmillian, 1966.

New Working Group on New Religious Movements, Vatican City. *Sects and New Religious Movements: An Anthology of Texts from the Catholic Church 1986–1994.* Washington D.C.: U.S. Catholic Conference, 1995.

Pontifical Council for Justice and Peace and Commission of the Churches on International Affairs, World Council of Churches. *Peace and Disarmament: Documents of the World Council of Churches and the Roman Catholic Church.* Geneva: Commission of the Churches on International Affairs, World Council of Churches/Vatican City: Pontifical Commission for Justice and Peace, 1982.

Reformed/Roman Catholic International Dialogue. *Towards a Common Understanding of the Church.* Pontifical Council for Promoting Christian Unity, *Information Service,* no. 74 (1990): 91–125.

Roberson, Ronald G., ed. *Oriental Orthodox-Roman Catholic Interchurch Marriages and Other Pastoral Relationships.* Washington D.C.: U.S. Catholic Conference, 1995.

Schere, James A., and Stephen B. Bevans, eds. *New Directions in Mission and Evangelization: Basic Statements 1974–1981.* Maryknoll, Orbis Books, 1992.

Stransky, Thomas, ed. *Declaration on Religious Freedom of Vatican Council II.* New York/Mahwah: Paulist Press, 1967.

5

Ecumenical Formation

Holy God, giver of peace, author of truth,
we confess that we are divided and at odds with one another,
that a bad spirit has risen among us
and set us against your Holy Spirit of peace and love.
Take from us the mistrust, party spirit, contention,
and all evil that now divides us.
Work in us a desire for reconciliation, so that, putting aside personal
    grievances,
we may go about your business with a single mind,
devoted to our Lord and Savior, Jesus Christ.
                        Worshipbook of the Presbyterian Church USA

The process of conversion is the process of being drawn more deeply into the mystery of the triune God. The full conversion of the human person involves the outward and the inward person and the congruity between the two. It involves works of love and interior experiences of God's own presence. It involves the sacraments and worship, and disciplines of thought, study, and prayer. And it involves increasing ability to see the many ways that God is at work reconciling the world to himself in the diversity of Christian communities. Conversion is essential to the ecumenical dimension of Catholic identity. In 1991 Pope John Paul reminded the Pontifical Council for Promoting Christian Unity that:

> Ecumenical relations are a complex and delicate reality which require study and theological dialogue, fraternal relations and contact, prayer and practical collaboration. We are called to work in all fields. Being limited to one or another of them while neglecting the others can never produce results. This global view of ecumenical activity must always be kept in mind when we present or explain our involvement. (IS no. 78 [1991], 140)

94

The early church rejected the Diatessaron, a melding of the four Gospels into one narrative. In the four Gospels that were eventually accepted, the same Lord is viewed through the differing emphases of the several Gospel communities. Similarly, it is the same will for our salvation which is witnessed to, lived, and imparted in the whole of the Christian community.

At the same time, it is clear that not all purported gospels were accepted by the early church. Recognizing the Master's voice in different liturgical, theological, and spiritual languages, learning to respect and admire, while resisting the impulse to be either overly and too quickly accepting or dismissive requires time, work, and a willingness to be molded by the Spirit. While the unity to which we are called is a unity-in-diversity this diversity is limited by the truth of revelation.

Catholic ecumenical formation requires a process of conversion. This process of conversion is a matter of interior transformation. It must also be tailored, however, to the character of international Catholic relations and the resources these provide for local and national developments; the unique character of each church and community and the manner in which relationships are best nurtured with each group; the specific local responsibility of parish and diocese depending on the groups and leadership present in each place; and the gifts of American opportunities and challenges for reconciliation to the global unity among Christians. Some of these factors will be noted with specificity when the dialogues are discussed in later chapters.

In each community the Holy Spirit has been active during the centuries of separation. Christians are called to know these gifts of the Spirit in other communities as the pilgrimage together toward full communion proceeds. As Pope John Paul testifies:

> I have said how we are aware, as the Catholic Church, that we have received much from the witness borne by other churches and ecclesial communities in certain common Christian values, from their study of those values and even from the way in which they have emphasized and experienced them....At this stage which we have now reached, this process of mutual enrichment must be taken seriously into account. (UUS 87)

Because ecclesiologies, soteriologies, biblical hermeneutics, and sacramental theologies vary considerably among the various churches and ecclesial communities, inevitably there are correlate differences in how the unity of Christians is understood. Anglicans, Lutherans, Orthodox, and Roman Catholics often share similar ecumenical program conceptions because they often share more similar understandings of ecclesiology and sacrament than some other groups and individual theologians share with them.

Among the classical Protestants, such as the Disciples, Methodists, and Reformed churches, one frequently finds a "denominational" understanding of the Church. In this ecclesiology one sees one's own church and each other church as expressions of the one true Church. In this ecclesiological understanding many Christians see one denomination as equal to any other. Holding this ecclesiology, many American Christians move easily from one church to the other depending on the congregation's ministry or communal temperament.

Many African American churches need to have a credible witness of biblical equality and openness from other churches before they are open to ecumenical engagement. It is only when there is an experience of baptismal equality and common social witness that classically framed discussions of theology and ecclesiology will become possible. But it is important to the process of ecumenical formation to come to see that the demand for baptismal equality and common social witness are sacramental, soteriological, and ecclesiological claims of great seriousness in their own right.

Pentecostal, Holiness, and many Evangelical churches affirm the biblical vision of unity as spiritual and not visible, and therefore are cool or even hostile toward the ecumenical movement as Catholics have understood it. Allowing time and opportunity for the Holy Spirit to guide the reconciliation of disparate biblical hermeneutics between partner churches is, therefore, an indispensable foundational process for crossing the wide gap between these communities.

The ecumenical movement is a privileged forum for discerning God's will for the Church. Such discernment is informed by the concrete partners that are experienced in each local and national context in which the Church is incarnate. In this chapter we will look briefly at four examples of ecumenical interaction and the opportunities for conversion at a variety of levels, from that of international dialogue between churches that had been out of communion for fifteen hundred years, to that of the meeting of pastoral needs at the parish level.

We will look first at the consideration of marriage and anointing of the sick in the international dialogue between the Roman Catholic Church and the Assyrian Church of the East. Second, we will look at a selection of passages from the spiritual autobiography of Jarena Lee, an early nineteenth-century African American Methodist woman. Third, we will look at some similarities and contrasts in contemporary Catholic and Lutheran biblical hermeneutics. Fourth, we will consider a variety of issues requiring ecumenical insight and sensitivity that might arise around a death and funeral in an American Catholic parish. In each case, the reader is inevitably required by the lived ecumenical situation to reach out in conversion to an enriched understanding of the key elements involved.

In the second portion of the chapter we will reflect theologically on personal and small group spirituality in praying for the unity of Christians. We will consider the need for openness to conversion on the part of the churches and ecclesial communities at the corporate level. And we explore the need for continuity between our personal and ecclesial spirituality.

The Assyrian Church of the East

The Assyrian Church of the East was separated from the wider church at the time of the Council of Ephesus (431). This ancient Persian Church, active through India and China in the Middle Ages, was always outside the Roman Empire. It has had a long, illustrious, but tragic history under Persian, Muslim, and most recently Iraqi and Turkish domination. The Patriarch now resides in Morton Grove outside of Chicago. As will be noted in chapter eight, a Common Declaration with Pope John Paul in 1994 claims resolution of the Christological issues that have divided the two churches for many centuries, opening the way for further communal theological exploration.

In the second session of the dialogue carried out by the

Mixed Commission for Theological Dialogue between the Catholic Church and the Assyrian Church of the East, the commission was able to recognize a deep similarity between the two Churches in the biblical foundation and theological understanding of marriage and the anointing of the sick. In the two churches, marriage is viewed as an indissoluble bond open to fertility. The mutual fidelity of the partners to the unity of their partnership and to family life is emphasized in both traditions. In the two churches the anointing of the sick is a sign and effector of the forgiveness of sins and the healing power of Christ. Such healing is understood by both traditions as a sign of the inbreaking of the Kingdom of God.

The Church of the East does not list marriage and the anointing of the sick as sacraments, as does the Catholic Church. The process of dialogue was able to articulate an underlying theological, soteriological congruity of ecclesial acts that could not be anticipated directly from the terms by which the acts were identified in the respective churches.

An African Methodist Episcopal Preacher

Conversion takes different forms in different Christian traditions. Jarena Lee, an early nineteenth-century African American Methodist Episcopal preacher, left an intimate account of her evangelical Christianity in *The Life and Religious Experience of Jarena Lee, a Coloured Lady, Giving an Account of Her Call to Preach the Gospel. Revised and Corrected from the Original Manuscript, Written by Herself,* selections from which are included in Amy Oden's *In Her Words: Women's Writings in the History of Christian Thought.*

Joel 2:28 serves as the opening text and apologetic for Lee's preaching career: "And it shall come to pass, that I pour out my Spirit upon all flesh; and your sons, and your *daughters* shall prophecy." Lee reports that under the influence of the preaching at a Methodist gathering she had a powerful affective experience:

> The text was barely pronounced, which was: "I perceive thy heart is not right in the sight of God" [Acts 8:21], when there appeared to *my* view, in the centre of the heart *one* sin; and

this was *malice,* against one particular individual, who had strove deeply to injure me, which I resented. At this discovery I said, *Lord* I forgive *every* creature. That instant, it appeared to me, as if a garment, which had entirely enveloped my whole person, even to my finger ends, split at the crown of my head, and was stripped away from me, passing like a shadow, from my sight—when the glory of God seemed to cover me in its stead. (277)

Lee leapt to her feet, she reports, so that she might, when acknowledged by the preacher, describe to the assembly her sense of the power of Christ to forgive sins at work in her experience and to give thanks for this gift. This event she describes as a twofold process of "conviction for sin" and "justification from sin."

A subsequent event, an "entire sanctification of the soul to God," followed several months later. Lee found that her initial conversion experience had not removed all her sinful tendencies, "there yet remained the root of pride, anger, self-will, with many evils, the result of fallen nature." She urgently petitioned the Lord in personal prayer, requesting him to "sanctify" her. "That very instant, as if lightening had darted through me, I sprang to my feet, and cried, 'The Lord has sanctified my soul!' There was none to hear this but the angels who stood around to witness my joy—and Satan, whose malice raged the more" (279). Classical Methodist theology speaks of two movements of grace in God's action with the soul, justification, and sanctification.

Lee reports that several years later she experienced a similarly vivid personal spiritual event in which "there seemed to sound a voice which I thought I distinctly heard, and most certainly understood, which said to me, 'Go preach the Gospel!'" She demurred and considered the propriety of following this call, but concluded with a Christological basis for her eventual positive response. "If a man may preach, because the Saviour died for him, why not the woman? seeing he died for her also. Is he not a whole Saviour, instead of a half one?" (280–81). This "call" she then took to the bishop for his consideration, approval, direction, and supervision.

Those not nurtured in the Evangelical Protestant culture may find Lee's account strange and foreign, but at the same time oddly familiar. The affective intensity of the spiritual experiences described can be found in a wide variety of spiritual writings from throughout Christian history. The impulse to approach, consider, and resolve a theological problem Christologically is also likely to be familiar, even if the conclusion reached is at variance with the conclusions reached on the question of women preaching the Gospel in other parts of the Christian world. The suddenness of the reported transformation, the localization of conversion and sanctification in a moment rather than a lifelong process, and the disconnection of these processes from recognizable sacramental activity will require more from the Catholic reader. They will see Lee's report in the light of the Council's teaching that the separated churches and communities "have been by no means deprived of significance and importance in the mystery of salvation. For the Spirit of Christ has not refrained from using them as means of salvation which derive their efficacy from the very fullness of grace and truth entrusted to the Catholic Church" (UR 3). Ecumenical formation entails entering into the experience of the other in order to understand how the grace of Christ is at work in fellow Christians.

Lutheran Biblical Hermeneutics

In the late twentieth century there is a widespread, although not universal, agreement among Christians that the use of historical-critical, literary-critical, and archeological methods in biblical studies is appropriate and beneficial. In many parts of the United States on a Sunday morning the local Catholic parish and the nearby Lutheran, Anglican, and Methodist churches will hear the same texts read and preached upon, often by preachers who have consulted the same commentaries. While the time for Eucharistic sharing seems distant, across much of the Christian world there is a deep communion already enjoyed at the table of the Word.

It can come as a surprise, therefore, to realize that hermeneutical structures for understanding Scripture and revelation shape differences even among churches that have been in long and successful dialogue. As will be explored in chapter nine, the Catholic Church has had extensive and productive discussion on the international and national levels with a large body of Lutheran churches. Although Lutherans and Catholics report basic agreement in *Scripture and Tradition: Lutherans and Catholics in Dialogue IX,* the different emphases continue.

Most obvious and familiar is the difference in the way the relationship between the Bible and the Church as a living interpretive tradition is explained and normatively presented. Lutherans emphasize the authority of the Scriptures in defining and norming the Church. Scripture, because it is from Christ and leads to Christ, is the final authority for followers of Christ. Catholic understanding emphasizes the authority of the Church's teaching office standing under and interpreting the Scriptures in a definitive and normative way. For Catholics the Scriptures and the Tradition that preserves and interprets them are a living unity of revelation.

More subtle differences may be seen in the ways that the study and interpretation of Scripture in the two traditions tend to relate to the broader theological and liturgical matrixes of the communities. Overall, Lutheran emphasis has historically been, and continues to be, on the preached Word and its salvific power. The books of Luther's own "canon within the canon," his hermeneutical key to the larger body of the Scriptures, consisted of the Gospel of John, the letters of Paul to the Romans and the Galatians, and 1 Peter. Each of these books is highly sermonic in literary style as compared, for instance, to the synoptic Gospels, with their briefer, more compact literary units.

One of the most important of the recurrent and underlying themes of the documents from the Second Vatican Council is that of inculturation. Not surprisingly, *Dei Verbum,* the Dogmatic Constitution on Divine Revelation, urges the study of the variety of literary forms used by the ancient writers and "customary and characteristic patterns of perception, speech and narrative which prevailed at the age of the sacred writer"—in short, the literary culture of the ancient writers.

The Catholic and Lutheran approaches, one putting special emphasis on one central liturgical form, the homily, and the other emphasizing cultural diversity of literary forms, are related to primary theological concerns. The two approaches are not mutually exclusive, but they are different. A just appreciation of the assets and limitations of the two requires one to see beyond the surface to the ecclesial presuppositions and implications.

Catholic Parish Funerals

In lived experience, one of the most challenging and important ecumenical contexts is that presented by the liturgical and pastoral needs and events surrounding a central moment in the life of the community and the family, such as a death. In our pluralistic culture, relatively few persons live their lives so completely within their own community that those who attend the wake and funeral will be uniformly of one faith community. Many families have members from other Christian communities within them. The needs for pastoral sensitivity and ecumenical information and formation can be both demanding and rewarding for those reaching out and ministering to the bereaved.

As is articulated in the *Catechism of the Catholic Church* and *The Order of Christian Funerals,* the Catholic understanding of the death of a Christian is grounded in an understanding of baptism. The death of a Christian person is seen in the perspective of sacramental participation in the redeeming death and rising to new life of our Lord. Having died with Christ in baptism, we rise with him in death. Even in the case of one who died before baptism, the funeral liturgies offer comfort to the bereaved through reference to baptismal faith of the Christian community and the glory of the Resurrection. There is, therefore, a unity among Christians in death for which we still work and pray in life.

There are, however, significant differences in the emphases which the various Christian churches and communities bring forward in their funeral and pastoral care styles. Ecumenical sensitivity is enhanced by an awareness that Christians from other communities may be surprised and disoriented by the emphases that are comforting and expected by grieving Catholics.

The instructions for the homilist in the *Order of Christian Funerals* indicate that a eulogy is never to be offered. At the same time the rites and the instructions teach that the body of the deceased is to be treated with reverence, as in life it served as the temple of the Holy Spirit; and the general intercessions include petition that the goodness of deceased friends and family members might receive reward. Ecumenical insight will enable one to develop an ability to see how in many Christian communities the use of a eulogy fills these latter theological and liturgical goals, approved by Catholic teaching but located differently in Catholic liturgical usage. A grieving family member, expecting a eulogy, might be enabled to take much deeper comfort in the funeral of the Catholic deceased if this congruity of intention, given form in different usage, is offered catechetically in the funeral preparations.

Ecumenical pastoral care is further complicated by the fact that some Christian communities have considerably different doctrines concerning the efficacy of the Church's prayers for the dead, the nature of the beatific vision, and the immediacy of judgment after death. The question of reception of communion at the funeral Mass will also raise needs for pastoral sensitivity, especially if the spouse, parents, siblings, or children of the deceased are not Catholic. Careful pastoral response might include the participation of clergy from the Christian communities of family members, the use of a Scriptural vigil or rosary at the wake, or the choosing of familiar hymns that have entered Catholic usage from other Christian traditions. The challenge to teach Catholic doctrine authentically and to respect the limits of our existing Christian unity, while recognizing the need to offer comfort in the Paschal Mystery in a way that other Christians may be able to hear as the hope of our redemption in the midst of grief, calls one to stretch the limits of one's pastoral sensitivity and deepen one's conversion.

Praying for Unity

Ecumenical conversion takes place on the level of and on the part of the separated churches and communities, on the level of and on the part of the individual Christian, and in the congruity of the two. During the twentieth century several religious communities, such as the communities of Chevetogne and Taize, have undertaken to be witnesses and pioneers in the process of uniting the conversion of the individual Christian and the conversion of the churches and separated communities. They offer insight out of their experience of life and prayer.

Dom Olivier Rousseau of the Eastern Catholic monastery of Chevetogne has written of the problem of praying for unity with true and noncondescending charity toward those who understand the truth of the Gospel differently from oneself, while remaining deeply committed to the faith of one's own church. He offers three motifs and motivations shaping such communal prayer. Each of these is imposed upon Christians by the love of Christ, by faith in His word, and by the example of the earliest Christian tradition.

First, communal prayer across the divisions among Christians is grounded in the will, the wish, the longing, of Christ. The Gospel of John reports that he himself prayed that his followers might be one (17:21). His action in this is to be followed by his followers, as in other things.

Second, crossconfessional communal prayer for unity is grounded in the promise that the prayer of two or three gathered in Jesus' name will be answered (Mt 18:19–20). During their prayer those gathered are not divided. These moments of unity become, as it were, an apprenticeship in the more pervasive unity for which those gathered are praying. These moments of prayer move Christians from being persons whose backs are turned towards each other, each confession facing away from the others, to Christians turned toward God and one another, beginning to recognize themselves as disciples of the same Lord. The act of gathering in Jesus' name to pray for unity is a moment of such unity.

Third, communal prayer is aimed at abatement of the heated passions, particularly the polemical passions, that have fed division. Such prayer fosters insight rather than blindness in looking at the real doctrinal disagreements. It leads to being able to distinguish between real issues and nonessentials. It leads to the ability to forgive, a necessary component of the ecumenical movement and of ecumenical formation.

Max Thurian of the ecumenical community of Taize spoke of the ordinariness of prayer for Christian unity. Like other prayer, it requires humility. And, like other prayer, it should include the elements of adoration, confession of sin, thanksgiving for God's works of grace on our behalf, and intercession.

The God whom we adore in prayer, the God in whose presence we self-consciously understand ourselves to be when in prayer, is both One and triune. The adoration of this God is directed to the Creator who, in wisdom and love, holds the entirety of creation in an ordered unity. The adoration of this God is directed to Christ, whose *kenosis* of redemption, accomplished in his life, death, and resurrection, is a work of unity on our behalf. And the adoration of this God is directed to the Holy Spirit, present in the Church but not exhausted by it. The Spirit blows where it wills, leading all toward the unity of the Kingdom of God.

Prayer for Christian unity requires searching, with humility and a repentant spirit, the ways that we have sinned against unity. It requires going beyond noting the sins of the past to newness of life in the present.

Prayer for Christian unity involves thanksgiving for God's actions in planting the desire for unity in human hearts. This thanksgiving extends to gratitude for those who have given leadership and ministry to the fulfillment of this desire.

Finally, prayer for Christian unity is a supplication for unity and for the unifiers. The tasks of charity and common actions for social justice and full human flourishing, of theological inquiry and dialogue, and of coming together to pray as one are not always easy. Prayer for Christian unity involves placing the difficulties of the task and the needs of those involved in these tasks before God. We pray not only for the unity of the churches but also for wisdom, patience, and zeal in contributing to that unity.

The Conversion of the Churches

Work by the Groupe des Dombes, an independent ecumenical group of Catholics and Protestants in France, has articulated thinking developed over five decades of prayer and theological discussion on the need for conversion, *metanoia,* on the part of the churches. They have noted that the conversion of the churches goes on in three arenas: symbolic gestures, theological dialogue, and corporate acts of approval and reception.

Drama-filled symbolic gestures of reconciliation and public statements expressing longing for unity on the part of the heads of communions and others in roles of ecclesial leadership change the context in which ecumenical dialogue is carried out. Theological dialogue makes further symbolic gestures of unity possible. But these symbols are embedded in the lives of churches and communities. Ecumenical conversion involves the conversion of the ecclesial bodies themselves.

The Second Vatican Council speaks of this need:

> Christ summons the Church, as she goes her pilgrim way, to that continual reformation of which she always has need, insofar as she is an institution of men [and women] here on earth. Consequently, if, in various times and circumstances, there have been deficiencies in moral conduct or in Church discipline, or even in the way that Church teaching has been formulated—to be carefully distinguished from the deposit of faith itself—these should be set right at the opportune moment and in the proper way. (UR 6)

The implication is clear: not only the personal failings in charity, wisdom, or moral conduct of individuals are to be appraised honestly, but the household of the church, the ways of articulating the faith, and of carrying out its tasks may need to be renewed.

In the encyclical *Ut Unum Sint,* Pope John Paul elaborates and demonstrates this principle. "Not only personal sins must be forgiven and left behind," he states, "but also social sins, which is to say the sinful 'structures' themselves which have contributed and can still contribute to division and to the reinforcing of division" (UUS 34). In a public gesture of great significance, he asks that the church leaders and theologians engage with him, under the guidance of the Holy Spirit, in the task of exploring the manner in which the ministry of unity of the Roman pontiff "may accomplish a service of love recognized by all concerned" (UUS 95–96). Ways of exercising the papal ministry are here opened to renewal so that the service of love which is the very intent of the ministry may be apprehended as such by others even before the theological issues are resolved.

In *For the Conversion of the Churches* the Groupe des Dombes has offered recommendations for furthering the conversion of the churches. In so doing they have challenged the churches in both specific and more general ways. They have summarized their concerned observations in pithy sentences and paragraphs. "Unhappily, each confession has arrogated to itself traditional designations that belong to the whole church as a distinctive label: but it is the whole church which is catholic, just as the church in its entirety is evangelical, orthodox and called upon to reform itself" (205). "In general terms Catholicism is so concerned about fullness that it tends to add and include even impurities and syncretism, while the Protestants are so concerned about obedience to Scripture that they tend to cut down and suppress, at the risk of falling into purism and abstractions" (199). The Groupe asks with pointedness "are the churches of the Protestant Reformation drawing all the consequences of their conviction that they belong to the one church of God instituted by Christ?" (203). "If the Roman Catholic Church sees itself as the sacrament of the mediation of Christ, while priding itself in the mystery of its origin, will it nevertheless accept, as a human and historical reality, that it recognize itself as an imperfect, sinful sacrament which contributes to division?" (211).

The answers to such questions are, of course, mixed. The results of the development within the ecumenical movement and of the particular actions and dialogues discussed in the subsequent chapters of this book indicate that the answers to such questions must, for the most part, be yes. The churches have engaged their differences and their need for conversion with some remarkable outcomes. Churches which held each other in excommunication have lifted these censures. Liturgies have converged. Communities have undertaken to consider together difficult questions and have stood together against social evils in the world. But this conversion, like the unity that is sought, is not yet complete.

An integral element of the conversion necessary for an ecumenical vision is an openness to a worldwide, history-long, catholic perspective. Christians are not only related to those they know, but also to all who have lived through the two thousand years of Christian history. In the current ecumenical movement this entails a sensitivity to the different ecumenical contexts in which the churches live. The pluralism, affluence, and educational levels of the North Atlantic churches is not the experience of other sectors of the world.

Of course, in addition to knowing the international complexity of the relations among the churches, it is important to recall the cultural and religious diversity of North America. While one may read about ecumenism in the abstract, it is important to know who lives in one's own religious environment and give particular focus to the study of one's Christian neighbors. While Methodists are spread evenly across the continent, one will find more Lutheran partners in the upper midwest and more Baptists in the south, for example. Those in pastoral ministry, especially, will need to tailor the pastoral and theological dimensions of their ecumenical formation to the Christians with which one is called to work.

Eastern Europe is emerging from decades of persecution and religious marginalization. Tensions are directed at one another and often exacerbate centuries of strife among the churches. Theological issues, for example, between Orthodox and Catholics become ideological legitimations for interethnic strife, so that the theological content of agreements cannot be dealt with objectively.

Like Orthodoxy in Eastern Europe, Catholicism in Latin American and Southern Europe has been the dominant force for centuries. Therefore the newly emerging pluralism and new affirmation of religious liberty are only gradually being acknowledged. Like Orthodoxy in Eastern Europe, Catholicism in Latin America often experiences pluralism and ecumenism as a threat to what was traditionally a religious hegemony. Both cultures have a difficult time distinguishing between ecumenical partner Christian churches, insensitive and nonecumenical Christian evangelicalism, and other aggressive non-Christian religious movements, all of which are identified with the culture of the North Atlantic, especially the United States.

In Asia and Africa the contexts for ecumenism are quite different again. In both of these contexts, the conflicts of Europe are not the experience of the local Christians. Asian Christians, with the exception of those in the Philippines, are minorities among the great non-Christian religions. Among the first ecumenical unions among Reformation churches were those that occurred in India. On the one hand, interfaith dialogue is often the living priority, and on the other hand, common Christian efforts toward unity and witness are culturally imperative.

In Africa Christianity is growing quickly, alongside of Islam, and replacing many of the traditional religions. On the other hand, there are many African Instituted Churches that include indigenous elements along with Christianity and take a variety of postures relative to the ecumenical movement. In all of these contexts, the reconciling impulse of the Gospel and the ecumenical program of the churches take on an important relationship to the culture, which must be part of the horizon of the global ecumenical movement.

Further, ecumenical symbolic gestures, deliberations, doctrinal dialogues, and commitments on the part of the ecclesial bodies are only a portion of the story. These commitments, teachings, and ecclesial gestures must be received. They must be enacted and lived by the entire community of faith.

Living Our Ecumenical Formation

Viewed from a certain perspective, communal action in charity and social justice is ecumenically easier than the tackling of theological issues with rigor and precision. While not all Christians agree on the priorities of social needs and some social issues are genuinely divisive for committed Christians, there are many more areas of agreement than disagreement among Christians about the demands to feed the hungry, visit the sick and those in prison, and care for the most vulnerable in society.

However, in lived experience, many have found that their ecumenical formation has been most seriously challenged in encounters in the hospital room, the soup kitchen, the refugee services office, the drug addiction treatment center, or the chance meeting with a neighbor on a street corner. As Pope John Paul notes, collaboration is the school for ecumenical formation.

Each of us carries within ourselves preconceptions and oversimplifications of what Christianity looks like. We have notions of what God's action on the human spirit and in the human psyche will produce. And we have expectations of how the Gospel can be offered as gift to others. When we engage in care of others outside our ordinary arenas of activity, these expectations can be challenged in surprising ways.

It can be in these unexpected places that a Protestant from a group suspicious of auricular confession may powerfully encounter a pastoral need that cries out for this form of ministry. The dialogues on the theological level between his or her group and the Catholic or Orthodox Churches, with rich sacramental tradition in this area, may be newly perceived as a response to a lived need in ministry.

A Catholic, unused to and uncomfortable with the free-form and sometimes impassioned pastoral prayers and preaching styles of Southern Baptists, Evangelicals, Holiness, and Pentecostal pastoral workers, may discover that these styles meet lived pastoral needs in unexpected ways. The warmth of these human communities and of their vision of God offered in such favored passages as John 3:16, "For God so loved the world that he gave his only Son, so that everyone who believes in him may not perish but may have eternal life," may offer hope to those in most desperate need, when ministrations using other approaches may have failed to connect.

It is in the face of the many unmet needs of our world that we may for the first time realize the extent to which we, as Christian persons and as Christian communities, need each other. We need each other to provide balance and new insights. We need each other to call ourselves to account for the extent to which we have not lived out what we profess to believe. And we need each other because the tasks of the Body of Christ for the world are too serious and too large for even the largest Christian community to meet alone.

The Church has no meaning, no purpose, separate from its place in relationship to God's love for us. In ecumenical conversion we are called to love one another with something of the love that has been shown to us in creation, redemption, and the sustaining and sanctification of the Spirit. We are called to be imaginative and resourceful in our loving. The process of ecumenical life is a context in which we need to learn how to recognize, value, and appropriate elements from other Christian groups that are gifts of the Spirit intended for all.

However, the unity of Christians is not, in the end, a human task, but a work of the triune God. The closing paragraph of *Unitatis Redintegratio* serves as reminder:

> This sacred Council firmly hopes that the initiatives of the sons of the Catholic Church, joined with those of the separated brethren [fellow Christians is a more contemporary phrase], will go forward, without obstructing the ways of divine Providence, and without prejudging the future inspirations of the Holy Spirit. Further, this Council declares that it realizes that this holy objective—the reconciliation of all Christians in the unity of the one and only Church of Christ—transcends human powers and gifts. It therefore places its hope entirely in the prayer of Christ for the Church, in the love of the Father for us, and in the power of the Holy Spirit. "And hope does not disappoint, because God's love has been poured forth in our hearts through the Holy Spirit who has been given to us." (Rom 5:5)

Study Questions

1. Pope John Paul has stated that ecumenical relations calls us to work in "study and theological dialogue, fraternal relations and contact, prayer and practical collaboration." Why does ecumenical formation require attention to so many fields of activity?

2. How would you explain theologically the results of the second round dialogue of the Mixed Commission for Theological Dialogue between the Catholic Church and the Assyrian Church of the East on marriage and on the anointing of the sick?

3. Review the spiritual experience of Jarena Lee. Recount some instances in your own experience or that of someone in the late twentieth century with whom you are familiar that parallel Jarena's story.

4. One of the most important tasks in ecumenical formation is becoming aware of what one does not yet know about other Christian groups. What questions about Biblical hermeneutics in communities other than your own do you have? How might you go about learning more on this subject?

5. What are some key theological and pastoral ecumenical issues that should be considered in the preparation and carrying out of wake and funeral rites in an American Catholic parish?

6. Review the theologies of prayer for Christian unity offered from the experience of the communities at Chevetogne and Taize.

7. What arenas of activity are identified by the Groupe des Dombes as loci for the conversion of the churches?

8. What tasks of conversion do you see as most pressing for your own church? For your own community, diocese, or parish?

Selected Readings

Bedell, Kenneth B., ed. *Yearbook of American & Canadian Churches.* Nashville: Abingdon Press, published each year.

Bobrinskoy, Boris. "The Theology of the Prayer for Unity," *One in Christ* 3/3 (1967): 262–90.

Campbell, Ted A. *Christian Confessions: A Historical Introduction.* Louisville: Westminster/John Knox, 1996.

Catechism of the Catholic Church. Washington D.C.: U.S. Catholic Conference, 1994.

Common Christological Declaration between the Catholic Church and the Assyrian Church of the East, November 11, 1994. Pontifical Council for Promoting Christian Unity, *Information Service*, no. 88 (1995): 1–6.

Davies, Rubert. "The Spirituality of Ecumenism." In *Christian Spirituality: Essays in Honor of Gordon Rupp*, Peter Brooks, ed. London: SCM Press LTD, 1975, pp. 307–28.

Groupe des Dombes. *For the Conversion of the Churches.* James Greig, trans. Geneva: World Council of Churches, 1993.

Hagen, Kenneth, Daniel J. Harrington, S.J., Grant R. Osborne, and Joseph A. Burgess. *The Bible in the Churches: How Different Christians Interpret the Scriptures.* New York/Mahwah: Paulist Press, 1985.

John Paul II. Address to the Plenary Assembly of the Pontifical Council for Promoting Christian Unity. Pontifical Council for Promoting Christian Unity, *Information Service*, no. 78 (1991): 139–41.

Kinnamon, Michael, and Brian E. Cope, eds. *The Ecumenical Movement: An Anthology of Basic Texts and Voices.* Grand Rapids: Eerdmans, 1997, pp. 497–525.

Melton, J. Gordon. *The Encyclopedia of American Religion, Religious Creeds.* Fourth edition. Detroit: Gale Research Incorporated, 1993.

Noll, Mark. *A History of Christianity in the United States and Canada.* Grand Rapids: Eerdmans, 1992.

Oden, Amy, ed. *In Her Words: Women's Writings in the History of Christian Thought.* Nashville: Abingdon Press, 1994.

Order of Christian Funerals–Study Edition. Chicago: Liturgy Training Publications, 1990.

Piepkorn, Arthur C. *Profiles in Belief: The Religious Bodies of the United States and Canada.* San Francisco: Harper & Row, 1977–1979.

Puglisi, James F., S.A. "On the Path to Christian Unity: Will Words Alone Suffice?" *Bulletin/Centro Pro Unione* N. 50 (Fall 1996): 18–23.

Sawyer, Mary R. *Black Ecumenism: Implementing the Demands of Justice.* Valley Forge: Trinity Press International, 1994.

Skillrud, Harold C., J. Francis Stafford and Daniel F. Martensen, eds. *Scripture and Tradition: Lutherans and Catholics in Dialogue IX.* Minneapolis: Augsburg, 1995.

Thurian, Max. "Conversion spirituelle et prière pour l'unité." *Verbum caro* 14 (1960): 265–85.

Wainwright, Geoffrey. "Ecumenical Spirituality." In *The Study of Spirituality*, Cheslyn Jones, Geoffrey Wainwright, and Edward Yarnold, S.J., eds. New York and Oxford: Oxford University Press, 1986, pp. 540–48.

Watley, William. *Singing the Lord's Song in a Strange Land: The African American Churches and Ecumenism.* Geneva: World Council of Churches, 1993.

6

The Nature, Goal, and
Reception of Dialogues

For meditation:
Lord, help me not to despise or oppose what I do not understand.

William Penn (Quaker)

Introduction

Dialogue is an essential element of human interaction in every dimension of life, from the family through the workplace to the government. In a society that treasures freedom of expression and guards with religious fervor pluralism of ideas, focusing on what is specific about religious and especially ecumenical dialogue is a challenge. In each parish and neighborhood dialogue is necessary to carry on the ministry of the Church, whether it is among members of the same church or between church members and others with whom they live. The "dialogue of life" is the experience of human existence in a pluralistic world.

Pope John Paul, in his encyclical *Ut Unum Sint* delineates four among the various dimensions of dialogue in the Christian community as ecumenically paramount: *dialogue of charity, dialogue of conversion, dialogue of truth,* and *dialogue of salvation.* These dimensions are not mutually exclusive but develop and deepen together. The dialogues of truth and salvation cannot be sustained in ecumenical encounter without commitment to charity and conversion.

The dialogue of charity demonstrates the love Christians have for one another and for all human beings. Indeed, this dialogue is necessary so that sufficient trust may exist in order to move forward toward deeper unity. In the Orthodox-Roman

Catholic dialogue, for example, there were almost fifteen years of *dialogue of charity* before sufficient trust was built up to move forward to a theological dialogue in 1980.

The *dialogue of conversion* entails a zeal for the unity of the Church, an openness to being changed by the other, and a receptivity to new dimensions of understanding and gifts of God's grace that can only emerge in the dialogue itself. Ecumenical dialogue is an essential of Christian life and a rich source of spiritual renewal. The dialogue of conversion is not merely an institutional interchange, but a Spirit-led encounter in Christ and with Christ that changes the heart. At the same time it is also a conversion which may call for institutional change in the structures and relationships of the churches. As the previous chapter explored, dialogue is a way of life, a way of being in the world, an openness to the Holy Spirit in community.

When there is conversion to the ecclesial path of ecumenism and sufficient trust rooted in love, one goes on to the *dialogue of truth*. Ecumenical dialogue is not one of compromise or negotiations, but of discerning the truth of the Gospel together by the study of the Scriptures, Christian history, the signs of the times and by speaking the truth to one another in love. The fruits of these fifty years of the churches together in the dialogue of truth will be taken up in subsequent chapters.

Finally, Pope John Paul speaks of the *dialogue of salvation*. Dialogue among Christians, within their church and among the churches in yet imperfect communion, is both an element in Christ's saving call to the Christian and a source for the saving mission of the Church in the world. To avoid this dialogue in Christ is to avoid the very mystery of Christ's death and resurrection for us, which is itself the great interchange, a dialogue between God and the human community that finds incarnation in dialogue among Christians.

The process of incorporating the fruits of ecumenical dialogue in the life of the community follows the pattern of the Incarnation and requires the aid of sociological and even political insights to complement the work of the Spirit operative in the quest and realization of Christian unity. It engages and requires the cooperation of the entire Christian Church.

This chapter will summarize three elements of dialogue: (1)

The Nature of Dialogue, (2) The Goal of Dialogue, and (3) The Reception of Dialogue. Careful study of specific dialogues and relationships will give flesh to the sketches provided here.

THE NATURE OF DIALOGUE

In this section, three aspects of the nature of dialogue will be discussed, namely, (A) The Notion of Dialogue, (B) Bilateral and Multilateral Dialogue, and (C) The Complementarity of Bilateral and Multilateral Dialogue.

A. The Notion of Dialogue

Dialogue presupposes some elements of commonality that serve as a basis for unity and other elements that are unfamiliar and/or are perceived as antithetical. The latter represent a foreign horizon that through the dialogue encounter can be incorporated into one's own horizon, permitted to express itself there, hence to be understood. When no common basis of core values and accepted unity exists, one is merely engaging in a two-way monologue.

In this process of understanding, where the "fusion of the horizons" denotes the opening up of an unfamiliar world, one must be prepared to take both horizons seriously. One does not disavow one's own vantage point, except under the conviction of having encountered a deeper truth or a more accurate formulation. On the other hand, one must be ready to allow unfamiliar or disquieting elements to come to be newly understood.

Genuine dialogue does not allow the shallow surrender of one's own or a partner's convictions. This would result in a false irenicism that does not contribute to lasting unity. In a 1996 paper prepared for the ongoing Roman Catholic/United Methodist dialogue, Margie Ralph utilized the work of Michael Kinnamon in *Truth and Community* (29–33) to articulate a list of principles which might be used to inform ecumenical dialogue. It addresses the needs and dynamics of ecumenical dialogue at a variety of levels of formality:

1. Ecumenical dialogue must have a spiritual orientation. A willingness to be transformed is essential.

2. In ecumenical dialogue, participants must be given permission to define themselves, to describe and witness to their faith in their own terms.

3. In order to be helpful to the group in an interdenominational dialogue, each participant needs to have a clear understanding of his or her own faith and present it with honesty and sincerity.

4. The integrity of each person must be treasured by all. As each speaks, he or she must be mindful not only of his or her own integrity, but of the integrity of the person with whom he or she may be disagreeing. Mutual growth, not victory, is the desired fruit.

5. Remember that dialogue, particularly at the congregational level, is between people and not just between churches or ideological positions.

6. Keep the dialogue in the present. No participant needs to represent or defend his or her denomination throughout history. Present issues are the ones that need discussion.

7. Be willing to separate essentials from nonessentials.

8. Do not insist on more agreement from your partner in dialogue than you expect from members of your own denomination.

9. Interpret the faith of the dialogue partner in its best, rather than in its worst, light.

10. As time goes on, don't avoid hard issues. You will undoubtedly not want to tackle these first, but once trust has been established, it is important, in the service of truth, to discuss even difficult issues.

11. Search for ways to turn the increased understanding achieved through dialogue into activities for renewal. An immediate way to do that is to have it lead to prayer. But as time goes on, other activities will occur to the group.

Dialogue is a spirituality before it is a theological method or a path toward institutional transformation and unity. As a consequence, conversion and renewal remain at the base of all ecumenical endeavor. This reality introduces a measure of hazard into ecumenical relationships, particularly for people and institutions who desire to control the process of Christian unity. In the process of ecumenical conversion one has to reckon with the grace of the Holy Spirit, which is not always amenable to human control.

The particular topics of ecumenical dialogue must be allowed to engage the partners in communal conversion and transformation in which they together rediscover the apostolic faith and the demands of the Gospel. The topics of dialogue must not be approached solely because they may offer opportunities for affirmation of the faith tradition of the partners, although this can be an important aspect of dialogue relationships between churches with little historical mutual interaction. Beyond such affirmations, however, lies the call to consider both traditions in the light of the apostolic faith.

The objective content of revealed truth, in its depth, breadth, and richness, is the norm of ecumenical dialogue. The temptation exists to attempt to "short circuit" the process by appealing to one's own confession as the norm of acceptance and by an unwillingness to accept anything beyond its boundaries. But any unity which might result from such a truncated process would be vitiated by a superficial reconciliation and would not represent the unity of the Church that God wills, a unity founded upon the reality of faith.

Each church claims to have remained faithful to the apostolic faith and to lack nothing that is necessary in God's design for the Church. To recognize these claims does not imply that one understands each church to possess all of ecclesial reality in total clarity and precision. Both theology and pastoral practice have been enriched and renewed as a result of dialogue. Through dialogue all of the churches are better able to discern between what are essential elements of the Gospel in the Church and what are the gifts—or liabilities—of culture and human traditions.

In ecumenical dialogue each communion is faced with elements foreign to its tradition and to which it must respond. As a result of dialogue with the Anglicans and Orthodox, the Roman

Catholic Church has been challenged to reassess the tradition of synodical decision making and the collegial exercise of the Petrine office. As a result of dialogue with the Western churches, the frequency of communion has been renewed among the Orthodox. Encounters with the Reformation churches has stimulated Biblical piety and a new balance of word and sacrament in Catholic devotion.

The unfolding effort to enter into communion with other churches will require of each church a careful scrutiny in regard to the faith and practice of its partners. Each will also need to explore its own formulations of the faith so that they are transparent to the truth they are intended to communicate. By its nature the dialogue process demands that ambiguous formulations which militate against the identity in faith of both churches be clarified in order to be understood. Through the dialogue relationship each partner church serves as challenge for the other.

The notion of ecumenical dialogue, then, is a complex idea which embraces both exterior elements and interior elements stemming from the spiritual center of the Christian life that is disturbed by the recognition of disunion as contrary to the will of God. Dialogue seeks, through charity, penance, and renewal, to articulate a catholic vision of truth that is based on the totality of the apostolic faith and is a foretaste of the eschatological unity to which the entire human race is summoned in the design of God.

B. Bilateral and Multilateral Dialogue

Formal dialogues between churches take two forms: bilateral, between two divided churches, and multilateral, including several churches. In these dialogues a variety of methods have served over the decades and are employed today both in informal parish and diocesan settings and in the formally commissioned dialogues of the churches.

The first of these is the method of *comparative ecclesiology*, where different churches compare their expressions of faith, worship life, decision-making structures, spirituality, and the like. In the early meetings of Faith and Order, for example, it was necessary for churches to know accurately how they differed in the interpretation of Scripture or the administration of the sacraments before they could go forward in reconciling the church-dividing differences. Such a method contributes to mutual understanding and appreciation and can often dispel stereotypes, but it does not necessarily lead to unity of faith or formulation.

Second, a methodology has developed since the Lund meeting of the Faith and Order Commission of the World Council of Churches (1952) called the *Christological method.* This method will be discussed in more depth in chapter seven. Briefly, the *Christological method* focuses on what is common in Christ and develops methods of biblical, historical, and contextual research that surface common understandings, transcending the divisions of the past, so that formulations that express the truth of the Gospel in accurate terms and are authentic to the sources can be made, using language different from that of past polemic. Pope John Paul has particularly praised this method in speaking to the Anglican Roman Catholic International Commission:

> Your method has been to go behind the habits of thought and expression born and nourished in enmity and controversy, to scrutinize together the great common treasure, to clothe it in language at once traditional and expressive of an age which no longer glories in strife but seeks to come together in listening to the quiet voice of the Spirit. (IS no. 44 [1980], 90)

This has been fruitful in bilateral conversations such as those Catholic, Eastern Orthodox, Oriental Orthodox and Assyrian Churches. Both bilateral and multilateral dialogues use this Christological methodology. Such classic ecumenical texts as *Baptism, Eucharist and Ministry* (1982) are examples of the fruitfulness of this approach.

More recently both the achievements of biblical scholarship and an increasing recognition of the variety found in cultures around the world have brought a third methodology into play that has important ecumenical consequences. This is the *contextual* or *intercontextual methodology.* In biblical studies there has been recognition of the diversity of theology, liturgy, and church order (polity) in the New Testament churches. There is a comparable diversity in the uses made of biblical material in supporting the theologies of the churches today. In ecumenical dialogue the *contextual method* allows the cultural concerns of the various churches and communities to be integral parts of the discussions. In the African American churches, for example, hymnody and the particular use of biblical texts are as important as the creeds in understanding the faith affirmations and theological concerns of the churches. In looking at theological questions raised in Latin America, Africa, and Asia one must recognize that they may come from contexts very different from those of the North Atlantic and Middle Eastern churches.

It is important to realize that anything perceived as church-dividing in ecumenical dialogue, whether *bilateral* or *multilateral,* has the function of being so, even if it is not a traditional theological formulation. Likewise, it is important to recognize that not everything that has been taught to be church-dividing may, in fact, be so, in the light of ecumenical research, renewal of the churches, or other more overriding causes for unity.

Multilateral dialogues take two forms: those serving *convergence* and not empowered to propose designs for union, and *church union discussions.* The Faith and Order movement represents the former. In the World Council, and through a multiplicity of Faith-and-Order-type discussions in national, regional, and local communities, formulations have been developed that serve as a common ground for unity without proposing action in the churches.

Church union discussions, such as those of the Consultation on Church Union in the United States, seek to use the theological methods of Christological research and contextual exploration to provide a *consensus* in faith, sacramental life, and church order for a united church, in this case the Church of Christ Uniting. In this conversation, the Episcopal, Presbyterian, Disciples, United Methodist, African Methodist Episcopal, African Methodist Episcopal Zion, Christian Methodist Episcopal Churches, the United Church of Christ, and the International Council of Community Churches have before them proposals based on more than thirty years of dialogue. These proposals will place those acting on them positively into full communion by Advent 2000. United churches based on multilateral dialogue have emerged around the world since the mid-twentieth century. The most dramatic of these are those of the Indian subcontinent, beginning with the Church of South India in 1948.

The *bilateral dialogues* use these same methodologies and can be focused on the goal of mutual understanding or on the goal of full communion or some intermediate level of communion. This form of dialogue has the potential of focusing in a concentrated manner on divisive and controversial issues between the two partners and on a limited number of topics, so that remarkable results can be achieved in a rather short time. These dialogues have been most fruitful among Orthodox, Catholic, and Reformation churches with explicit confession statements and formulated ecclesiologies.

Nevertheless, other communities, lacking a pronounced dogmatic tradition, doctrinal formulations, and clearly defined liturgical forms have also entered quite successfully into this form of dialogue. At present only a small section of world Christianity is not involved in bilateral dialogue. The bilateral dialogue form can enable the local churches to engage in constructive dialogue in their turn. The relationship between international and national dialogues and the local church is very important, not only as holding out the hope and promise of full communion, but also in nourishing ecumenical understanding and spirituality through study, prayer, and evaluation.

C. Complementarity of the Dialogues

The subject matter of the dialogues has concentrated upon vertical *koinonia* in discussing the Trinity, Christology, pneumatology, and ecclesiology. Much of this discussion has required a correlate attention to horizontal *koinonia* in such issues as apostolic succession, authority, baptism, common witness, councils, episcopacy, Eucharist, invocation of saints, Mariology, marriage, ministry, ordination, papacy, laity, priesthood, Scripture, tradition, and worship. Some important dialogues have touched on ethical themes such as conscience, abortion, euthanasia, human rights, and moral formation. For the most part, the subject matter of the dialogues has concentrated on church-dividing issues in the various arenas in which they occur.

The dialogues are all interrelated, sometimes by conscious study, but most frequently by the common context of *koinonia* theology that has emerged in both the bilateral and multilateral contexts. The two styles of dialogue have found ways of reinforcing each other by a theological common ground and by study and synthesis of the full range of dialogue results.

The work of the World Council of Churches has assisted some bilateral and multilateral church union proposals. Learnings from one bilateral conversation have had positive influences on others. Proposals that cannot be realized, for example, between Lutherans and Catholics at the present time may serve to stimulate action between Anglicans and Lutherans. There is a regular forum among ecumenical leaders from the Christian World Communions on the bilateral dialogues that helps to coordinate this journey and share its fruits. These dialogues present a complementary contribution to the one pilgrimage toward Christian unity.

THE GOAL OF DIALOGUE

Christians realize that the unity of the Church is the gift of God and cannot be attained by recourse to human effort alone. Such a realization, while anchoring one firmly in the spiritual richness of one's own tradition, nonetheless releases one from undue attachment to one's own efforts or one's own tradition. It enables one to welcome the genuine gifts and ministrations of the Spirit in other churches and to enjoy the plethora of charisms with which the Holy Spirit endows the entire Christian community, thus upbuilding the Church and continuing its mission.

In the Catholic understanding and that of many of the ecumenical partners, the fostering of ecumenism, while emanating from an interior disposition of repentance and renewal, cannot remain a purely invisible endeavor, but must express itself in a visible and organic manner. The culmination of such a spiritual and social *koinonia* occurs in the Eucharist, as the World Council stated in 1961, speaking of the Church in the form of "one fully committed fellowship, holding the one apostolic faith, preaching the one Gospel, breaking the one bread, joining in common prayer, and having a corporate life reaching out in witness and service to all."

The cause of Christian unity should not remain an intramural exercise devoted to the ecclesial sphere alone, but must embrace the entire human community in its racial, social, economic, and cultural diversity. Unity is the ultimate goal of God's plan for humanity, to "gather together in unity the scattered children of God."

> The calling of the church is to proclaim reconciliation and provide healing, to overcome divisions based on race, gender, age, culture, color, and to bring all people into communion with God. Because of sin and the misunderstanding of the diverse gifts of the Spirit, the churches are painfully divided within themselves and among each other. (Canberra 1.2)

Unity of disciples is a sacramental anticipation, in baptism and Eucharist, of the unity of all God's children, who receive the summons to unity by means of the Gospel proclamation and mission of the disciples. Ecclesial unity, then, anticipates eschatological unity, and manifests the presence of the Kingdom. The goal of ecumenism, in this respect, is to render the Church more "catholic," and to demonstrate how the Church can be an inclusive community that reaches out to people everywhere.

As noted in chapter three, the churches are beginning to enumerate together the elements that will need to be reconciled if this goal of full *koinonia* is to be realized. Obviously, churches will move by stages toward the goal, and some churches will be able to move more quickly than others. However, the goal of Christian unity can only be reached by the patient and tedious process of dialogue.

Dialogues themselves surface new issues that need to be resolved. Centuries of division and independent development have created concerns that must be resolved if the communion now realized is to be perfected. Dialogues that have as their goal the full visible unity of the Church are not permanent. Their results reach a level of maturity when they can be submitted to the sponsoring churches for evaluation and eventual action.

However, as they are acted upon through the magisterial structures of the churches, they are also tested in the spiritual lives of the community. The following section will deal with the reception of dialogue results.

THE RECEPTION OF DIALOGUE

From the very beginning of the life of the Church, the penetration of formulations of faith and forms of life in the Christian community—reception—has been a key process. Reception moves forward under the direction of the Holy Spirit. A basic spiritual attitude of the Christian is a receptivity to what the Spirit is doing in the Church. The ecumenical dimension of Christian spirituality calls for zeal for the unity of the Church and a receptive enthusiasm about each step forward on this pilgrimage.

The particular books that were included in the biblical canon, the formulations of the Incarnation, the Trinity, and the creeds that became the testimony to the faith of the early councils only gradually came to be received as normative by the Christian community. Scholars of early Christian literature who study the reception and nonreception of the councils of Chalcedon and Ephesus among the churches and the more recent authoritative statements in the churches find no one course for reception. Today this study of earlier patterns of reception is complemented by the study of ecumenical reception.

Pope John Paul highlights the urgency of the study of the dialogues and their reception in his encyclical: "...a new task lies before us: that of receiving the results already achieved" which "must involve the whole people of God." Results are not to remain "statements of bilateral commissions but must become a common heritage" (UUS 80).

None of the churches has yet developed an authoritative explanation of reception. We are only beginning to learn about ecumenical reception as the churches become more deeply engaged, and as historians and theologians reflect. Cardinal Willebrands defines reception, in regard to the ecumenical movement thus:

In *Catholic understanding* reception can be circumscribed as a process by means of which the People of God, in its differentiated structure and under the guidance of the Holy Spirit, recognizes and accepts new insights, new witnesses of truth and their forms of expression because they are deemed to be in line of the apostolic succession and in harmony with the *sensus fidelium* of the Church as a whole. Because such witnesses of new insights and experiences are recognized as authentic elements of apostolicity and catholicity, they basically aim at acceptance and inclusion in the living faith of the Church....In its full form reception embraces the official doctrine, its proclamation, the liturgy, the spiritual and ethical life of the faithful, as well as theology as systematic reflection about this complex reality. Reception therefore involves the *kerygma,* the *didaché,* and the *praxis pietatis.* Inasmuch as the entire People of God partakes in the search for and the unfolding of the truth of God's word, all the charisms and services are involved according to their station: the theologians by means of their research activities, the faithful by means of their preserving fidelity and piety, the ecclesial ministries and especially the college of bishops with its function of making binding decisions. One can also say that ministry and charism, proclamation and theology, magisterial ministry and sense of faith of the People, all act together in the reception process. The Church and all her members are therefore involved in a learning process that by its very nature is not exclusively concerned with theological documents, but also considers developments in the domains of liturgy, pastoral care, canon law, discipline, forms of piety, etc. It is an important task of the bishops to ensure that all domains and levels of Christian ecclesial life participate in this process in depth. (*Origins* 14:44 [April 18, 1985], 722)

Thus, the parish community, the catechetical program, the preaching of the Church, the teaching of theology, all have a role in the assimilation of the ecumenical movement and the results of the dialogues it has produced for the churches.

The churches, including the Catholic Church, are in the early stages of the move from dialogue to reception and eventual institutional action. Only a few dialogue texts have come before the Catholic Church for institutional action at the level of the Holy See. While this official response and action is only one element in reception, it is key. Care will need to be taken that every action deepens communion both within the Church and between the churches acting on the dialogue results.

In addition to the Common Declarations with Eastern and Oriental Orthodox patriarchs, three dialogues that have begun to be acted on by the Catholic Church are: (1) the World Council *Baptism, Eucharist and Ministry (BEM)* (1982–1987); (2) the Anglican Roman Catholic International Commission *Final Report* (ARCIC I) (1982–1991); and (3) the Lutheran World Federation/Roman Catholic Joint Declaration on Justification by Faith (JD) (1998).

In these three cases different processes have been followed, but in each, new levels of commitment have been displayed and new learnings about ecumenical reception have emerged. Careful study of these dialogues, the processes of evaluation, and the particular actions proposed will be important if one is to assess the present state of ecumenical evaluation and reception. Other churches in the United States, such as the nine churches of the Consultation on Church Union; the Evangelical Lutheran and Episcopal Churches; and the ELCA and three Reformed Churches, Presbyterian Church, Reformed Church in America and the United Church of Christ; face decisions on proposals for full communion during this last decade of the twentieth century.

The World Council of Churches' Faith and Order Commission's *Baptism, Eucharist and Ministry* is a multilateral convergence document that does not claim full consensus among the churches. It is a contribution to ecumenical agreement, but has not been proposed as a basis for any final action. It has been the most extensively studied text in the modern ecumenical movement, and has elicited responses from almost two hundred Orthodox, Anglican, and Protestant Churches, and the Catholic Church.

In 1982, the Commission on Faith and Order of the WCC invited all churches to respond to *BEM* at the highest level of authority. The Pontifical Council for Promoting Christian Unity (PCPCU), in response, inaugurated a threefold program: (a) broad consultation in the Catholic Church at large, (b) preparation of a draft text, (c) a response, in consultation with the Congregation for the Doctrine of the Faith (CDF).

In the course of this process, the PCPCU sent *BEM* to all the Catholic episcopal conferences, and requested them, in conjunction with their theological and seminary faculties, to study the document and to respond to it. Reports from twenty-six episcopal conferences were returned, along with responses from theological faculties, seminaries, theological associations, ecumenical organizations, individual dioceses, and individual theologians. Next, the PCPCU, in conjunction with a team of theological consultants, examined the reports and prepared a critical draft of a Catholic response to *BEM*. Then, the PCPCU and the CDF examined the draft and produced a mutually agreed response. The final draft was submitted to the Pope, and the response was released in August 1987. Pope John Paul II made a number of positive statements about *BEM* before, during, and after the official Catholic response process.

The mandate and results of the ARCIC are different from *BEM*. The restoration of full communion is the goal, and the claim is that this is a *consensus,* not merely a *convergence* text. Substantial agreement is claimed on Eucharist and ministry, and convergence on authority. Upon the completion of the ARCIC I *Final Report,* it was sent to all the Catholic episcopal conferences in March 1982 with the request to discern whether "it is consonant in substance with the faith of the Catholic Church on the matters discussed." The CDF forwarded its reflections to the Catholic episcopal conferences. The consultation in the Catholic community continued and several episcopal conferences, especially those with a sizable Anglican presence, communicated their evaluation to the PCPCU. The PCPCU composed a response in collaboration with the CDF. The final official response was published in December 1991.

While the Roman Catholic response was basically positive, the tone and method of the response were not well received in the community of ecumenical scholars. The response raised specific issues which required greater clarification from the Catholic point of view. ARCIC II responded by appointing a small committee of persons who were associated with the composition of the *Final Report,* and sent a document containing the clarifications to the Holy See, where it was studied by the PCPCU and the CDF. Cardinal Cassidy, in 1994, responded positively to the "Clarifications" and stated that "the agreements reached on Eucharist and Ministry is thus greatly strengthened and no further study would seem to be required at this stage" (IS no. 87 [1994], 237).

The complexity of this process and the misunderstandings it produced, signal the fact that the Roman Catholic Church, like other churches involved in the ecumenical pilgrimage, is only gradually developing structures and processes to facilitate ecumenical communication, collaboration, and response.

A final example involves the Lutheran World Federation (LWF). As will be noted below, progress in the international dialogue and in Germany and the United States has provided a context to move from theological dialogue to ecclesial action. The U.S. work on "Justification by Faith" and the German work on the "Condemnations of the Sixteenth Century," were brought together through the international leadership of the LWF and the PCPCU to produce a draft Joint Declaration. After various stages of revision, with the participation of episcopal conferences and Lutheran churches around the world, the text was submitted to member churches of the Lutheran World Federation and the Holy See for formal ratification in 1998. The agreement, like the Common Declarations with Anglican and Orthodox leaders, is a formal confessionally-binding witness to the faith that will place the churches affirming it on a new basis. The condemnations connected with the doctrines of justification articulated by the Council of Trent and in the *Book of Concord* will be seen as not applying to the present day churches affirming the Declaration.

As the churches move forward in their journey together toward full communion, reception becomes an increasingly important part of their life together. At this time there is no consensus among the churches and within the Roman Catholic Church on how reception will proceed. The diverse results need to be kept in harmony with one another, the collegial and consultative convictions of the Church need to be honored, and continued theological reflection is needed to enrich our understanding as the Church responds to this movement of the Holy Spirit. Dialogue, while a spiritually nourishing Christian discipline, is not an ecumenical end in itself. The results of the dialogue are for the support of the communion that exists and the building of deeper levels of communion toward full unity.

Conclusion

The development of dialogue has enriched both the daily life and the hopes for the future of all the churches in the ecumenical movement. The nature and goal of the dialogues and their reception in the lives of the churches become intrinsic to all Christian formation. The spirit of dialogue permeates the Christian life, as the Roman Synod for Africa affirms:

> The church family has its origin in the Blessed Trinity, at the depths of which the Holy Spirit is the Bond of Communion. It knows that the intrinsic value of a community is the quality of relations which it makes possible. This synod launches a strong appeal for dialogue within the church and among religions. (*L'Osservatore Romano,* English ed., 19/7 [11 May 1994] no. 20)

The accomplishment of the ecumenical task requires the power of the Holy Spirit. Augustine counseled the community to pray as if everything depends upon God and to act as if everything depends upon ourselves. The ecumenical process requires one to heed such counsel. The reports and results of dialogues can nourish the spirituality, catechesis, and intellectual life of the whole people of God. The nature, goal, and reception of dialogue combines the dual obligation, to rely trustingly on God and to utilize all the hermeneutical and theological tools available to contribute to the divine and human union which ecumenical efforts espouse.

Study Questions

1. What is the ultimate goal of ecumenical dialogue? What are some of the principles and methods of dialogue?

2. What are some of the pastoral and spiritual fruits of ecumenical dialogue as it pursues its goal?

3. What are the principles that ecumenical partners bring to the dialogue?

4. What are some of the dimensions of dialogue enumerated by Pope Paul VI and Pope John Paul II?

5. What are the differences between multilateral and bilateral dialogues and the contributions of both?

6. What is meant by the theological concept of reception? What are some of its classical examples and its contemporary ecumenical challenges?

7. What are the opportunities for dialogue in parish pastoral life?

8. What are the challenges for reception before the churches as institutions? In their catechesis and formation?

Selected Readings

Cassidy, Edward Idris, Cardinal. "Letter." Pontifical Council for Promoting Christian Unity, *Information Service*, no. 87 (1994): 237.

——. "The Measure of Catholic Ecumenical Commitment." *Origins* 22:43 (April 8, 1993): 736–44.

Evans, G. R. *Method in Ecumenical Theology: The Lessons So Far.* Cambridge: Cambridge University Press, 1996.

Falconer, Alan D. "Towards Unity through Diversity: Bilateral and Multilateral Dialogues." *One In Christ* 29 (1993): 279–85.

Ford, John T., and Darlis J. Swan. *Twelve Tales Untold: A Study Guide for Ecumenical Reception.* Grand Rapids: Eerdmans, 1993.

Ford, John T. "Bilateral Conversations and Denominational Horizons." *Journal of Ecumenical Studies* 23 (Summer 1986): 518–28.

——, ed. "A Report of the Bilateral Study Group of the Faith and Order Commission of the National Council of Churches." *Mid-Stream* 28 (1989): 115–36.

Gassmann, Günther. "Nature and Function of Bilateral and Multilateral Dialogues and their Interrelation." *Mid-Stream* 25 (1986): 299–308.

John Paul II. "Address to the Members of the Anglican/Roman Catholic International Commission." Pontifical Council for Promoting Christian Unity, *Information Service*, no. 44 (1980): 90–91.

Kinnamon, Michael. *Truth and Community: Diversity and its Limits in the Ecumenical Movement.* Grand Rapids: Eerdmans, 1988.

Kinnamon, Michael. and Brian E. Cope, eds. *The Ecumenical Movement: An Anthology of Basic Texts and Voices.* Grand Rapids: Eerdmans, 1997, pp. 129–210.

Lanne, Emmanuel, O.S.B. "Two Decades of Bilateral Conversations and their Impact on the Ecumenical Movement." *Mid-Stream* 25 (1986): 309–21.

Nilson, Jon. *Nothing Beyond the Necessary: Roman Catholicism and the Ecumenical Future.* New York/Mahwah: Paulist Press, 1995.

Puglisi, J. F., and S. J. Voicu. *A Bibliography of Interchurch and Interconfessional Theological Dialogues.* Rome: Centro Pro Unione, 1984.

Radano, John A. "Response and Reception in the Catholic Church." *Mid-Stream,* 35 (1996): 71–103.

Rusch, William G. *Reception: An Ecumenical Opportunity.* Philadelphia: Fortress Press, 1988.

Secretariat for Promoting Christian Unity. "Reflections and Suggestions Concerning Ecumenical Dialogue." *In Doing the Truth in Charity: Statements of Pope Paul VI, Popes John Paul I, John Paul II and the Secretariat for Promoting Christian Unity, 1964–1980: Ecumenical Documents I.* Edited by Thomas F. Stransky and John B. Sheerin, pp. 75–88. New York/Mahwah: Paulist Press, 1982.

Willebrands, Johannes Cardinal. "The Ecumenical Dialogue and its Reception." *One In Christ* 21 (1985): 217–25.

7

The Contribution of the World Council of Churches

O God, holy and eternal Trinity,
  We pray for your church in the world.
    Sanctify its life; renew its worship;
      Empower its witness; heal its divisions;
        Make visible its unity.
Lead us, with all our brothers and sisters,
  Toward communion in faith, life and witness
    So that, united in one body
      By the one Spirit,
        We may together witness
    To the perfect unity of your love. Amen
              Fifth World Conference on Faith and Order

Conversion to the ecumenical vision of the Gospel takes place on the personal level in the human heart and mind and on the ecclesial level by decisions for renewal and dialogue taken by the churches themselves through their normal teaching and decision-making offices. Ecclesial reconciliation takes place in every dimension of church life—in the local congregation and at the centers of decision making, on the national, regional, and international levels. One means the churches have developed for giving form to their commitment to one another is to live and work together in councils and conferences of churches. These agencies, which exist at every level from the local to the international, each have their own organization and mission, according to the will of the churches that constitute them.

It is important for those working in ecumenism locally to know of the international, national, and regional support for their efforts available from their own church and from the councils that bring churches together. In the United States there are ministerial organizations, neighborhood congregational clusters, citywide councils of churches and state-level conferences. The Roman Catholic dioceses are encouraged, where appropriate, to take membership in these local agencies, as are parishes in their very local clusters.

In many countries of the world there are national councils. These are particularly important because, unlike the Catholic Church, the Protestant, Anglican, and Orthodox churches are often national churches with juridical and magisterial authority located within the appropriate national leadership. In over forty national councils, the appropriate Catholic episcopal conference is a full member. In the Western hemisphere this is true in Brazil, in the regional conference of the Caribbean and some nations within it, and in Canada. In the United States, the Catholic Bishops' Conference works closely with the National Council, with regular meetings between the General Secretaries, and has full membership in the National Council's Faith and Order Commission. While there are no theological obstacles to Catholic membership in such councils, in some cases, issues of size, finance, and history make collaboration rather than membership seem the appropriate relationship for this time.

On the worldwide level, over three hundred Orthodox, Protestant, Old Catholic, and Anglican churches belong to the World Council of Churches. While the World Council and the various national, regional, and local councils have no institutional connection, the very presence of the churches together in commitment to unity engenders reconciliation at every level of the churches' life. Pope John Paul notes with appreciation: "Today I see with satisfaction that the already vast network of ecumenical cooperation is constantly growing. Thanks also to the influence of the World Council of Churches, much is being accomplished in this field" (UUS 43).

The Roman Catholic Church, through a Joint Working Group, a full membership on the Faith and Order Commission, the providing of staff in the mission and social justice sections, and by a presence at all Assemblies and most meetings of the Council, is as active as many of the member churches of the Council. As the Pope reminds us in his encyclical, the Catholic Church is fully committed to the WCC's constituting goal "to call the churches to the goal of visible unity in one faith and in one Eucharistic fellowship expressed in worship and in common life in Christ" (UUS 24).

This chapter will review the structure and self-understanding of the World Council, the history of its Faith and Order dialogues, and their results and significance for the churches. It will be important to study this chapter along with the Faith and Order texts and those of the Joint Working Group between the Holy See and the WCC.

Especially important will be the study of the 1950 *The Church, the Churches and the World Council of Churches*. This foundational text is helpful in diocesan and local discussions about councils and conferences, and offers language that is useful in interpreting what a council can be. It will also be important to read the documents of the Faith and Order movement, especially *Baptism, Eucharist and Ministry; Scripture, Tradition and the Traditions;* and *Confessing One Faith*.

What Does the World Council Look Like?

The Council itself is the relationship among its member churches. It does not replace them, nor does it speak for them. It provides a forum for common witness in the world, often taking its clues from the struggles of member churches in their particular contexts. Over the decades before the fall of apartheid in South Africa, the churches together were outspoken critics of this inhuman and unchristian system of racial oppression. During the period before the fall of Marxism the World Council provided one of the few places in which the churches from Eastern Europe could meet fellow Christians and keep alive the hope of survival and solidarity. In this context, common witness took the form of personal and ecclesial support as well as quiet pressure and diplomacy. There are thousands of examples from every sector of the globe where this common witness has held up the witness of Christ and of Christ's reconciling love for the human community.

The Council emerged in 1948 from the confluence of three streams of ecumenical life. The mission movement was the most dramatic challenge to Christian divisions, especially among Protestants, or where Protestants were in tension with Catholics and Orthodox. In the wake of World War I, the need for solidarity in social service and Christian witness to justice and peacemaking gave rise to the Life and Work movement, with its focus on social ethics, church, and society. The third stream will be the primary focus of this chapter, the Faith and Order movement, which seeks to marshal the theological resources of the churches to explore and heal the divisions that have kept the churches apart.

The history of the Council has been a gradual movement of the churches out of isolation, mutual polemic, and distrust, to collaboration, dialogue, and deeper communion *(koinonia)*. The early history of the ecumenical movement has to be seen in the light of the two world wars that so divided Europe, and the memories of hostility and wars of religion that are etched in the monuments and borders of the European landscape. The experience of resistance to Hitler, the survival in the East behind the Iron Curtain, the organization and mutual support of Protestant churches in Asia, Africa, and Latin America all provided the backdrop for the emergence of the World Council in 1948, and the gradual entry of the Catholic Church into the ecumenical movement.

The movement flourished in the period of decolonialization, when many of the Protestant churches, like the nations to which they had sent missionaries, became independent and self-governing in the Third World. At the same time, Middle Eastern tensions were leading Orthodox in that area to reach out to the West. Eastern European isolation made Orthodox solidarity with Protestant, and later Catholic, fellow Christians a lifeline in despair.

Yet the enthusiasm about release from the burdens of war and the conversion to ecumenical openness that came in the foxholes, resistance movements, and postwar collaboration in relief, rebuilding, and resettlement challenged these newly found partners to find a theological understanding to undergird the Council. It was in a historic 1950 meeting of the Central Committee that the foundation was articulated in *The Church, the Churches and the World Council of Churches*. To this day, this text reminds the churches of how far we have come on the road to unity, and how far we have to go in realizing full communion.

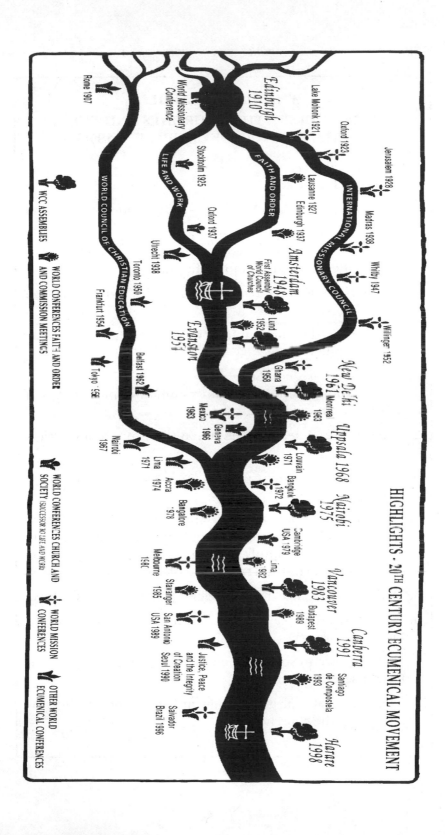

HIGHLIGHTS · 20TH CENTURY ECUMENICAL MOVEMENT

WHAT IS A COUNCIL?
THE CHURCH, THE CHURCHES AND THE WORLD COUNCIL OF CHURCHES (1950)

What a Council is not:
1. A "super church."

2. A negotiator of church unions—it promotes contact and study.

3. Based on any particular conception of Church—ecclesiology is under discussion among the churches.

4. Membership does not relativize a church's own conception of the Church.

5. Membership does not imply acceptance of a particular doctrine of Church unity.

Assumptions underlying a Council:
1. Conversation, cooperation, and common witness are based on recognition of Christ.

2. The New Testament confesses that the Church of Christ is one.

3. The Church of Christ is more inclusive than one's own church.

4. The relationship of member churches to the one, holy, catholic Church is a subject of mutual consideration. Membership does not imply recognition of one another as churches in the full and true sense of the word.

5. Members recognize in others elements of the true Church.

6. Members seek to learn of Christ what witness to the world they can bear.

7. Members are in solidarity and assist in need and refrain from insensitive actions.

8. Members relate spiritually and learn from one another, for renewal of the churches.

The churches meet approximately every seven years in an Assembly, bringing together representatives from around the world to pray, deliberate, elect officers, and make policy for the years to come. Most Assemblies have relied on the theological work of Faith and Order for the deepening and clarification of views on the nature of the unity sought. At the first Assembly the churches committed themselves to "stay together," which itself was a historic gesture after the centuries of division, the ravages of the Second World War, and the tensions of decolonization. The 1968 Assembly delineated a vision of the Church as mystery and prophetic sign; the 1975 Assembly put forth the vision of a Conciliar Fellowship; and greater detail was given to that vision of *koinonia* in the 1991 Assembly, quoted at length in chapter three.

As an example of how this emerging clarification of unity developed through the decades, we can look at the 1961 Assembly, which took place on the eve of the Vatican Council. This Assembly saw the first official Catholic observers, the entry of virtually all of the Eastern European Orthodox, and the first Pentecostal members from Latin America. Its text emphasized the universal and local character of the unity we seek, a foretaste of the collegiality and subsidiarity that would be articulated in the ecclesiology of the Vatican Council:

> We believe that the unity which is both God's will and his gift to his Church is being made visible as all in each place who are baptized into Jesus Christ and confess him as Lord and Savior are brought by the Holy Spirit into one fully committed fellowship, holding the one apostolic faith, preaching the one Gospel, breaking the one bread, joining in common prayer, and having a corporate life reaching out in witness and service to all and who at the same time are united with the whole Christian fellowship in all places and all ages in such wise that ministry and members are accepted by all, and that all can act and speak together as occasion requires for the tasks to which God calls his people. (New Delhi, 116)

The World Council is not an institution with a particular headquarters, rather it is the relationship between the Protestant and Orthodox Christians down the street, through their churches. And it is the churches, in their various stages toward unity, living together. Yet, to serve this web of relationships, this pilgrimage toward unity, this common witness to the Gospel in the world, this solidarity in service, the churches have pooled some of their resources to share a common staff to provide for the Assemblies and the vast numbers of meetings, publications, systems of communication, and interchanges that are necessary to nurture this journey together.

There is an office in Geneva, with a General Secretariat and four organizational units. These units are: (1) Unity and Renewal; (2) Mission: Health, Education, and Witness; (3) Justice, Peace, and the Integrity of Creation; and (4) Sharing and Services. Among these units, some churches emphasize certain of their values while others have different emphases. Likewise, within each dimension of church life there are those who bring one charism or another. Therefore, there are continuing tensions among the elements of the World Council, as there are tensions among the still divided churches. These tensions are the sign of the unity not achieved and of the dynamism of the Holy Spirit urging those who serve the common mission to promote the particular gift they see as primary.

Those engaged in advocacy for justice, peace, and the integrity of creation are sometimes impatient with the painstaking theological work necessary in unity and renewal. Those concerned with evangelism sometimes find it difficult to understand the urgency of interreligious dialogue. The dialogue between the churches is augmented by the dialogue within the dimensions of emerging ecumenical solidarity. A careful study of the World Council's common reflection on social teaching and ethics, the nature of mission and dialogue, and its contribution to social service and resource sharing is an important addition to the review of the theological dialogue toward unity in this chapter.

THE FAITH AND ORDER DIALOGUES: THE BEGINNING

As noted in chapter one, the movement toward full visible unity was pioneered by the U.S. Episcopal Church and the Anglican Communion in its 1888 Chicago-Lambeth Quadrilateral, the American Society for Church History founded the same year, and more general movements toward unity which had earlier roots in such groups as the Evangelical Alliance. However, it would wait for the early twentieth century for these theological and historical impulses to find institutional expression in the modern ecumenical movement.

The Faith and Order initiative, under Anglican and Disciples leadership, became a datable institutional reality with the first World Conference on Faith and Order meeting in Lausanne, Switzerland, in 1927. The preparations laid a firm foundation for careful exploration and mutual understanding of the honest theological differences the churches faced in affirmation of the Christian faith, in the variety of approaches to the sacramental life, especially the ordained ministry, and in confessing the nature of the Church. This Conference and the second World Conference in Edinburgh in 1937 were historic, but seem very superficial, given the great progress made since them.

The churches were just beginning to know one another. For many, especially in the Protestant West, the depth and importance of the divisions were not recognized until careful discussion took place over the nature of apostolicity, continuity in ministry, Eucharistic ecclesiology, and the nature of conciliarity as understood by the Orthodox. Orthodox and Anglicans brought commitment to a doctrine of ministry that seemed excessive to some Protestants. Lutherans and Orthodox brought commitment to confessional agreement in the content of the faith that seemed unenlightened to the modern critical minds of some. The scientific tools of critical biblical and historical scholarship seemed reductive and secularist to many in the East.

The method used in these first two conferences was that of *comparative ecclesiology*. That is, theologians of the various Protestant, Anglican, and Orthodox churches articulated the positions of their churches in honest, open, and irenic ways. In this fashion the churches began to know one another, to identify their common elements of faith, their differences of practice, and the fundamental differences that kept them divided. This method was necessary, and is often the first step when new individuals and communities enter into the ecumenical conversation.

However, as the movement matured, a new method was introduced at Lund in 1952. When the question was asked, "Where do we stand?" the participants in the conference asserted: "Christ has made us His own and Christ is not divided. In seeking Him we find one another." This *Christological methodology* was the great turning point in ecumenical discourse that has made the subsequent bilateral and multilateral progress possible. In this new context scholars from the various traditions look together at the biblical, historical, and contextual dimensions of the doctrines under question and work together to formulate the faith in accurate ways that transcend the polarizations of the past:

> We have seen clearly that we can make no real advance toward unity if we only compare our several conceptions of the nature of the Church and the traditions in which they are embodied. But once again it has been proven true that as we seek to draw closer to Christ we come closer to one another. We need, therefore, to penetrate behind our divisions to a deeper and richer understanding of the mystery of the God-given union of Christ with His Church. We need increasingly to realize that the separate histories of our Churches find their full meaning only if seen in the perspective of God's dealings with his *whole* people. (Vischer, 85–86)

Already in the Lund meeting progress was made on such issues as worship and intercommunion; in addition, the famous challenge to the churches, known as the Lund principle, was formulated: "The churches should do together all those things which their consciences do not require them to do separately." It was also in this conference that the so-called "nontheological" factors, such as culture, race, gender, and class were considered and made an essential part of the church unity agenda with serious theological and methodological implications. These considerations came to be part of what is called the *contextual methodology*.

In preparation for the fourth World Conference on Faith and Order, held in Montreal in 1963, there was an extensive preparatory process. In the United States there was a 1957 conference on Faith and Order at which Roman Catholic participants were present with authorization for the first time. This conference proposed that a Faith and Order Commission be developed in the United States and situated within the National Council of Churches of Christ.

The National Council itself had a more practical origin as a *cooperative agency* of its member churches, with an agenda in society and in the churches that originally did not include unity in faith and sacraments. The history of the World Council and the National Council have been quite different, even though all of the Orthodox, Anglican, and Protestant members of the National Council are also members of the World Council. The theological work of Faith and Order has only gradually begun to influence the National Council and to develop a higher profile among the U.S. churches. The bilateral dialogues and the success of the World Council *Baptism, Eucharist and Ministry* text have made important contributions to the entry of the National Council into the church unity movement in a serious way. Study of the results of the National Council Faith and Order discussions are an important element in understanding the U.S. contribution to global ecumenism, and to the Catholic experience of ecumenism in the United States.

The Major Contributions of Faith and Order

Following the dramatic breakthrough at the Lund meeting, there has been steady progress in the contribution of the Faith and Order Commission. In this section about the Faith and Order dialogues, we will review the work on Scripture and tradition, conciliar fellowship, the sacraments, unity and renewal, *koinonia,* and the apostolic faith. It must be remembered that Faith and Order is dealing with a whole host of issues not treated here, and is influenced by and influences factors within the lives of the churches, bilateral progress, and church union negotiations. All of these relationships, influences, and developments are part of the one ecumenical movement.

One of the thorniest issues separating the churches of the Reformation from Orthodoxy and Roman Catholicism is the issue of the relationship between Scripture and tradition. Renewal of biblical and historical scholarship in the early twentieth century, new approaches to understanding the development of doctrine over time, and commonality in the use of the critical tools of scholarship across confessional differences, all contributed to a renewed understanding of the common ground underlying all of the Christian churches. The new Christological methodology enabled scholars to look together at the texts of the Bible, councils, and confessions with fresh perspectives:

> The oral and written tradition of the prophets and apostles under the guidance of the Holy Spirit led to the formation of Scriptures and to the canonization of the Old and New Testaments as the Bible of the Church. The very fact that Tradition precedes the Scriptures points to the significance of Tradition, but also to the Bible as the treasure of the Word of God. (Kinnamon, 139)

This World Conference, held in Montreal in 1963, fell during the midst of the period when the Roman Catholic bishops were meeting in Council at the Vatican. Issues of revelation, Scripture, and tradition was also being debated there. Many of the ecumenical observers at Vatican II were delegates to Montreal. For the first time, Roman Catholics were officially present, although not delegates to the Conference. Some of these Catholic representatives were also advisors at the Council. It is useful to study the statement *Scripture, Tradition and Traditions* side by side with the Council's Decree on Divine Revelation *(Dei Verbum)* to note the dramatic convergence that emerged.

The affirmation of the "traditional" character of Scripture at Montreal is further amplified by its explication of the "traditioning" process in the Church:

> Our starting point is that we are all living in a tradition which goes back to our Lord and has its roots in the Old Testament, and we are all indebted to that tradition inasmuch as we have received the revealed truth, the Gospel, through its being transmitted from one generation to another. Thus we can say that we exist as Christians by the Tradition of the Gospel (the *paradosis* of the *kerygma*) testified in Scripture, transmitted in and by the Church through the power of the Holy Spirit. Tradition taken in this sense is actualized in the preaching of the Word, in administration of the Sacraments and worship, in Christian teaching and theology, and in mis-

sion and witness to Christ by the lives of the members of the Church. (Kinnamon, 140)

This dramatic breakthrough does not, of course, solve all of the problems of church divisiveness centering around biblical interpretation, the theology and administration of teaching authority in the Church, or the process of discernment between the traditions (with a small *t*) and the Tradition of the Gospel (with a large *T*). The latter is seen to be normative for all within a united Church, the former are expressions of the appropriate diversity of the churches.

This convergence on Scripture and tradition, however, is important for the future work of Faith and Order, where it provides the foundation for the use of the Bible and history as proposals are put forward for the structure of a united church, sacramental reconciliation, and common confession. It is clear, from the churches' responses to *Baptism, Eucharist and Ministry*, for example, that many of them have yet to receive this important agreement. Likewise, new developments in biblical interpretation and inculturation require the reformulation of this agreement in each new generation.

There was not another World Conference for thirty years, but the work of Faith and Order within the churches, in the bilaterals, in national councils, and through the World Council Commission continued to develop and deepen. During the late 1960s and 1970s the Commission faced the great task of integrating the variety of Orthodox voices from Eastern Europe, the Roman Catholic members after that Church joined in 1968, the emerging Third World voices with their particular theological concerns, and increased numbers of women's voices. These perspectives brought the gifts of their cultural, theological, and concrete experiences. It is during this period that greater attention was given to the contextual method, especially through such studies as *The Unity of the Church and the Renewal of Human Community* and *The Community of Women and Men in the Church*.

Of particular importance were the studies on patristics, authority, and church order. As a result of these studies, and taking account of the rich resources of the bilateral dialogues of this period, the World Council was able to put before the churches a vision of a united church as a *Conciliar Fellowship (Koinonia)* that is grounded in an understanding of Acts 15 and of the early ecumenical councils. This vision lays forth an ecclesiological content and an agenda for areas where dialogue must develop:

> The one Church is to be envisioned as a conciliar fellowship of local churches which are themselves truly united. In this conciliar fellowship, each local church possesses, in communion with the others, the fullness of catholicity, witnesses to the same apostolic faith, and therefore recognizes the others as belonging to the same Church of Christ and guided by the same Spirit...they have received the same baptism and share in the same Eucharist; they recognize each other's members and ministries. They are one in their common commitment to confess the gospel of Christ by proclamation and service to the world. To this end, each church aims at maintaining sustained and sustaining relationships with her sister churches, expressed in conciliar gatherings whenever required for the fulfillment of their common calling. (Fifth Assembly, Nairobi 1975, in Kinnamon, 110)

In fulfilling this agenda, the Faith and Order Commission produced a convergence text on *Baptism, Eucharist and Ministry* in 1982, which has become the most widely studied text in the ecumenical movement. In 1992 the Commission produced an ecumenical commentary on the Nicene Creed, *Confessing One Faith.* As was discussed in chapter three, at the Fifth World Conference in 1993 the theme of *koinonia* was taken up following the Canberra statement, *The Unity of the Church as Koinonia: Gift and Calling.* In the 1993 Conference, among other things, the universal ministry was put on the program of the ecclesiology study, indicating that the papacy will be part of this World Council agenda.

As also noted in chapter three, the elements of full communion: (1) unity in faith; (2) unity in sacraments, including ministry; (3) unity in decision making, including conciliarity and papacy; and (4) unity in mission are increasingly seen as a common agenda for a common ecclesiology toward which the churches move. Faith and Order continues to make substantive contributions to all of these areas.

The most dramatic ecclesiological event in the modern ecumenical movement, beyond the founding of the World Council and the Roman Catholic entry into the ecumenical movement with the Vatican Council, is the challenge to the churches involved in response and reception of the ecumenical results.

On the basis of the theological work beginning in 1927 on the sacraments and culminating during the 1970s, when the churches were asked to circulate and contribute to the revision of a draft, the Commission published the *Baptism, Eucharist and Ministry* convergence text in 1982. It was sent to the churches asking "the extent to which your church can recognize in this text the faith of the Church through the ages," and other questions pressing the ecumenical agenda beyond the dialogue of experts into the very heart of church life, worship, and decision making. Today the text and the responses are essential elements in the study of the sacraments in all of the churches in the ecumenical movement. We know more today about the common ground on these issues, and the places where differences—real or perceived—lie, than at any time since the Reformation.

The theological affirmations of the text and the responses cannot be elaborated in detail here, but are essential for fully understanding the development of ecumenical relationships at this stage of the ecumenical movement and for laying out the agenda for the future of the dialogue on these three themes.

Traditionally the divide between those churches which baptize infants and those which baptize only adults has been a major ecumenical hurdle. The *BEM* text affirms the common theology of baptism, its foundational character for the Church and the ecumenical movement, and offers the commentary that "both forms of baptism embody God's own initiative in Christ and express a response of faith made within the believing community," inviting that they be regarded as "equivalent alternatives" ("Baptism," *Commentary* 12).

In the responses from the churches, the most positive have been to the "Eucharist" section, which spells out a common liturgical and theological foundation grounded in Scripture, but taking full account of the Christian heritage and the emphases and debates that have formed the churches.

The text surveys most succinctly the institution, meaning, and celebration of the sacrament. The themes of thanksgiving, memorial or *anamnesis,* invocation of the Holy Spirit or *epiklesis,* communion of the faithful, and meal of the kingdom are delineated. The text obviously builds on the twentieth-century biblical, liturgical, and patristic renewal without filling the text with theological and historical reference. In fact, it has given rise to thousands of commentaries and specialized studies. It is particularly helpful, though not providing full consensus, in resolving the divisive issues of real presence and sacrifice.

> The words and acts of Christ at the institution of the eucharist stand at the heart of the celebration; the eucharistic meal is the sacrament of the body and blood of Christ, the sacrament of his real presence. Christ fulfills in a variety of ways his promise to be always with his own even to the end of the world. But Christ's mode of presence in the eucharist is unique. Jesus said over the bread and wine of the eucharist: "This is my body...this is my blood...." What Christ declared is true, and this truth is fulfilled every time the eucharist is celebrated. The Church confesses Christ's real, living and active presence in the eucharist. While Christ's real presence in the eucharist does not depend on the faith of the individual, all agree that to discern the body and blood of Christ, faith is required. ("Eucharist," *Commentary* 13)

Movement toward reconciliation in the doctrine of the real presence of Christ and of the relationship of the Lord's Supper to the "unique sacrifice of the cross" has been made possible through the reclaiming of biblical and patristic concepts of memorial/*anamnesis* and of the role of the Holy Spirit/*epiklesis.* The multilateral character of the dialogue, with Reformed and Orthodox emphasis on the Spirit's role and the Lutheran and Catholic emphasis on the incarnational dimension of Eucharistic theology, have enhanced the churches' ability to move forward in this issue.

The responses of nearly two hundred churches indicate that more work will need to be done on the issues of ecclesiology;

sacraments and sacramentality; and Scripture and tradition. Some of the churches' responses show the need for further study of earlier agreements made during the long course of the ecumenical movement. In some contexts, this common text has enabled church union negotiations and bilateral dialogues to move forward more rapidly.

The section in *BEM* on ministry is the longest, but the responses of the churches indicate that it has proved the most difficult section for the churches to receive. Nevertheless, its characterization of the authority of ministry as collegial, personal, and communal; explication of a concept of apostolic succession in terms of doctrinal as well and episcopal continuity; and suggestions of routes to the recognition and reconciliation of ordained ministries summarize important progress in the bilateral dialogues and lay the ground work for further progress. From the beginning of Faith and Order, ministry has been a thorny issue, so the wide range of common ground identified in this section of *BEM* represents a hopeful marker on the pilgrimage.

Other elements of the Faith and Order agenda also warrant local study as the experts continue to work at common formulations. The study, Toward a Common Confession of the Apostolic Faith Today, producing the *Confessing One Faith* commentary on the Nicene Creed and a study guide, is of particular importance. Such studies create a multilateral context in which to explore church dividing issues, such as Marian teaching, the *filioque*, and Justification by Faith.

In the U.S. this is of particular importance. Many of the churches that use the creed in worship take it for granted, while the majority of Protestant Christians, Baptist, Methodist, and Pentecostal, do not regularly use the creed. On the other hand, many of the conservative Evangelical Christians, who are not traditionally connected with the ecumenical movement, are more concerned with orthodoxy in the Trinitarian faith than are some of the Christians within the member churches of the councils. The fact that the World Evangelical Fellowship produced a positive response to *Confessing One Faith* is itself historic. Faith and Order in the National Council has been able to do some important studies that linked noncreedal churches into this discussion.

Conclusion

As Pope John Paul has noted in his encyclical, the World Council has made a particular and important contribution to the ecumenical movement. Its Faith and Order Commission has developed texts that move the churches closer to common ground. All ecclesiology, sacramental theology, social ethics, and dogmatic theology in the future will need to be taught in the light of these developments, using these texts as sources for understanding, pastoral action, and ecumenical hope.

The Christological methodology developed in Faith and Order; the foundation laid in convergences on Scripture and Tradition, Conciliar Fellowship, Baptism, Eucharist and Ministry, the Apostolic Faith, the Church and the World; as well as identifying for the churches together the elements necessary for full *koinonia* provide a theological matrix for the widest ecumenical circle. It is within this wider circle that particular relationships intensify toward full communion.

It remains to study these texts, bring them into the catechetical and pastoral lives of the churches, and to proceed with dialogue and research furthering the recommendations they provide. "With regard to other Christians, the principle documents of the Commission on Faith and Order and the statements of numerous bilateral dialogues have already provided Christian communities with useful tools for discerning what is necessary to the ecumenical movement and to the conversion it must inspire" (UUS 17).

> From this basic but partial unity it is now necessary to advance toward the visible unity which is required and sufficient, and which is manifested in a real and concrete way, so that the churches may truly become a sign of that full communion in the one, holy, catholic and apostolic church which will be expressed in the common celebration of the eucharist. (UUS 78)

Study Questions

1. What are the four streams of ecumenical life that contributed to the foundation of the World Council and how has the Roman Catholic Church contributed to them?

2. What is the significance and content of the 1950 Toronto Statement for the ecumenical movement? What are some of the key themes of the World Council Assemblies?

3. What are the important methodological contributions of the Faith and Order movement to the ecumenical dialogues? What is the significance of the shift from comparative ecclesiology to a Christological methodology?

4. What are some of the key theological contributions of the Faith and Order dialogues?

5. What is the content of the *Scripture, Tradition and the Traditions* statement and how does it relate to the Vatican Council's Declaration on Divine Revelation?

6. What is the content and significance of the *Baptism, Eucharist and Ministry* text and its contribution to the churches? What has been the response of the churches to this text?

7. What is the vision of the united Church as a *Conciliar Fellowship* and what have been its implications for the ecumenical movement?

8. What contribution can Faith and Order or similar dialogue structures make in a city or state context on the local level? What are the national and local conciliar structures and their contributions in your community?

Selected Readings

Baptism, Eucharist and Ministry: 1982-1990: Report on the Process and Responses. Geneva: World Council of Churches, 1990.

Bent, Ans Joachim van der. *Historical Dictionary of Ecumenical Christianity.* Metuchen: Scarecrow Press, 1994.

Best, Thomas, and Günther Gassmann, eds. *On the Way to Fuller Koinonia.* Geneva: World Council of Churches, 1993.

Brinkman, Martien E. *Progress in Unity?: Fifty Years of Theology Within the World Council of Churches, 1945–1995.* Louvain: Peeters, 1995.

Burgess, Joseph, and Jeffrey Gros, eds. *Building Unity: Ecumenical Dialogues with Roman Catholic Participation. Ecumenical Documents IV.* New York/Mahwah: Paulist Press, 1989, pp. 449–90.

——. *Growing Consensus, Church Dialogues in the United States, 1962–1991. Ecumenical Documents V.* New York/Mahwah: Paulist Press, 1995, pp. 581–673.

Confessing the One Faith: An Ecumenical Explication of the Apostolic Faith As It Is Confessed in the Nicene-Constantinopolitan Creed (381). Geneva: World Council of Churches, 1991.

Gassmann, Günther, ed. *Documentary History of Faith and Order: 1963–1993.* Geneva: World Council of Churches, 1993.

Gros, Jeffrey, ed. *The Search for Visible Unity: Baptism, Eucharist, Ministry.* New York: Pilgrim Press, 1984.

——. "The Vision of Christian Unity: Some Aspects of Faith and Order in the Context of the Culture of the United States." *Mid-Stream* 30 (January 1991): 1–19.

——, and William G. Rusch, eds. *Deepening Communion.* Part VIII. Washington D.C.: U.S. Catholic Conference, 1998.

Kinnamon, Michael, and Brian E. Cope, eds. *The Ecumenical Movement: An Anthology of Basic Texts and Voices.* Grand Rapids: Eerdmans, 1997, pp. 211–62, 325–92.

Link, Hans-Georg. ed. *Apostolic Faith Today: A Handbook for Study.* Geneva: World Council of Churches, 1985.

Vischer, Lukas, ed. *A Documentary History of the Faith & Order Movement: 1927–1963.* St. Louis: Bethany Press, 1963.

Visser't Hooft, W. A. *The Genesis and Formation of the World Council of Churches.* Geneva: World Council of Churches, 1982, pp. 112–20.

——, ed. *The New Delhi Report: The Third Assembly of the World Council of Churches, 1961*. New York: Association Press, 1962.

Wainwright, Geoffrey. *The Ecumenical Moment: Crisis and Opportunity for the Church*. Grand Rapids: Eerdmans, 1983.

8

Ecumenical Developments with the Eastern Churches

O Sovereign and almighty Lord,
  Bless all thy people, and all thy flock.
Give thy peace, thy help, thy love unto us thy servants,
  The sheep of thy fold,
That we may be united in the bond of peace and love,
  One body and one spirit, in one hope of our calling,
  In thy divine and boundless love.

Liturgy of St. Mark

Introduction

The Eastern Churches, the Assyrian Church of the East, and the Eastern and Oriental Orthodox churches, present a challenge to the comprehension of the Western Christian observer not acquainted with the culture of these communities. Part of the challenge resides in history. The Eastern churches have a keen sense of remembrance, particularly in reference to Western aggression, and in some cases a sense of superiority in their confidence of apostolic fidelity. Latin Catholics have often considered the divisions between East and West to be a matter of schism, with differences of church order alone separating the churches, while the Orthodox tend to consider it a matter of doctrine, often speaking of Protestants and Catholics as heretics.

National background and ethnicity will be an important factor in understanding these churches. Eastern Orthodoxy has condemned ethnocentric reductionism as heretical. However, each of these churches has a particular cultural history that is a gift to its liturgical, spiritual, and ethical tradition, but can also be a burden that isolates the community from other Christians, and sometimes even from sister churches with whom full communion is shared. The Assyrian Church of the East grew up in the Persian Empire beyond the borders of the Roman Empire; the Oriental Orthodox Churches were in Africa, Asia Minor, and Armenia on the borders of the Roman world; and Rome and Constantinople separated as Latin, Greek, and Slavic cultures began to diverge during the first centuries of Christianity.

In the present day, the words *schismatic* and *heretic* are seldom used by Western Christians, but the differences of perception between West and East are not less real and profound. The Catholic Church recognizes the sacramental character of these *sister churches* and insists that any study of the nature of the Church take full account of developments of both East and West. Pope John Paul continually reminds Catholics that the Church must learn to breath again "with both lungs," and that the first thousand years of full communion is a common resource for reform and renewal. For the Roman Catholic Church this means taking account of the Eastern synodical tradition, the early relationships among the five patriarchates, and the collegial relationships among the autocephalous Orthodox churches when renewing its own collegial, synodical, papal, and episcopal conference life to better serve the unity of the churches.

The Eastern Orthodox churches consider the West to have broken away from the common Tradition. This view has factual support in the events of 1054 and 1204. Likewise, such developments as the addition of the *filioque,* papal centralization, infallibility, the Marian dogmas in Catholicism, and the ordination of women in Protestantism are seen as unilateral developments moving away from the Apostolic heritage. Sacramental theology has also developed under different patristic emphases, leaving Orthodox less easily able to recognize the sacraments of the Catholic Church than Catholics are able to do in regard the sacraments of the Orthodox Churches.

The theological disputes and their resolution are explored in detail when one studies Christology, patristics, and Trinitarian theology. Likewise, the ecclesiology of the Eastern churches and their contrast and complementarity with Western developments in Catholicism and Protestantism are explored in depth when one is studying the nature of the Church. In this chapter a very summary overview will be given of the present state of relationships between the Catholic Church and (1) the Assyrian Church of the East; (2) the Oriental Orthodox Churches; and (3) the Eastern or Byzantine Orthodox Churches. All of these churches have extensive relationships with the Protestant world, through the World Council and in bilateral dialogues. Important progress has also been made between the Eastern and Oriental Orthodox Churches on the Christological issues, and they have before them similar proposals to those with the Catholic Church.

The Assyrian Church

The Catholicos of the Persian Church, who was later to receive the title of patriarch, lived first at the royal capital, Seleucia-Ctesipon, later moved to Baghdad, and now resides outside of Chicago. The disagreements that gave rise to this church emerged in the fifth century, when the Church was defining the humanity and divinity of Christ, and the role of Mary as the Mother of Christ and the Mother of God *(theotokos)*. A careful study of the theological developments of the schools of Alexandria and Antioch, and the theological position of Nestorius, who claimed that Mary should be called the Christ bearer *(Christotokos)* or Mother of his humanity *(antropotokos)*, will be important to understand the background of the Council of Ephesus (431) which was not received by this church.

The church flourished in largely Zoroastrian Persia, and by reason of the transportation system, was enabled to send missionaries to India, Tibet, China, and Mongolia. Living in lands which did not profess Christianity, the Assyrian Church of the East experienced persecution, particularly during the invasion of Tamburlaine in the late fourteenth century, when the majority of these Christians were killed, and the rest fled to Kurdistan and were reduced to a small community in Eastern Turkey. A large segment of this Church came into communion with the Roman Catholic Church as the Chaldean Catholic Church. In 1996 the Chaldean and Assyrian patriarchs established a Joint Commission for Unity to promote the reunification of their churches.

A major breakthrough occurred in 1994 when the Patriarch, Mar Dinkha IV, and Pope John Paul II signed a Common Christological Declaration that stated that the two churches are united in the confession of the same faith in Christ and envisioned broad pastoral cooperation between the churches in areas of catechesis and in the formation of future priests.

The Joint Declaration echoes the language of Chalcedon, in regard to "person" and "nature," as well as the four qualifications of Chalcedon, "no confusion, no change, no division, no separation," but it respects Assyrian sensibilities by not insisting on the Mariological title *Theotokos* as absolutely necessary:

> [Christ's] divinity and humanity are united in one person, without confusion or change, without division or separation....The humanity to which the Blessed Virgin gave birth always was that of the Son of God himself....In the light of this same faith the Catholic tradition addresses the Virgin Mary as "the Mother of God" and also as "the Mother of Christ." (IS no. 88 [1995], 2)

The Pope and Patriarch, furthermore, established a committee for theological dialogue and charged it with overcoming the obstacles that still prevent full communion.

The Assyrians accept only the first two ecumenical councils. They have asked not to be called Nestorian, because of the pejorative associations of the past. They are not in communion with any other church.

The Oriental Orthodox Churches

The Council of Ephesus did not resolve all the conflicts over the nature and person of Christ. The schools of Antioch and Alexandria continued with different emphases, and there were several attempts to come to common formulations of the orthodox faith in the Incarnation. The affirmation that Christ is truly human and truly divine was a common commitment, but the formulation of the two natures in one person of Christ used by the Council was not received by the churches of Alexandria and much of Antioch. The Church of Armenia was absent from the event, but also rejected the formulations of the Council. While the intervention of Pope Leo in Chalcedon (451) provided the formulation used by the Council, the major theological controversies took place among theologians and patriarchates in the East.

Debates continued through the subsequent centuries, with the emperor Justinian proposing compromise formulations as late as 532, with the hopes of reconciling his Syrian and Egyptian subjects into one orthodox faith for the empire. However, until the twentieth century these differences in Christology were not able to be reconciled.

The Armenian, Coptic, Ethiopian, Syrian, Malankara Syrian, and Eritrean churches are in full communion, but have developed in cultural isolation, without an ecclesiology that requires structures of decision making together, such as the councils that were important in Eastern Orthodoxy and Catholicism. Their rich liturgical and spiritual lives witness to a level of inculturation in African, Asian, and Middle Eastern environments that contrast with the relative uniformity of the Latin West or the Byzantine East.

These churches are members of the World Council of Churches and, through contacts there, have a wide range of relationships with the Eastern Orthodox and Protestant Churches. The Chalcedonian problem has moved toward resolution, first in World Council dialogues, then with the Eastern Orthodox, and finally with the Catholic Church. Because of the diversity of these churches, and the different cultural situations with their local Catholic counterparts, the Pontifical Council for Promoting Christian Unity fosters bilateral relationships with each of them individually.

The Pro Oriente Foundation in Vienna has sponsored a series of very important dialogues between Catholic and Oriental Orthodox theologians from all of these churches. They have been able to come together and explore the Christological, ecclesiological, and sacramental concerns that will provide the necessary foundation in faith for full reconciliation. Study of these texts will be important for both ecclesiology and Christology. After discussions in 1971, the participants were able to affirm together:

We believe that Our Lord and Savior, Jesus Christ, is God the Son Incarnate; perfect in his divinity and perfect in his humanity. His divinity was not separated from his humanity for a single moment, not for the twinkling of an eye. His humanity is one with his divinity without commixtion, without confusion, without division, without separation. We in our common faith in the one Lord Jesus Christ regard his mystery inexhaustible and ineffable and for the human mind never fully comprehensible or expressible. We see that there are still differences in the theological interpretation of the mystery of Christ because of our different ecclesiastical and theological traditions; we are convinced, however, that these differing formulations on both sides can be understood along the lines of the faiths of Nicaea and Ephesus. *(Communiqué)*

The resolution of the Christological differences has proceeded through the means of dialogues with particular churches, and Common Declarations between the pope and particular patriarchs. The Armenian Catholicos Khoren I of Cilicia visited Pope Paul VI in May 1967, and the two church leaders agreed that the disputes over Christological terminology no longer prevented common profession of faith in Christ. This and other common declarations with the Eastern churches are a demonstration of the fruitfulness of the *Christological methodology* and the search for new language, transcending old controversies, but transparent to the Apostolic Faith.

In 1967, Pope Paul VI visited His Beatitude Snork Kaloustia, Armenian Patriarch of Constantinople, in Istanbul. The Pope emphasized the importance of the teaching of the Council of Ephesus as the basis of unity of the two Churches. During the visit of Armenian Catholicos Vasken I of Etchmiadzin in May 1970, Pope Paul VI stated that the different expressions of the one faith were due to nontheological factors. The Pope quoted a twelfth-century Armenian Catholicos, who maintained that the term "two natures" would be acceptable insofar as it indicates the absence of any confusion of the humanity and divinity in Christ, as opposed to Eutyches and Apollinarius, and asked, "Has not the time not come to clear up once and for all such misunderstandings inherited from the past?" (IS no. 11 [1970], 6).

In the *Common Statement* issued on this occasion, both Churches made a common commitment to encourage theological research into the remaining difficulties.

In regard to ecclesiology, Catholicos Vasken I, on the occasion of his visit to Pope Paul VI, said: "We have remembered as in a reawakening that we have been brothers for the past two thousand years." The Pope responded: "Let us give thanks to the Lord together that day by day the profound sacramental reality existing between our Churches is made known to us, beyond the daily differences and the hostilities of the past." In their *Joint Declaration,* the hierarchs affirmed that research must continue in regard to "mutual recognition of the common Christian faith and the sacramental life, on mutual respect of persons and their Churches" (IS no. 11 [1970], 10).

The *Joint Communique* issued on the occasion of the visit of Armenian Catholicos Karekin II of Cilicia in April 1983, encouraged cooperation in areas of the theological formation of clergy and laity, catechetical instruction, pastoral concerns, and cultural and humanitarian service. In December 1996 Pope John Paul and Catholicos Karekin, now of Etchmiadzin, offered a *Common Declaration,* aimed at putting to rest remaining Christological differences.

The Coptic patriarch of Alexandria, who also carries the title Pope, holds a historic primacy among the churches of Ethiopia and Eritrea. In May 1973, Coptic Pope Shenouda III visited Pope Paul VI. The following is a profession of faith contained in the *Common Declaration* that they signed at the end of the meeting:

> We confess that Our Lord and God and Savior and King of us all, Jesus Christ, is perfect God with respect to His divinity, perfect man with respect to His humanity. In Him His divinity is united with His humanity in a real, perfect union without mingling, without commixtion, without confusion, without alteration, without division, without separation. His divinity did not separate from His humanity for an instant, not for the twinkling of an eye. He who is God eternal and invisible became visible in the flesh, and took upon Himself the form of a servant. In Him are preserved all the properties of the divinity and all the properties of the humanity,

together in a real, perfect, invisible and inseparable union. (IS no. 22 [1973], 9)

The *Declaration* also went on to an ecclesiological affirmation:

These differences cannot be ignored. In spite of them, however, we are rediscovering ourselves as Churches with a common inheritance and reaching out with determination and confidence in the Lord to achieve the fullness and perfection of that unity which is His gift. (IS no. 22 [1973], 10)

It proceeded to affirm a large degree of ecclesial mutuality in stating: "We have to a large degree, the same understanding of the church, founded upon the Apostles, and of the important role of ecumenical and local councils."

Out of this dialogue important recommendations have been made both with respect to the relationships of the Coptic Orthodox and Coptic Catholic Churches in Egypt to decrease tensions and increase collaboration, and with a view to a united church in Egypt with the Coptic Pope as its patriarch.

The Syrian or Jacobite Church, represents the portion of the patriarchate of Antioch that did not receive Chalcedon, and whose patriarch now resides in Damascus. This Church has lived much of its history under Muslim rule. The early days of Muslim occupation were characterized by religious tolerance and justice, when the Syrian Orthodox Church enjoyed a position of great influence and prestige under the Caliphs. During this period, the Arabs also profited from the learning and culture of the Syrian Orthodox Church. The Church expanded as far East as Afghanistan and now has a large number of faithful in India. Following the Crusades, religious toleration gave way to alienation and open persecution.

Syrian Patriarch Ignatius Jacoub III visited Pope Paul VI, October 25–27, 1971, and Pope John Paul II, May 13–16, 1980. Syrian Patriarch Ignatius Zakka I Iwas visited Pope John Paul II, June 20–23, 1984. The *Common Declaration* between Pope Paul VI and Patriarch Mar Ignatius Jacob III, on October 27, 1971, states that they are in agreement in regard to the ancient Christological difficulties: "that there is no difference in the faith they profess concerning the mystery of the Word of God made flesh and become really man, even if over the centuries difficulties have arisen out of the different theological expressions by which this faith is expressed" (IS no. 16 [1972], 5). They continued to exhort clergy and faithful to seek to remove the obstacles which still prevent full communion between them.

In the *Common Declaration* of June 1984 between Pope John Paul and Patriarch Ignatius Zakka I Iwas, several dramatic affirmations created a new basis for unity between the two churches:

> We find today no real basis for the sad division and schisms that subsequently arose between us concerning the doctrine of Incarnation. In words and life we confess the true doctrine concerning Christ our Lord, notwithstanding the differences in interpretation of such a doctrine which arose at the time of the Council of Chalcedon.... Sacramental life finds in the holy Eucharist its fulfillment and its summit, in such a way that it is through the Eucharist that the Church most profoundly realizes and reveals its nature....The other Sacraments...are ordered to that celebration of the holy Eucharist which is the center of sacramental life and the chief visible expression of ecclesial communion. This communion of Christians with each other and of local Churches united around their lawful Bishops is realized in the gathered community which confesses the same faith....Anxious to meet [our faithful's] needs and with their spiritual benefit in mind, we authorize them [when access to their own priest is impossible] to ask for the sacraments of Penance, Eucharist and Anointing of the Sick from lawful priests of either of our two sister Churches, when they need them. (IS no. 55 [1984], 62–3)

This is the first occasion when a common declaration makes such a connection among Church, Eucharist, and bishop, and encouraged Eucharistic hospitality in cases of need.

Important developments have also taken place with the two Syrian Malankara Orthodox Churches of India and the Ethiopian Church. The Eritrean Orthodox Church became an independent church in 1993 with the concurrence of Coptic Pope Shenouda III and Ethiopian Patriarch Paulos.

It is only in the United States where all of these churches are able to meet together with Catholic counterparts in theological and pastoral dialogue. Such dialogue is important for these churches as a context for consideration of their differences, for example, on marriage and other sacramental practices.

The Catholic Church has much to learn in its other relationships from the dramatic developments in theological dialogue which are enabling the Christological divisions of centuries to be transcended. Application of these principles to the ecclesiological differences that remain will be as much of a challenge to the Catholic Church as to its Oriental counterparts. The understanding of the nature of councils, the exercise of collegiality, the notion of primacy, the synodical governance of the Church, and the limits of theological and liturgical inculturation will all be enriched in this conversation.

The Eastern Orthodox Church

The early history of the Church is dominated by the patriarchates of the eastern part of the Roman Empire, Alexandria and Antioch. To these was added the preeminence of Constantinople, especially after the move of the imperial capital there in the early fourth century, and Jerusalem later in the century, after imperial patronage of the city had fostered its redevelopment. With the invasion and eventual evangelization of the barbarians in the West, Rome's focus and culture emerged in a more gradual and quite different fashion. The high Greek culture, heir of ancient Greece and Rome, presided over by a successful Christian emperor during the pre-Islamic period and surviving until the fall of Constantinople in 1453, and a successful mission to central and eastern Europe, left the East as the center of both creativity and conflict in theology. The West was marginalized during much of the period of the Turkish advance, and was an ineffective ally of the East during the period of siege and fall.

As noted above, the break between East and West was a gradual development with theological and cultural antecedents before 1054 and significant bonds of *koinonia* continuing until the brutal fourth crusade of 1204. The ineffective reunion councils of 1274 and 1439, followed by a Roman policy of proselytism and uniatism created a permanent alienation and deep levels of resentment, yet to be healed. The student of this relationship will need to study carefully not only the history, but also the present situations of tension in Eastern Europe, the Middle East, and the anti-Roman theological pressures emerging from the monastic community of Mount Athos, and of some of the national churches, particularly that of Greece. One can see in the daily papers the Croatian Catholic and Serbian Orthodox tensions, and the Romanian hostilities played out in the streets of their cities.

Careful study of the variety of Orthodox reactions to the invitation they received to send observers to Vatican II, the response of the Orthodox to the Catholic Church opening its sacraments to the Orthodox Churches in its Decree on the Eastern Churches, and the linkages that have developed with the West through the history of the World Council of Churches will add insight to the present complicated situation. The years of Slavic Orthodox repression under Marxism and centuries of domination by Islam add to the complexity of the relationships.

While the meeting of Patriarch Athenagoras and Pope Paul VI in Jerusalem in 1964, and their commending of the 1054 anathemas to oblivion (1965) gave a dramatic start to this process of reconciliation after centuries of estrangement, it took fifteen years of a *dialogue of charity*, and the beginning of an annual exchange of delegates on St. Andrew's and St. Peter's feasts before a theological *dialogue of truth* became possible in 1980.

In this section we will briefly review the results of this dialogue, recognizing that a more careful study of the texts themselves and of the events of history, will be necessary to penetrate the importance and depth of this relationship and its challenges.

The first meeting of the theological dialogue on Patmos in 1980 outlined a plan and method. There was a suggestion to begin with those areas which divide the churches, given the great common life of faith and sacraments that are shared. However, it was finally decided to use the *Christological method* of the other dialogues, beginning with areas that can be affirmed together first, only gradually approaching the more dramatic, church-dividing issues on the basis of these shared convictions. This method has proved fruitful, despite the deep difficulties that have emerged, especially since 1989, and the fact that the meetings have frequently been postponed because of the inability of the full Orthodox complement of churches to provide representatives. The dialogue group itself is large, as each of the autocephalous and autonomous churches is represented by a bishop and a theologian.

In 1982 a statement emerged from the dialogue: "The Mystery of the Church and of the Eucharist in the Light of the Mystery of the Holy Trinity":

I. CHRIST AND THE EUCHARIST
    1. Christ and the new creation
    2. Christ in Eucharist event
    3. Sacrament of Christ in the Holy Spirit
    4. Church and Eucharist
        a) Pentecost completion of Paschal Mystery
        b) Church realized in baptism, chrismation, and Eucharist
        c) Church and Eucharist in eschatological perspective
    5. Spirit at work through the Eucharist
        a) The coming of Christ prepared by Spirit
        b) Spirit manifests Christ in Eucharist (*anamnesis*)
        c) Spirit transforms the gifts (*epiclesis*)
        d) Spirit makes communion among the faithful
    6. Trinitarian mystery in the Church by Eucharist
II. THE CHURCH
    1. The Church as local
    2. The local church as Eucharistic *koinonia*
    3. The bishop in the Eucharistic assembly
    4. Apostolic succession
III. THE UNITY OF THE CHURCH
    1. The Church local and universal
    2. Unity and diversity
    3. Conditions for ecclesial communion
        a) Catholicity in time link with apostolic church
        b) Catholicity among the churches
    4. Bonds of communion in the New Testament
(IS no. 49 [1982], 107–112)

This text does not resolve issues of the relationship between local and universal church, a discussion that will be necessary for a common understanding of the role of councils, patriarchs, and popes. Likewise, the formulations of the procession of the Holy Spirit and the *filioque* debate are not resolved. Nevertheless, common theological convictions are enunciated that provide a groundwork in theology of the Trinity, Eucharist, and the episcopate upon which a resolution of these issues can develop.

In 1987 an agreement was finished in Bari, Italy, on "Faith, Sacraments and the Unity of the Church":

INTRODUCTION (1–4)
 I. FAITH AND COMMUNION IN THE SACRAMENTS (5–6)
     1. True faith is a divine gift and free response of the human person (7–12)
     2. The liturgical expression of faith (13–14)
     3. The Holy Spirit and the sacraments (15–17)
     4. The faith formulated and celebrated in the sacraments: the symbols of faith (18–20)
     5. Conditions for communion of faith (21–24)
     6. True faith and communion in the sacraments (25–33)
     7. The unity of the church in faith and sacraments (34–36)
 II. THE SACRAMENTS OF CHRISTIAN INITIATION: THEIR RELATION TO THE UNITY OF THE CHURCH (37–53) (IS no. 64 [1987], 82–87)

The several elements of the sacraments in East and West are described, with their accompanying accentuations and differences. The baptism of infants, and the pastoral practices which govern the minister, manner of baptism, and sequence of the sacraments of initiation form the remainder of the document. The final paragraph implies that a certain diversity in the practice of Christian initiation is not incompatible with mutual recognition and Church unity:

> Finally it is to be recalled that the Council of Constantinople, jointly celebrated by the two churches in 879–880, determined that each See would retain the ancient usages of its tradition. (87)

Nonetheless, the Statement stops short of making a specific judgment concerning the legitimacy of the present differences in practice. It does not include the profession of the mutual recognition of sacraments that some Catholics and Orthodox had hoped would be forthcoming.

A third statement was finished at Valaamo, Finland, in 1988: "The Sacrament of Order in the Sacramental Structure of the Church, with Particular Reference to the Importance of Apostolic Succession for the Sanctification and Unity of the People of God":

INTRODUCTION (1–5)
  I. CHRIST AND THE HOLY SPIRIT (6–14)
 II. THE PRIESTHOOD IN THE DIVINE ECONOMY OF
     SALVATION (15–23)
III. THE MINISTRY OF THE BISHOP, PRESBYTER, AND
     DEACON (24–43)
IV. APOSTOLIC SUCCESSION (44–55)
(IS no. 68 [1988], 173–78)

The Statement surveys the specific means whereby communication among the Churches has been maintained in the course of Church history, concentrating in particular upon the Council of Bishops and upon the place of the first bishop within the conciliar structure:

> The synodal structure of episcopal activity showed itself especially in questions under discussion which interested several local churches or the churches as a whole....Their forms could change according to different places and times, but their guiding principle is to manifest and make efficacious the life of the Church by joint episcopal action, under the presidency of the one whom they recognized as the first among them....It is in this perspective of communion among local churches that the question could be addressed of primacy in the Church in general and in particular, the primacy of the bishop of Rome, a question which constitutes a serious divergence among us and which will be discussed in the future. (53, 55)

The further elaboration entitled, "Ecclesiological and Canonical Consequences of the Sacramental Structure of the Church: Conciliarity and Authority in the Church" was scheduled for discussion by the Joint Commission at the 1990 Freising meeting. There are many lessons for the other churches of the ecumenical movement from the experience of autocephalous churches in full communion, from the Orthodox theology of local churches, and from the synodal governance at the center of Orthodox ecclesial identity.

However, factors associated with the political condition of life in the former Soviet Union and Eastern Europe and issues of uniatism forestalled for the present a consideration of the planned agenda. The dialogue was only able to proceed by dealing with the pressing contemporary issues, which it did by producing a statement in 1993 at Balamand in Lebanon: "Uniatism, Method of Union of the Past, and the Present Search for Full Communion":

INTRODUCTION (1–5)
  I. PRINCIPLES (6–18)
 II. PRACTICAL RULES (19–35)
(IS no. 83 [1993], 96–9)

The statement rejects uniatism as a method of seeking unity, "because it is opposed to the common tradition of our Churches" and further proscribes it as a form of missionary apostolate that "can no longer be accepted either as a method to be followed nor as a model of the unity our Churches are seeking" (12).

At the same time, the Balamand statement supports the existence of the Eastern Catholic Churches as part of the Catholic communion and addresses practical issues connected with meeting the spiritual needs of the faithful. The statement speaks to the hope that the Oriental Catholic Churches will "be inserted, on both local and universal levels, into the dialogue of love, in mutual respect and reciprocal trust...and enter into the theological dialogue, with its practical implications" (16). The statement ends: "by excluding for the future all proselytism and all desire for expansion by Catholics at the expense of the Orthodox Church, the commission hopes that it has overcome the obstacles which impelled certain autocephalous churches to suspend their participation in the theological dialogue and that the Orthodox Church will be able to find itself altogether again for continuing the theological work already so happily begun" (35). The Balamand text has received different levels of reception among the Orthodox and Eastern Catholic churches.

In the United States there has been a theological dialogue between the Eastern Orthodox Churches and the Catholic Church for over thirty years as well as an annual conference among bishops of the two traditions. The fifteen texts of these consultations provide important responses to the Joint International Commission, other ecumenical statements, particular pastoral concerns, especially regarding marriage and family, and theological issues not yet treated by the International Commission. The U.S. consultations have been able to continue even when ecclesio-political concerns have made the international meetings impossible.

Conclusion

The inevitable tensions that exist between *sister churches* that have lived and developed in estrangement, and sometimes animosity, for so many centuries cannot obscure the fact of the deep affinity among the great traditions of the East and the churches of the West. The progress on the Christological issues with the Assyrian and Oriental Orthodox churches, and the beginning of the pilgrimage toward reconciliation with the Eastern Orthodox churches, open out a hope for global reconciliation that presses Christians for greater ecumenical energy and understanding in each local situation where they encounter one another.

For the Roman Catholic Church, an integral element of its reform in the years following the Council is the reappropriation of the Eastern dimension of the common Tradition, and an appreciation of traditions that complement its own. As reflection on collegiality, the conciliar and synodal character of the Church, episcopacy and primacy as signs of communion and servants of unity, the sequence and catechesis of Christian initiation, and Eucharist-centered ecclesiology, again come into church life, both the patristic heritage and the living Eastern traditions are integral to Western theological and pastoral thought.

As Pope John Paul invites Christians in his Apostolic Letter *Orientale Lumen:*

> ...considerations now need to be broadened so as to embrace all the Eastern Churches in the variety of their different traditions. My thoughts turn to our brothers and sisters of the Eastern Churches in the wish that together we may seek the strength of an answer to the questions man is asking today in every part of the world. I intend to address their heritage of faith and life, aware that there can be no second thoughts about pursuing the path of unity, which is irreversible as the Lord's appeal for unity is irreversible. (3)

Study Questions

1. Comment on the Christology of the Assyrian Church of the East and the Joint Declaration between Pope John Paul and Patriarch Mar Dinkha IV.

2. Enumerate the Oriental Orthodox Churches and describe the characteristics of the agreements that have been reached on Christology.

3. What are some of the agreements reached in the dialogues between the Roman Catholic and Eastern Orthodox Churches on the local Church, unity and diversity, and the sacraments?

4. What is meant by the term *sister church* as used between Orthodox and Roman Catholic Churches?

5. What are some of the difficulties between Catholic and Orthodox over the history of uniatism, and what are some of the proposals for resolving the issue?

6. What are some of the riches of the Eastern Churches that have come as gift to the churches of the West? How can Orthodox spirituality and history further enrich Catholic life?

7. What are some of the pastoral issues that contribute to Orthodox/Catholic tension and promises for unity in the local situations in this country? What are concerns that need to be dealt with and resolved in the dialogue?

8. What areas of the world require more care and study if Ortho-dox/Catholic tensions are to be healed? How can Christians in this country contribute to that reconciliation?

Selected Readings

Borelli, John, and John Erickson. *The Quest for Unity: Orthodox and Catholics in Dialogue; Documents of the Joint International Commission and Official Dialogues in the United States 1965–1995.* Crestwood: St. Vladimir Seminary Press/Washington D.C.: U.S. Catholic Conference, 1996.

Davey, Colin. "Orthodox-Roman Catholic Dialogue." *One In Christ* 20 (1984): 346–64.

———. "'Clearing a Path Through a Minefield': Orthodox-Roman Catholic Dialogue, 1983–1990." *One In Christ* 26 (1990): 285–307.

———. "'Clearing a Path Through a Minefield': Orthodox-Roman Catholic Dialogue 1983–1990 (2)." *One In Christ* 27 (1991): 8–33.

Evans, Gillian R. "Orthodox and Roman Catholic Ecclesiology: The Recent Scene and the Residual Difficulties." *One In Christ* 30 (1994): 34–49.

Fortino, Eleuterio F. "The Catholic-Orthodox Dialogue." *One In Christ* 18 (1982): 194–203.

Fries, Paul, and Tiran Nersoyan. *Christ in East and West.* Macon: Mercer University Press, 1987.

Gregorios, Paulos, William H. Lazareth, and Nikos A. Nissiotis, eds. *Does Chalcedon Divide or Unite? Towards Convergence in Orthodox Christology.* Geneva: World Council of Churches, 1981.

John Paul II. *Orientale Lumen. Origins* 25:1 (May 18, 1995): 1–13.

McPartlan, Paul, ed. *One in 2000?: Towards Catholic-Orthodox Unity: Agreed Statements and Parish Papers.* Slough: St. Paul's, 1993.

———. "Towards Catholic-Orthodox Unity." *Communio* 19 (1992): 305–20.

Meyendorff, John. *Vision of Unity,* Crestwood: St. Vladimir's Seminary Press, 1987.

Pro Oriente Consultation Between Theologians of the Oriental Orthodox and the Roman Catholic Churches, "Communiqué." *Wort und Wahrheit: Revue for Religion and Culture,* Supplement (December 1972):182.

Roberson, Ronald G. *The Eastern Christian Churches: A Brief Survey.* Rome: University Press of the Pontifical Oriental Institute, 1995.

————, ed. *Oriental Orthodox-Roman Catholic Interchurch Marriages and Other Pastoral Relationships.* Washington D.C.: U.S. Catholic Conference, 1995.

Stormon, E. J., S.J., ed. *Towards the Healing of Schism: The Sees of Rome and Constantinople: Public Statements and Correspondence Between the Holy See and the Ecumenical Patriarchate, 1958–1984. Ecumenical Documents III.* New York/Mahwah: Paulist Press, 1987.

"Syrian Orthodox Church." Pontifical Council for Promoting Christian Unity, *Information Service,* no. 16 (1972): 3–5.

Tarasar, Constance, ed. *Orthodox America 1794–1976: Development of the Orthodox Church in America.* Syosset, NY: Orthodox Church in America, 1975.

Vischer, Lukas, ed. *Spirit of God, Spirit of Christ: Ecumenical Reflections on the Filioque Controversy.* Geneva: World Council of Churches, 1981.

"Visit of His Holiness Amba Shenouda III." Pontifical Council for Promoting Christian Unity, *Information Service,* no. 22 (1973): 3–10.

"Visit to Rome of his Holiness Vasken I." Pontifical Council for Promoting Christian Unity, *Information Service,* no. 11 (1970): 3–10.

Ware, Kallistos. *The Orthodox Way.* Crestwood: St. Vladimir's Seminary Press, 1979.

9

Anglican, Lutheran, and Catholic Relations

A mighty fortress is our God, a bulwark never failing;
Our helper he amid the flood of mortal ills prevailing:
For still our ancient foe
Doth seek to work us woe;
His craft and power are great,
And, armed with cruel hate,
On earth is not his equal.
Did we in our own strength confide, our striving would be losing,
Were not the right man on our side,
the man of God's own choosing:
Dost ask who that may be?
Christ Jesus, it is he;
Lord Sabaoth, his name,
From age to age the same,
And he must win the battle.

Martin Luther

Introduction

Roman Catholic ecumenism builds on the premise that all baptized Christians are in real but imperfect communion, that all are equally called to unity, and therefore Catholics reach out to all Christians and all churches in ecumenical seriousness. However, the unity of the Church is based on the dialogue of truth, which is oriented toward a common confession of the Apostolic Faith, common sacramental life, common structures of communion, and common witness in the world.

In a variety of ways the vision of unity is shared by member churches of the World Council: "The goal of the search for full

173

communion is realized when all the churches are able to recognize in one another the one, holy, catholic and apostolic church in its fullness. This full communion will be expressed on the local level and the universal levels through conciliar forms of life and action" (Canberra, 2.1). Among the World Council member churches, there are common ecclesiological elements and hermeneutical perspectives that make pilgrimage easier between and among some churches.

Catholics share the most common faith with the Orthodox, though historical and cultural features make progress on those theological matters that still divide us more gradual. With the churches of the Reformation we share distinct elements with different churches, making the progress of the dialogue take a varied pace and character with each. In these next three chapters we will take up three categories of churches with which the Roman Catholic Church is in dialogue. In ecumenism there is no partisanship. Therefore, progress with any two or more churches is the occasion for rejoicing, prayer, and study for all Christians.

This chapter will take up three dimensions of the ecumenical journey. First to be considered is the dialogue with the Anglican Communion, with which Roman Catholics share a common claim to apostolic continuity and a common affirmation of catholic universality. Next we will treat the Roman Catholic-Lutheran relationship, which has been the most theologically productive because of similar commitments to doctrinal clarity and common methods of historical and biblical scholarship. A final section of this chapter will briefly survey Anglican-Lutheran relationships, which have important impact for the whole of the ecumenical family in pilgrimage to full communion. Both Anglicans and Lutherans, through the Lambeth Conference and the Lutheran World Federation, have affirmed the six elements of full communion enumerated by the World Council and noted in chapter three.

The following chapter will deal with Roman Catholic relations to other churches committed to full communion through World Council membership and bilateral dialogue. Chapter eleven will touch on the wide range of Christians and their communities that stand on the margin of the classical ecumenical movement, whose ecclesiologies do not envision zeal for the visible unity of the

Church as central to their identity, but who as fellow Christians are important partners in Christ.

More in-depth study of Lutheranism and Anglicanism, both in the United States and worldwide, will need to take place in the context of the study of the history of Christian thought and the story of the Church. It will be especially important to take account of the extensive Roman Catholic Luther scholarship, especially that which has developed in Germany over the last half century. In studying Anglicanism, attention will need to be given to its historical, spiritual, and liturgical developments; the variety of theological influences that make up the Anglican theological complex; and Roman Catholic studies on Anglican canonical and sacramental developments.

Anglican/Roman Catholic Relations

It is important to study the gifts of Anglicanism in the variety of contexts in which it has been inculturated. Its influence on the united churches of South Asia, where it has introduced the historic episcopate into ecumenical churches, the leadership roles of its bishops in various parts of Africa, and the development in styles of decision making in the U.S. make its reality much richer than might be expected were one only to attend to developments in England. For instance, one might find among Anglicans in Asia and Africa similar attitudes and appraisals of British history and colonialism to those one can find, for example, among Irish Roman Catholics. Reconciliation of memories is as important among those who share a common language and culture as across what might appear greater cultural barriers.

The Anglican Church stems from the civil and religious personages, institutions, and formulations associated with the reign of Elizabeth I (reigned 1558–1603), when Matthew Parker became Archbishop of Canterbury. A *via media* between Rome and Geneva was the policy. The Thirty-Nine Articles and the *Book of Common Prayer,* the fruit of the theological and liturgical work of Archbishop Thomas Cranmer (1489–1556), became normative and created a rich doctrinal system, the formularies of which, in substantially their present form, originate from this period.

Richard Hooker (1554–1600), was the apologist *par excellence* of the Elizabethan settlement of 1559. In his treatise *Of the Laws of Ecclesiastical Polity,* published in eight books between 1594 and 1662, long after his death, he sought to justify episcopacy and to oppose the Puritans who maintained the absolute authority of Scripture to the extent that whatever was not expressly commanded in the Scriptures was unlawful.

Anglicanism lost its leadership and establishment for a while in the seventeenth century during the Puritan revolt. Significant accommodations were necessary with the restoration of the episcopacy and monarchy. And theologically there has been a strong Calvinist influence among the streams that characterize Anglican thought. However, with the ancient theological centers of Oxford and Cambridge and their strong liturgical and literary lives, there is also a deep appreciation of patristic and scholastic heritage and an openness to the renaissance and Enlightenment contributions. To understand Anglicanism it will be important to study both the evangelical revivals of the eighteenth century and the Oxford movement of the nineteenth century, which produced a very strong catholicizing party within Anglicanism and illustrious figures recognized by both of our churches, such as John Henry Cardinal Newman. The evangelical movement, with its Calvinist influences in theology and strong missionary zeal, remains a significant strain alongside the catholic elements, especially in Britain and parts of the Third World.

While medieval canon law persists in Anglicanism, in the nineteenth and twentieth centuries this basis was amplified, providing a larger place for the all baptized in decision making, providing for autonomy in the national provinces much like Orthodox autocephaly, and developing nonjuridical sacramental and consultative structures for international communion. The resulting bonds of communion are the Anglican Consultative Council, the Lambeth Conference of bishops, which meets every ten years, and the ministry of the Archbishop of Canterbury as primate.

In 1998 the issue of differences over authority and primacy are at the center of the Anglican/Roman Catholic relationship, as Archbishop Carey and Pope John Paul noted in December, 1996: "At present the international commission is seeking to further the convergence on authority in the church. Without agreement in this area we shall not reach the full visible unity to which we are both committed."

There was a prehistory to the Vatican II relationship with the Anglican communion. Initiatives to improve Anglican/ Roman Catholic relations in the late nineteenth century proved ironic when the Vatican issued a historical judgement on Anglican orders in *Apostolicae Curae* of 1896. While this text claims that Anglican orders were "absolutely null and utterly void," it did not sound the death knell to hopes of union, but encouraged further dialogue between the churches. This eventually developed in the 1920s, when Cardinal Mercier sponsored a series of important, informal conversations at Malines, Belgium. These conversations did not produce official results, but they began a relationship that was never quite broken off, and which bore fruit in the 1960s. The Decree on Ecumenism referred to the Anglican Communion as having "a special place" among Churches issuing from the Reformation, one "in which Catholic traditions and institutions in part continue to exist" (13).

The national dialogue between Anglicans and Catholics began in the U.S. in 1965 and was followed by the international dialogue, involving the entire Anglican Communion. In March 1966, the Archbishop of Canterbury, Michael Ramsey, paid a visit to Pope Paul VI, and the two churchmen stated their intention "to inaugurate...a serious dialogue which, founded on the gospels and on the ancient common traditions may lead to that unity in truth for which Christ prayed." The program of the dialogue and its method where crystallized in the Malta Report of 1968.

Of all of the dialogues in which Roman Catholics are involved, this relationship seemed to move the most rapidly. Through the course of the 1970s a series of reports were issued on Eucharist, ministry, and authority. These were put together in the *Final Report,* formulated in the context of an ecclesiology of communion/*koinonia,* and formally placed before the churches in 1982. As noted in chapter six, in a complex process of careful evaluation, this report placed a bilateral proposal before the Roman Catholic Church and one of its partners for the first time since Florence (1439). The *Final Report* now has become part of the inner life of these two churches. Those preparing for orders or for teaching the faith should find it integral to their formation. It claims substantial agreement on the doctrines of ordination and the Eucharist, and proposes substantial progress on the question of authority, including papacy, infallibility, and reception. Again, the method, commended by John Paul II in 1980, is the Christological one, going behind the polemical formulations of the past to the biblical and historical sources together.

On the basis of the report Cardinal Willebrands was able to note that there was a new context from the Roman Catholic side for the evaluation of Anglican orders. With the positive evaluations of the claimed substantial agreement on Eucharist and ministry provided by the Lambeth Conference in 1988 and the Pontifical Council for Promoting Christian Unity, in collaboration with the Congregation of the Doctrine of the Faith in 1991, and with subsequent clarifications, Cardinal Cassidy was able to say for the Roman Catholic Church that further work was not necessary on these issues at that stage in the dialogue process.

The clarifications on Eucharist dealt with Roman Catholic concerns about the continuing real presence of Christ, the necessity of an ordained minister presiding, the propitiatory character of Christ's sacrifice, the fruits of which are present in the Eucharist for the living and the dead, and the reality of bread and wine being truly changed into the body and blood of Christ.

The fact that the Anglican Roman Catholic International Commission (ARCIC) and now the Roman Catholic Church and the bishops of the Anglican Communion can formally affirm that we are in substantial agreement on the Eucharist and on the areas of ordained ministry treated in *Final Report,* does not mean that our people all understand this common faith, or more to the point, know that we hold a common faith in these matters. Indeed, Anglican and Roman Catholic catechesis, seminary training, and theological writing will need to begin with this common affirmation and its content as a base line by which the churches move forward. The *Catechism of the Catholic Church,* for example, will have to be interpreted in the light of these developments, and not vice versa.

Likewise, agreement on the theology of ordination and of Eucharist does not mean that there is formal recognition of Anglican orders, even with the "new context." As the dialogue has moved forward, the emergence of the question of the ordination of women has provided a new challenge within both churches and has intensified the importance of agreement on authority. The affirmation of the Anglican Communion is that there are no biblical, sacramental, or confessional barriers to taking this step, if done with the proper magisterial authority. The Roman Catholic Church, on the other hand, affirms that it has no authority to make a decision to change sacramental practice in this way. This issue has had a particular ability to raise feelings in the two churches, as they both move forward with integrity. The level of intimacy already experienced between the churches and the level of conviction with which this issue is held give a strong emotional tone to this discussion. On the other hand, it indicates how deeply churches have to listen to one another in order to begin to feel for and understand different spiritualities, modes of decision making, and ways of confessing fidelity to the Tradition.

In this context developments such as the 1968 encyclical *Humanae Vitae* or the 1995 Congregation of the Doctrine of the Faith historical judgement that the teaching on the ordination of women can be seen as infallible are often interpreted, even by church leaders, as "new obstacles." However, some of the dialogue texts have preferred to see these developments as new challenges which emerge out of the intimacy we experience as the inner life of the partner church becomes essential to one's own ecclesial identity. Clearly, as popes and archbishops have continued to remind us, we are at a stage in our pilgrimage together where we can be neither surprised nor deterred at the challenges we encounter together.

Since the publication of the *Final Report,* ARCIC has produced three significant texts in addition to the clarifications provided for the Roman Catholic Church. *Church as Communion* (1990) sketches the ecclesiological context in which all of the further issues in need of resolution are to be discussed. It has become a key ecumenical text in focusing the theology of *koinonia.*

Salvation and the Church (1986) is an important contribution to the major Roman Catholic/Protestant difference over justification by faith, and has been essential in reconciling Evangelical Anglicans, with their strong Calvinist influence, to the ecumenical process. Evaluations of this text from both sides will

be a significant step in the resolution of this central Reformation concern. The Joint Declaration with the Lutherans will
probably be the first effort at the level of the magisterium of a
Reformation church. However, this text will enhance the
Lutheran/Anglican/Roman Catholic common ground as all
three of these churches pursue their common goal.

Finally, *Life in Christ: Morals, Communion and the Church*
(1993), building on the prior statement *Church as Communion,*
maintains that life in communion is constituted by the acceptance of the same basic values. Genuine Christian unity
demands a unity of life as well as of faith. Anglicans and Roman
Catholics share the same basic moral values.

These values stem from a "shared vision," so that the fundamental moral question becomes not "What ought we to do?" but
"What kind of persons are we to become?" It affirms that the
Christian calling empowers one for communion with God and
each other in a *koinonia* that entails responsibilities to God,
nature, and society, whereby the seriousness of these responsibilities is not only a crisis of, for instance, sexual ethics, but involves
humanity itself. The text goes on to discuss two instances of disagreement, marriage after divorce, and contraception, and suggests the common ground which does not allow these
differences to be church-dividing. It suggests these principles as
a basis for looking at other contentious issues such as abortion
and homosexuality.

This text will be an important one for anyone studying the
ethical tradition of the church. While Anglicans and Roman
Catholics did not divide over ethical issues, their cultural, theological, and ethical development in separation have given rise to
quite distinct traditions that will need to be taken into account as
unity progresses. Likewise, along with some World Council
work, this provides one of the few international dialogues that
has given attention to the moral tradition.

The ARC dialogues in the United States, Canada, and other
parts of the world where these two churches proclaim the Gospel
in a common culture, are a rich resource for study and expanding the content of the common faith. In the United States intensive studies have been done by the diocesan ecumenical officers
of the two churches, exploring the pastoral dimension of the

relationship and the reception of the ARCIC texts. Covenants, joint episcopal pilgrimages, and common pastoral guidelines characterize this relationship in many situations.

Lutheran-Roman Catholic Relations

The visit of a delegation of the Lutheran World Federation to the Vatican in 1964 precipitated an international bilateral dialogue to maintain and develop the contact with the Catholic Church that had been initiated by the presence of Lutheran observers at the Second Vatican Council. The preparations for such a dialogue were conducted by a Roman Catholic-Lutheran Working Group, which met at the Strasbourg Ecumenical Research Institute in August 1965 and April 1966. These negotiations led to the official appointment of a Joint Lutheran-Roman Catholic Study Commission on "The Gospel and the Church." The first stage of the dialogue began in October 1967 and ended in February 1971, with the adoption of the "Malta Report" of 1972. In 1996 this Joint Commission was changed to a Commission on Christian Unity, to signal the commitment of both of these churches, after thirty years of dialogue, to the arduous path of full communion together.

This dialogue, internationally, in its U.S. expression, and in Germany, has been the most theologically productive of any of those in which the Roman Catholic Church has been engaged. Any student of late-twentieth-century Christianity will find this theological and historical contribution essential for recognizing the change of direction in western developments since the sixteenth century.

The U.S. dialogue has touched on all of the issues outlined as part of the Roman Catholic agenda, noted in Pope John Paul's encyclical, *Ut Unum Sint*. In nine rounds of dialogue, agreements have been reached on justification by faith, Mary and the saints, Scripture and tradition, papacy, infallibility, Eucharist, ordained ministry, and the confessional nature of the Church.

While none of these claim full resolution of the issues treated, they focus the question precisely as to how much agreement is necessary for full communion and whether or not these agreements provide a sufficient basis for moving forward. The 1983 U.S. agreement on Justification by Faith provided sufficient positive basis that it was not necessary for the international dialogue to provide new Biblical or theological work as it moved toward a Joint Declaration on the theme.

The international dialogue has made substantial contributions to the questions of Eucharist, ministry, the reevaluation of Martin Luther's role, and the nature of the Church. Of all the texts of this dialogue, it will be particularly important to note the 1993 text *The Church and Justification,* which summarizes all of the work done to that date, and the 1985 *Facing Unity,* which will be discussed below.

During Pope John Paul's 1982 visit to Germany, he raised with his Lutheran colleagues the prospect of a study to determine whether the condemnations of the sixteenth century, included in the Lutheran *Book of Concord* and the Council of Trent, were still applicable to one another in light of the results of the dialogue. This German project has produced five volumes of results, with positive recommendations to the churches about reassessing the condemnations of the past. The 1998 Joint Declaration, discussed below, is the fruit of the success of this German, American, and international work.

From among the many important texts from this dialogue, two will be singled out—the international dialogue *Facing Unity* and the proposed Joint Declaration on Justification by Faith. As a result of the positive work on Justification by Faith in the U.S. and on the condemnations of the sixteenth century, including those on Justification, a Declaration was proposed at the highest appropriate level of authority in the member churches of the Lutheran World Federation and the Roman Catholic Church.

This Declaration, planned for some time after the 1997 celebration of the 450th anniversary of the decrees on Justification of the Council of Trent, is a short text based on the dialogues, but not a dialogue report. It has the effect of placing these churches in a new relationship:

> The doctrinal condemnations of the 16th century, in so far
> as they relate to the doctrine of justification, appear in a new
> light: The teaching of the Lutheran churches presented in

this Declaration does not fall under the condemnations from the Council of Trent. The condemnations in the Lutheran Confessions do not apply to the teaching of the Roman Catholic Church presented in this Declaration. (41)

The Declaration articulates the agreement of the churches on the central content of the Gospel, touching the most profound truth of our salvation in Jesus Christ. At the Reformation, when the churches were still united in 1530, the princes and theologians from those parts of Germany which would be known after 1555 as "Evangelical" or Lutheran, presented a confession of faith at Augsburg, known to posterity as the Augsburg Confession. In it they affirmed that it was sufficient for maintaining peace with the papacy and the bishops of their dioceses that it be allowed that the formulation "Justification by grace through faith" be preached. This effort to maintain unity was not successful, and subsequent efforts at reconciliation broke down. When the Council of Trent convened and finally began to clarify the Roman Catholic position, after 1546, the rift was already too deep to be healed.

Theological study of Christology, Mariology, and soteriology will be informed by the dialogues standing behind this Joint Declaration. Lutherans added other confessions to the ancient common ecumenical creeds and the Augsburg Confession, to maintain unity among them and to clarify their position in polemics with the Calvinists, Anabaptists, and Roman Catholics. These confessions are gathered together in the *Book of Concord,* finalized in 1580. Since that time Lutherans have not added new creeds or confessions to their life together. Catholics, on the other hand, have continued to develop, with the two Vatican Councils, and the papally pronounced Marian dogmas, all of which claim confessional status. This difference in developmental patterns offered a challenge to the dialogue and creates a background of added significance to the evolving ecumenical reconciliation.

At the heart of the agreement on the Joint Declaration is the affirmation:

Together we confess: By grace alone, in faith in Christ's saving work and not because of any merit on our part we are

accepted by God and receive the Holy Spirit, who renews
our hearts while equipping and calling us to good works.
(15)

It is important to note that not all Lutherans have moved forward
in making this common confession with Catholics. The large
Lutheran Church—Missouri Synod, though a full member of the
dialogue, is not able at this time to make this affirmation, and
cannot yet recognize the Catholic Church as one where "the
Gospel is rightly preached."

The Joint Declaration goes on briefly to explicate how certain differences within the doctrine of grace are resolved, both
from the Lutheran side and the Catholic side: human powerless-
ness, forgiveness of sin and making righteous, the relationship of
faith and grace, sin and concupiscence, law and Gospel, the assur-
ance of salvation, and the role of good works. This doctrine has a
particular importance, not only in reconciling our churches, but
in bringing the good news of God's free love to our people.

Reassessing condemnations of the past on the basis of common agreement on the apostolic faith is only one element in the
stages toward full communion enunciated by the churches
together. The Joint Commission of the Lutheran-Catholic dialogue issued a document in 1985 entitled *Facing Unity: Models,
Forms and Phases of Catholic-Lutheran Church Fellowship,* in which
was delineated an approach to full visible unity on the part of the
Lutheran and Catholic churches. The study enumerates six
essential elements of full communion, consonant with those
World Council documents noted in chapter three.

Facing Unity proceeds into unexplored territory in delineating a sketch of the manner in which separated Churches could
approach the realization of fellowship in a common ministry.
Church leadership would first be exercised in a coordinated
manner, which would lead to an initial act of mutual ecclesial
recognition predicated upon consensus in faith, sacramental
life, and the understanding of ministry.

A transitional act would follow in which the two churches
would recognize that "in the other church the church of Jesus
Christ is actualized," while "at the same time pointing to a lack of
fullness of the ordained ministry as a *defectus,* which, for the sake

of church fellowship, has jointly to be overcome" (124). Up to this time Lutherans have been able to recognize Catholic priests as ministers without recognizing the Catholic Church, while the Catholic Church could only recognize a ministry within an ecclesial community whose churchly character had been affirmed. Therefore, in different ways, both churches would have to move beyond their present lack of mutual recognition, while committing themselves to the further changes necessary for full communion to take place.

Thereafter, a phase of common ministry would begin, leading to collegiality. The critical transition that would seal Lutheran-Catholic relations would be the concelebrated ordination of new pastoral ministers by bishops who already exercise local, collegial *episcopé*.

An outline of part two of the *Facing Unity* proposal, "Forms and Phases of Catholic-Lutheran Church Fellowship," details this carefully constructed plan:

ON THE WAY TO CHURCH FELLOWSHIP (46–49)
GROWTH OF CHURCH FELLOWSHIP THROUGH MUTUAL
RECOGNITION AND RECEPTION (50–54)
A. Community of Faith (55–69)
    1. Joint Witness to the Apostolic Faith (56–60)
    2. Unity of Faith in the Diversity of Its Forms of Expression (61–66)
    3. Removal of Doctrinal Condemnations (67–69)
B. Community in Sacraments (70–85)
    1. Growth in Sacramental Life in Our Churches (71–74)
    2. Increasing Agreement in Understanding and Celebration of the Sacraments (75–82)
    3. Open Questions, Remaining Differences, Basic Agreements (83–85)
C. Community of Service (86–149)
    1. Commitment to a Structured Fellowship (Community of Service) (87–91)
    2. Structured Church Fellowship and a Common Ordained Ministry (92–103)
    3. Joint Reflection on the Early Church (104–111)
    4. The Signification of Reflection on the Early Church

A careful study of this text shows that it takes account of both Lutheran and Roman Catholic theological concerns, provides for an orderly integration of the episcopacy and papacy into a reunited fellowship, and maintains the positive heritages of the two traditions into the future united Church. Since there are many stages in this ambitious ecclesiological proposal, one must work patiently. The Joint Declaration, for example, is one major step that would remove some doctrinal condemnations along this carefully articulated journey. Studying proposals between other churches, such as those between the nine member churches of the Consultation on Church Union in the United States, or the three Lutheran-Anglican initiatives outlined in the next section, one realizes that the common journey to *koinonia* is enriched by the ecclesiological creativity and theological research of all of the dialogues.

Lutheran/Anglican Relations

In 1996 the Anglican churches of the British Isles—Scotland, Wales, England, and Ireland—and the Lutheran churches of Scandinavia and the Baltics—Estonia, Latvia, Lithuania, Norway, Finland, Iceland, and Sweden—signed an agreement of full communion, known as the Porvoo Declaration. This declaration is based on theological agreement in the apostolic faith, a common commitment to the threefold ordained ministry, common collaboration in ministry, and consultation in decision making.

The Finns and Swedes claim apostolic succession, never questioned by Anglicans nor evaluated negatively by Roman Catholics. The Danes and Norwegians had a break in episcopal ordinations at the Reformation, but maintained the ancient sees, orderly transmission of ministry, episcopal government, and a consistent confession of the faith from ancient times.

On the basis of a wider understanding of apostolic succession, including continuity of communities, faith, episcopal oversight, and presbyteral ordinations, these churches have found it possible to recognize one another and to participate in ordinations together in the future. If one were to follow the progress of this particular conversation as it developed, one could note the kind of ecumenical conversion, theological imagination, and common fidelity to both tradition and the eschatological call to reconciliation that is at the heart of the dialogue of truth.

In 1997 the Evangelical Lutheran Church in America and the Episcopal Church have before them a Concordat of Agreement which would place them in full communion, after an interim stage of Eucharistic fellowship begun in 1982. This Concordat is based on agreement in the apostolic faith, the threefold ministry, collaboration in ministry, and coordinated decision making. The separate institutional structures would remain as in the Porvoo agreement, but all future episcopal ordinations would include three bishops from each of the churches. The Episcopal Church would suspend the preface to its *Ordinal* for the time being, recognizing Lutheran pastors not ordained by bishops in the apostolic succession to function as priests for Episcopal congregations. This proposal is based on thirty years of dialogue, a carefully worked out theological understanding of the nature of full communion and the implications of the Gospel, and a fifteen-year period of interim Eucharistic fellowship.

In Germany there is an agreement between the Lutheran churches and the British Anglicans to collaborate in ministry, celebrate interim Eucharistic fellowship, and work toward full communion. This proposal does not offer a resolution to the question of bishops in the apostolic succession as the others do, but it does introduce a process much like the 1982 U.S. stage of movement toward full communion.

These three proposals incorporate most of the six elements enumerated in the World Council's vision of full communion, and many of those traced out in the stages suggested in *Facing Unity.* The Lutheran-Catholic proposal is much more gradual, not providing for mutual recognition of ordained ministers until all are ordained by bishops recognized by both churches. Likewise, there is a strong emphasis on magisterium and the role of the Petrine ministry which one would not expect to emerge in the Anglican-Lutheran reconciling proposals.

However, in the pilgrimage toward visible unity, each step for any church is a grace and challenge to all of the partners. There is a prospect of common faith deepening and common sacramental life enriching a wider common circle. In each step forward all rejoice, and at each new challenge or unsuccessful venture, all are called to deepen their commitment and zeal to find a way through to the unity Christ wills for all Christians.

Conclusion

The theological achievement of the Anglican, Lutheran, and Roman Catholic churches within the one ecumenical movement makes a substantial contribution to the whole. All three of these churches are in bilateral dialogue with the Orthodox churches and a variety of relationships with other Reformation churches, some of which will be treated later. The common sacramental, ethical, and creedal core of the Christian relationship leads these churches to include the history, theological development, and present-day contribution of one another in their catechesis and ministry preparation.

The common liturgical work on the *Book of Common Prayer,* the *Lutheran Book of Worship,* and the *Roman Missal* demonstrates the fruits of the modern liturgical renewal and points the way toward common sacramental understanding and celebration. The spiritual resources of these three traditions offer rich resources, with the English mystics, the Scandinavian and German spiritual leaders, and the Roman Catholic saints providing a common array of spiritual guides.

The seriousness of these churches in dealing with the remaining issues of authority, ministry, and structures of communion becomes an impetus for the whole ecumenical movement in approaching the difficult issues of episcopacy, collegiality, conciliarity, and primacy.

Indeed, the primacy of grace and of God's free and loving initiative in the Christian life is amply attested to by Christian saints, like Thérèse of Lisieux:

> After earth's exile, I hope to go and enjoy you in the fatherland, but I do not want to lay up merits for heaven. I want to work for your *love alone*.... In the evening of this life, I shall appear before you with empty hands, for I do not ask you, Lord, to count my works. All our justice is blemished in your eyes. I wish, then, to be clothed in your own *justice* and to receive from your *love* the eternal possession of *yourself*.

Study Questions

1. What are the features of Anglicanism that set it off from the other Reformation churches? What are some of its contributions to the ecumenical movement?

2. What were the factors in the 1896 evaluation of Anglican orders in *Apostolicae Curae* and what has been the role of contemporary scholarship in reevaluating that judgement?

3. What have been the key achievements of ARCIC I and II? What has been the evaluation of ARCIC I in the two churches? What are the implications of this positive judgement for Catholic life and education?

4. What has been the contribution of the Lutheran tradition to Christianity worldwide? How has Catholic life been enriched by this contribution?

5. What are some of the most significant results of the Lutheran Catholic dialogue? What is the import of the agreement on justification

for the Catholic writing of history, teaching of grace, and recognition of the Lutheran communities?

6. Outline how *Facing Unity* can be a viable model for union of Catholic and Lutheran churches.

7. How do the Lutheran Anglican proposals for full communion relate to Roman Catholic hopes with both of these churches?

8. What priorities should there be for bringing these agreements to life in parishes and dioceses? What are some examples of this common life that already exist?

Selected Readings

Burgess, Joseph, and Jeffrey Gros, eds. *Building Unity: Ecumenical Dialogues with Roman Catholic Participation. Ecumenical Documents IV.* New York/Mahwah: Paulist Press, 1989, pp. 11–34, 83–290.

———. *Growing Consensus, Church Dialogues in the United States, 1962–1991. Ecumenical Documents V.* New York/Mahwah: Paulist Press, 1995, pp. 173–338, 374–484.

Falardeau, Earnest, ed. *ARC Soundings: A U.S. Response to ARCIC I.* Lanham, MD: University of America Press, 1990.

Franklin, R. William. ed. "Anglican Orders: A Centenary of *Apostolicae Curae 1896–1996*: Essays on the Centenary of Apostolicae Curae." *Anglican Theological Review* 78 (Winter, 1996): 1–149.

Gros, Jeffrey, Rozanne Elder and Ellen Wondra, eds. *Common Witness to the Gospel: Documents on Anglican-Roman Catholic Relations (1983–1995).* Washington D.C.: U.S. Catholic Conference, 1997.

Gros, Jeffrey, and William G. Rusch, eds. *Deepening Communion.* Washington D.C.: U.S. Catholic Conference, 1998, Part I.

Hill, Christopher, and Edward Yarnold, S.J. *Anglicans and Roman Catholics: The Search for Unity, the ARCIC Documents and Their Reception.* London: SPCK/CTS, 1994.

John Paul II and Archbishop of Canterbury George Carey. *Common Declaration. Origins* 26:27 (December 9, 1996): 441–42.

Lehmann, Karl, and Wolfhart Pannenberg, eds. *The Condemnations of the Reformation Era: Do They Still Divide?* Margaret Kohl, trans. Minneapolis: Fortress Press, 1990.

Meyer, Harding, and Lukas Vischer, eds. *Growth in Agreement. Reports and Agreed Statements of Ecumenical Conversations on a World Level. Ecumenical Documents II.* New York/Mahwah: Paulist Press, 1984, pp. 12–34, 61–130, 167–276.

Purdy, William. *The Search for Unity: Relations Between the Anglican and Roman Catholic Churches.* London: Geoffrey Chapman, 1995.

Raem, Heinz-Albert. "The Third Phase of Lutheran-Catholic Dialogue, 1986–93." *One In Christ* 30 (1994): 310–327.

Reumann, John. "A Quarter-Century of Lutheran-Roman Catholic Dialogue in the United States." *One In Christ* 27 (1991): 185–91.

Rusch, William. "How May the Reformation Best Be Continued? Lutheran-Roman Catholic Relations Today." *One In Christ* 30 (1994): 301–9.

Tavard, George H. *Justification: An Ecumenical Study.* New York/Mahwah: Paulist Press, 1983.

——. *A Review of Anglican Orders: The Problem and the Solution.* Collegeville: The Liturgical Press, 1990.

——. "The Work of ARC-USA: Reflections Post-factum." *One In Christ* 29 (1993): 247–59.

Wicks, Jared, S.J. "Ecclesiological Issues in the Lutheran-Catholic Dialogue (1965–1985)." In René Latourelle, ed.; *Vatican II Assessments and Perspectives: Twenty-five Years After (1962–1987).* Vol. II. New York/Mahwah: Paulist Press, 1989, pp. 305–46.

Wright, J. Robert, and Joseph W. Witmer, eds. *Called to Full Unity: Documents on Anglican-Roman Catholic Relations, 1966–1983.* Washington D.C.: U.S. Catholic Conference, 1986.

10

Relations with the Classical Protestant Churches

Come, to the supper come,
  Sinners, there still is room;
Every soul may be his guest,
  Jesus gives the general word;
    Share the monumental feast,
      Eat the supper of your Lord.
In this authentic sign
  Behold the stamp Divine:
Christ revives his sufferings here,
  Still exposes them to view;
    See the Crucified appear,
      Now believe he died for you.

Charles Wesley

Christians encounter Christ and come to salvation in the midst of interpersonal and community relationships where Christ's saving love is witnessed to in Scripture, worship of the triune God, and lived spirituality and praxis. The initiation and formation of the still divided communities bring them to understand the gifts of their own churches. For most, it is only gradually that conversion to Christ and to his Church is amplified into an understanding of the history of one's own church in relation to other Christian communities and to the Gospel summons to unity.

In these two chapters we will survey the churches which have brought the Gospel to the majority of Americans and which form the backbone of U.S. Christian community. In this chapter we will focus on those churches with which Catholics and Orthodox share a common vision of the ecumenical movement and common hopes for full unity. In the next chapter we will concentrate on those churches whose vision of the Church does not emphasize visible unity, and who are often cool or hostile to the classical twentieth-century ecumenical movement and sometimes to the Catholic Church in particular.

It will be important to keep in mind the history reviewed in chapter one and the present situation of the U.S. churches. A careful study of American history and of Protestant theology will help to situate these churches in their appropriate ecumenical context. The brief introductions to the theology and spirituality of these churches offered here can indicate only the broad outlines of a complex cultural and ecclesial situation.

The Catholic Church is open to, and serious about relating to, both those churches more distant from the ecumenical movement and the classical ecumenical Protestant churches. As indicated by their membership in the World Council of Churches, the latter group are formally committed to the quest for visible unity and to the theology of *koinonia* emerging in the ecumenical movement. It will be rewarding to study their responses to the World Council *Baptism, Eucharist and Ministry* document, while one studies the dialogues they have had with the Roman Catholic Church and with one another. Along with the Lutherans and Episcopalians, these churches are the leaders in local ecumenism and form the core of the National Council of Churches.

MEMBER CHURCHES OF THE NATIONAL COUNCIL

African American Churches
    African Methodist Episcopal Church
    African Methodist Episcopal Zion Church
    Christian Methodist Episcopal Church
    National Baptist Convention of America
    National Baptist Convention, USA, Inc.
    Progressive National Baptist Convention
Eastern Orthodox Churches
    Antiochian Archdiocese of North America
    Greek Archdiocese of North America
    Orthodox Church in America
    Russian Orthodox Church, Patriarchal Parishes

Serbian Orthodox Church in the USA & Canada
Ukranian Orthodox Church in America
Peace Churches
Church of the Brethren
Friends United Meeting (Quaker)
Philadelphia Yearly Meeting (Quaker)
Oriental Orthodox Churches
Diocese of the Armenian Church of America
Coptic Orthodox Church
Syrian Orthodox Church of Antioch
Reformation Churches
Christian Church (Disciples of Christ)
Evangelical Lutheran Church in America
Hungarian Reformed Church
International Council of Community Churches
Korean Presbyterian Church in America
Mar Thoma Church
Moravian Church in America
Presbyterian Church
Reformed Church in America
Swedenborgian Church
United Church of Christ
United Methodist Church
Polish National Catholic Church

This chapter will focus with particular emphasis on the United Methodist, Presbyterian and Reformed, and Disciples of Christ dialogues with the Catholic Church. African American Methodists and Baptists are also members of the World and National Councils and, through the international dialogues, participate with their United Methodist and American and Southern Baptist partners in dialogue with the Catholic Church.

It seems clear, however, that African American theological ecumenism will only be successful if the African American members of the dominant churches, such as the Catholic Church, are ecumenically active, and parishes and dioceses show Christian leadership in the communal mission of building justice and peace. With these churches, *koinonia* in practice may need to precede *koinonia* in formulations of the faith and worship.

There are several important, smaller ecumenically oriented churches not covered in detail in this chapter, but which should be the subject of dialogue and study in a comprehensive view of Catholic ecumenism. The American Baptist Churches are members, with the Catholic Church, in the Faith and Order of the World and National Councils and have completed one round of U.S. bilateral conversations. They are part of the Baptist World Alliance international dialogue with the Vatican.

The historic peace churches: Mennonite, Church of the Brethren, and Friends (Quakers), are each quite ecumenical in their own way. Nevertheless, because of their size, their localization around the United States, and their own style of modesty, service, and nonviolence, they require particular attention, outreach, and contact as important communities of faith among us that retain and nurture certain specific and often unaccentuated Christian attributes. The history of persecution of these Christians by Catholics and Reformation Protestants make reconciliation with these churches a particular urgency.

Presbyterian/Reformed Catholic Dialogue

The term "Reformed" refers to those churches—presbyterian, congregational, and some episcopally ordered—whose roots are in the Swiss, Dutch, and Scottish Reformation, and the theological tradition of Calvin, Zwingli, and Knox. In Britain, which gave rise to the majority of the Reformed churches in the United States, the Scottish reformers developed a church order in which assemblies of presbyters, ministers, and ruling lay elders replaced bishops in the exercise of *episcopé*, thus the name *presbyterian*. English dissenters vested ecclesial authority in the local congregations. In 1957 the New England Puritan Congregationalists united with the German Evangelical and Reformed Church to form the United Church of Christ, one of the first and most dramatic ecumenical unions celebrated in North America. The Dutch Reformed who settled New Amsterdam (now New York) are now the Reformed Church in America. The Reformed churches are important ecumenical partners. They have a rich heritage of ecumenical cooperation. Many of the classical theologians of America, such as Jonathan Edwards, Philip Schaff, and Richard and Reinhold Neibuhr, are from the Reformed churches. The contributions these churches have made to the public order of American society are considerable.

During the period of European expansion and colonialism, Reformed churches were established in many parts of the world, so that in 1992 the World Alliance of Reformed Churches represented 172 churches of seventy million members in eighty countries. It is this World Alliance that cosponsors the international dialogue with the Catholic Church, and its North American department conducts the dialogue with the U.S. Bishops' Conference.

These churches of the Reformation originally did not intend to establish a new Church, but to "reform" the old Church. They adhered to the doctrine of the Apostles' and Nicene Creeds, and sought to expound the key themes of the Scriptures and the centrality of Scripture as the rule of faith and life, including sacramental life. Their theological emphasis on the sovereignty of God and the vastness of the distance between the human and the divine, bridged by God's own loving initiative in the life, death, and resurrection of Jesus Christ and the sending of the Holy Spirit, has been accompanied by a self-understanding of the local church as heir and fulfillment of the Old Testament community of Israel. In significant ways the ecclesial forms of the Reformed tradition continue the conciliar tradition of the pre-Reformation Western church, which had atrophied. Since the Second Vatican Council these have begun to be reintroduced in the Catholic Church. There are, therefore, areas of similarity, areas of contrast, and areas of reappropriation between the Reformed Churches and the Catholic Church.

The international and U.S. dialogues have made an important contribution. While they have treated some of the classical church-dividing themes such as Scripture and tradition, episcopacy and authority, and the sacraments, they have also explored new ground, instructive to all ecumenical relations. The U.S. dialogue has pioneered work on ethical issues and on methodology in moral decision making, and has produced statements on abortion, human rights, peace, and education. The abortion text, in particular, is a model for its methodology and the common ground it provides on this contentious issue. The U.S. dialogue was one of the first to suggest concrete goals and stages for a process of unity that would bring together the Catholic Church and a Church without bishops in the apostolic succession.

The international dialogue has been particularly creative in the areas of mission, hermeneutics, approaches to the reconciliation of memories and the writing of the history of painful periods in our past, justification, and identification of the Church as both sacrament and creature of the Word. The first dialogue in 1977 is entitled, *The Presence of Christ in Church and World*. The second stage of this dialogue produced the statement, *Towards a Common Understanding of the Church* (1990).

The latter statement consists of four chapters that provide a most helpful vision of a way forward for the Catholic Church with its Reformed partners:

INTRODUCTION (1–11)
1. TOWARD A RECONCILIATION OF
   MEMORIES (12–63)
   The partners attempt to read the sixteenth-century history of the Reformation and of their separation with "greater objectivity and more balanced judgment" (14).
2. OUR COMMON CONFESSION OF FAITH (64–88)
   A common confession of faith is proposed to stimulate further reflection.
3. THE CHURCH WE CONFESS AND OUR
   DIVISIONS IN HISTORY (89–144)
   The Church pertains to the confession of faith. Yet, the two Churches entertain agreements and divergences in reference to the relationship between the Church and the Gospel.
4. THE WAY FORWARD (145–165)

The report indicates some practical steps which may lead to greater communion. One of the most significant suggestions of this dialogue is the common writing of our separate histories:

We need to set ourselves more diligently, however, to the task
of reconciling these memories, by writing together the story
of what happened in the sixteenth century, with attention not
only to the clash of convictions over doctrine and church
order, but with attention also as to how in the aftermath our
two churches articulated their respective understandings into
institutions, culture and the daily lives of believers. But above
all, for the ways in which our divisions have caused a scandal,
and been an obstacle to the preaching of the Gospel, we need
to ask forgiveness of Christ and of each other. (63) (IS no. 74
[1990], 102)

The U.S. dialogue has produced six rounds of reports:
Reconsiderations (1966–1967), "The Ministry of the Church"
(1968–1971), *The Unity We Seek* (1976), *Ethics and the Search for
Unity* (1980), *Partners in Peace and Education* (1985), and the *Laity*
(1996). The churches that have been involved most directly
among the U.S. Reformed churches are the Presbyterian, the
United Church of Christ, and the Reformed Church in America.

The Reformed-Catholic dialogues are less well known than
Catholic dialogues with Anglicans and Lutherans. One of the
reasons may be the fact that these dialogues have sought to make
"the reports on each session...more descriptive than prescrip-
tive" so that "the value of these discussions does not lie only in
their necessarily provisional 'results'" but rather that "the read-
ers may let themselves be drawn into inner dynamic of the movement which gripped us" (*The Presence of Christ in Church and
World,* 9, 12, in Meyer and Vischer, 436–7).

Methodist-Roman Catholic Dialogues

In the United States, Methodism emerged as a cluster of
churches from its previous status as a movement within Anglicanism after the Revolution (1794), and prospered on the frontier by its itinerant circuit-rider evangelism in an early
nineteenth-century America that was very unchurched. Methodism can be particularly confusing for the beginning ecumenist
because of its dual character as movement and church.

U.S. Methodism draws from the successful evangelism of the

frontier circuit riders and elements retained from the Anglican tradition, and therefore has a certain tension within it between the evangelistic and social action dimensions, the sacramental and practical emphases, and the theological and experiential bases in understanding the faith. Awareness of the experiential dimensions of Methodism discussed in chapter five will be important to understanding the United Methodist-Roman Catholic dialogue and will also offer insight into the Evangelical, Holiness, and Pentecostal churches which have been influenced in a variety of ways by Methodism and are discussed in chapter eleven.

During the first half of the nineteenth century American Methodism experienced several divisions, the most large-scale of which was between North and South before the civil war. Other important divisions had already occurred, however, in the early nineteenth-century separation of the African Methodist Episcopal Church (1816) and the African Methodist Episcopal Zion Church (1821) from the broader Methodist movement. After the Civil War, the Black and White members of the Methodist Episcopal Church, South, separated to form the Colored (now Christian) Methodist Episcopal Church (1870).

The divisions among these three churches and the United Methodist Church, which is the result of two important church mergers in the twentieth century (1939 and 1968), and which has a significant African American membership, do not entail sacramental or doctrinal differences. All four are members of the Consultation on Church Union and are in conversation about Methodist reunion.

Because of its even distribution across the country, its structures of ministry and episcopacy, and its keen sense of spirituality and social ministry, the United Methodist Church shares Catholicism's sense of unity in cultural diversity, discipline, spirituality, canonical accountability, and social engagement. The United Methodist Church considers itself to share in the episcopal ministry of the Anglican, Orthodox, and Catholic Churches, but claims no unique divine rights for this form of church order. It teaches the doctrine of the priesthood of all believers and follows principles laid down in the eighteenth century for pastoral oversight by John Wesley. In contrast to the Reformed tradition, ministers are appointed, not "called" by the congregation. The highest authority of pastoral *episcopé* is invested in the Conference. The conference system, at local, regional, and national levels, is composed of lay and ordained members, and functions as the magisterium for the church.

Methodists have been among the most dedicated ecumenical participants and have contributed some of the great leaders and theologians of the ecumenical movement. Methodists' self-perception as being a "bridge" community between the Evangelical world and the classical Protestant world, and between the Protestant world and the older episcopally ordered churches has enabled them to productively engage a wide variety of ecumenical partners.

Methodism is spread throughout the world, with churches in Europe, North and South America, Africa, Asia, and Oceania. Methodists have participated in church unions which transcend confessional barriers, such as the Churches of South and North India. On the international level, dialogues with other churches are carried on through the World Methodist Council. The U.S. dialogues are sponsored by the General Commission on Christian Unity of the United Methodist Church.

The dialogue between the World Methodist Council and the Catholic Church has adopted a different style from other dialogues in attributing equal value to doctrine as such and religious experience. In this regard, it has not created the theological specificity of the dialogue with the Lutherans. Yet, it by no means occupies a secondary status in the mind of the Catholic Church. It will be helpful for the student to keep in mind that in Wesleyan theological method, the "quadrilateral" of Scripture, tradition, reason, and religious experience constitute the sources of theology. The choice of doctrine and spirituality as the bases for ecumenical discussion, therefore, reflects a respect for the theological practices as well as the devotional processes of the dialogue partners.

The dialogue between the World Methodist Council and the Roman Catholic Church functions on a quinquennial basis, renewing its membership, and changing its topic every five years, on the occasion of the plenary meetings of the World Methodist Council. Since its beginning in 1967, it has produced six reports:

INTERNATIONAL: WORLD METHODIST COUNCIL-PONTIFICAL COUNCIL FOR PROMOTING CHRISTIAN UNITY

Denver Report, 1971
    General Retrospect
    Christianity and the Contemporary World
    Spirituality
    Christian Home and Family
    Eucharist
    Ministry
    Authority
    The Way Ahead

Dublin Report, 1976
    Introduction
    Common Witness and Salvation Today
    Spirituality
    Christian Home and Family: Interchurch Marriages
    Moral Questions—Euthanasia
    Eucharist
    Ministry
    Authority
    Church Union Negotiations

Honolulu Report, 1981
    Toward an Agreed Statement on the Holy Spirit
    The Holy Spirit, Christian Experience, and Authority
    Christian Moral Decisions
    Marriage

Toward a Statement on the Church, Nairobi, 1986
    Nature of the Church
    Sacraments
    Called to Unity
    Ways of Being One
    Structures of Ministry
    Petrine Office

The Apostolic Tradition, Singapore, 1991
 Faith: Teaching, Transmission, and Reception
  Word and Church
  Spirit and Church
  Pattern of Faith
  Pattern of Life
  Pattern of Community
 Service: Ministry and Ministries
  Service of the Word
  Gift of the Spirit
  The Church, a Living Body
  Ordained Ministry
  Convergences and Divergences

The Word of Life: A Statement on Revelation and Faith, Rio,
    1996
 Revelation
  God's Self-Giving
  Revelation in History
  Trinitarian Revelation
 Faith
  Faith by Which We Believe
  Faith Which Is Believed
  Fruitfulness of Faith
 Mission
  Mission of the Church Comes from God
  Word and Act
  Mission and Community
  Apostolic Mission
  Mission and Ecumenism
  Mission and Cultures
 Sacramental Life
 Communion—*Koinonia*
  Communion through Apostolic Witness
  Basic Expressions of Communion
  The Church Universal

UNITED STATES: UNITED METHODIST CHURCH-NATIONAL CONFERENCE OF CATHOLIC BISHOPS

Shared Convictions about Education, 1970

Holiness and Spirituality of the Ordained Ministry, 1976

Eucharistic Celebration: Converging Theology–Divergent Practice, 1981
   Converging toward the Unity God Wills
   Structure of the Eucharistic Celebration
   Theological Understanding Emerging from the Structure
       Presence of Christ
       Sacrifice of Christ
       Faith and the Eucharist
   Work Begun and Unfinished: Questions toward the Future

Holy Living and Holy Dying, 1988
   Theological and Ethical Principles
   Pastoral Care
   Social Dimension
   Implications for Action

Denver (1971), Dublin (1976), Honolulu (1981), Nairobi (1986), Singapore (1991), and Rio (1996).

In the Denver Report the aim of the dialogue was to reach a consensus on the part of the two communions in regard to the common mission of Christians in the world. The dialogue makes reference to the fact that Methodists and Catholics do not possess a history of formal separation; notes John Wesley's "Letter to a Roman Catholic" of July 18, 1749, an openness to "Spiritual Ecumenism" and an emphasis on holiness of life found in both traditions; and explores the role of hymnody in the two churches. It seeks practical measures to promote ecumenism: in cooperation in theological training of ministers; in the use of common prayer in the liturgy and common use of hymns; in dialogue in regard to moral matters; in efforts to thwart the inroads of secularism upon Christians; in cooperation in social endeavors such as programs of world peace and development, family life, poverty, race, and immigration.

The dialogue emphasizes the compatibility of forms of spirituality in the two communions. These relate to both liturgical prayer and personal piety. Much is being learned from one another in ecumenical exchange on spiritualities. Topics discussed include traditional and contemporary devotional practices; the relation of spiritual life to the pursuit of good works; growth in holiness; sanctification of everyday life; the disciplined life; life in the Spirit; theology of the heart; the spiritual life as an outgrowth of the justification that emanates from faith and finds expression in affective patterns of moral and spiritual discipline, charismatic gifts, and sacrificial love, and as effective signs of the profession of faith, which sometimes generates a pious feeling; and the way in which the death and resurrection of Jesus is experienced in the Church.

In the fifth chapter of the report, on the Eucharist, "Points of Agreement," "Points of Difference," and "Points for Further Study" were offered. In regard to "Points of Agreement," the Real Presence, The Sacrifice, and Communion were explored, while in reference to "Points of Difference," the Presence and Intercommunion were offered. For Methodists the presence of Christ in the Eucharist is not different from Christ's presence in other means of grace, especially preaching. Methodists do not understand the transformation of the sacred species in the same way that Catholics understand this and as a result do not worship the Blessed Sacrament. Methodists admit to the Eucharist any Christian who is comfortable in accepting the invitation. "Points for Further Study" include the ministry and apostolic succession; common faith; and the relation between the Eucharist and ecclesiastical fellowship.

Discussion of "Ministry" provided a number of areas of agreement, which included ministry as participation in Christ's ministry; the work of the Holy Spirit; full-time, lifelong, dedication to Christ in teaching, preaching and pastoring; a mystical extension of the Incarnation; the recognition of prophetic and special ministries; and the recognition of ministry by virtue of "connectional" character, which in Methodist theology corresponds generally to the Catholic conception of "character" in the presbyterate. High standards of educational and spiritual training for ministry are provided for in each tradition. Theological factors in the authorization of ministry and the extent of mutuality in which ministers of the two communions can now share are noted as unsettled issues.

The particular contribution of the Dublin Report, deepening some of the issues begun in the Denver dialogue, is the agreement reached on salvation. Addressing "Common Witness and Salvation Today," the Dublin Report comments on general themes which pervaded the dialogue. The fundamental obligation of the Church to witness in words and life to God's saving gift in Christ is noted. Such a witness can only be effective when it is performed for the sake of truth. Salvation entails inseparable individual and social dimensions. God's salvation in Christ embraces the entire created order. Christian witness today must be aware of "inculturation." Finally, the Church is still commissioned to preach the Good News to all.

"Salvation" is multivalent, signifying the effort to survive, deliverance from an empty life to one of greater human enrichment, and the enjoyment of the "divine discontent." Salvation is not escape from the "world." Methodists and Catholics can affirm together a complex of theological themes related to the notion of salvation: the reality of sin; the grace of God; social concerns as solicitude for human dignity; a strong missionary impulse; concern for sanctification; sensitivity to the riches of other world religions; and the call to unity.

The Honolulu contribution emphasizes the basis in the Holy Spirit, an important Methodist emphasis, and takes up many of the earlier themes including authority, in this new context. Catholics especially will be intrigued by the results of the Nairobi Report, which touches on papacy and authority and draws on some of the Lutheran-Catholic dialogues. In light of the Pope's 1995 invitation, one affirmation is particularly striking:

> Methodists accept that whatever is properly required for the unity of the whole of Christ's Church must by that very fact be God's will for his Church. A universal primacy might well serve as focus of and ministry for the whole Church. (58)

The Singapore and Rio reports are particularly important in deepening the common ground among the churches on the questions of tradition, episcopacy and *episcopé,* revelation, authority, and *koinonia.*

The U.S. Methodist dialogues are important because some very practical polarizations in the public policy arena can easily obscure the profound spiritual, theological, liturgical, and ethical common ground. Two of the dialogues touch on these tense issues: *Shared Convictions in Education* and *Holy Living, Holy Dying.* The long Methodist commitment to public education and the concern of Catholic parents for public support of parochial education, while not church-dividing of itself, has created the necessity of beginning the U.S. dialogue with education. United Methodists and Catholics have the largest church-sponsored health care systems in the country, so their agreement on ministry to the sick and dying is a natural topic for agreement. However, within that wide area of agreement, different approaches toward euthanasia are discussed frankly and dispassionately in the dialogue. This dialogue is an important resource in the current contentious debate in American society on public policy approaches to end-of-life issues.

Two theological themes have also been taken up: *Holiness and Spirituality of the Ordained Ministry* (1976), and *Eucharistic Celebration: Converging Theology-Divergent Practice* (1981). Both of these merit further study, especially among those responsible for liturgical and ministerial formation.

The results of this dialogue suggest some very positive conclusions. Both churches are irreversibly committed to full communion and full ecumenical collaboration on the way to that goal. Responses to the World Council's *Baptism, Eucharist and Ministry* show even deeper convergences than the formal bilateral dialogue. Spiritual ecumenism and collaboration in social witness are central for both churches. These churches share a similar sense of disciplinary accountability. Each church has both hierarchical authority in the appointment of ministers and collegial structures of decision making. The two communions provide unique ecumenical leadership because of their numbers and their shared conviction that the present state of division is contrary to the will of Christ. An extensive list of positive, pastoral, practical initiatives for the local situation are suggested by these dialogues.

Disciples of Christ-Catholic Dialogue

In the sixteenth century Anabaptists churches affirmed a *restorationist* approach to church reform. In this understanding the true Church is one that restores the New Testament community of the biblical witness. The intervening years—or at least those after Constantine in the fourth century—were regarded as a departure from, rather than a development of, the apostolic faith. Some Baptists came to believe that from John the Baptist there was a line of martyrs, underground during Imperial days, that continued believers' baptism and congregational ecclesiology through the centuries in spite of the dominant Byzantine and Roman, "apostate" churches. Some of the Holiness, Adventist, and Pentecostal churches accept this restorationist understanding of church and history. A restorationist point of view of this type makes ecumenism based on the historic creeds, an acceptance of the many centuries of common history, and a mutual contemporary historical-critical reading of the Scriptures very difficult.

However, among the restoration movements which attempted to return to the original biblical testimony by transcending the intervening centuries was the early-nineteenth-century movement of Barton Stone and Alexander Campbell. They sought to reject denominations, confessions, and traditions so as to be simply Christian, with believers' baptism, weekly Eucharist, no other creed than Christ, and open communion and membership. Three communities have emerged from this movement: the Disciples of Christ, who have taken the ecumenical call as their leitmotif; the Churches of Christ, who have conjoined restorationism with a Biblical literalism; and the Independent Christian Churches.

The Disciples of Christ are a worldwide communion of Christians, originating in nineteenth-century Kentucky, where Barton W. Stone (1772–1844) led a revival of twenty thousand people which convinced him of the necessity of Christian unity. The community assumed the title "Christian," seeking to avoid nonbiblical names. Thomas (1763–1854) and Alexander (1788–1866) Campbell, Presbyterians from Ireland and founders of the Disciples of Christ, joined with Stone's frontier "Christian" movement to found the Christian Church (Disciples of Christ) in 1832. The Campbells' concern was to place Scripture above creedal statements, and to keep the Eucharist, the Lord's Supper, open to all who confessed Jesus Christ. Throughout their history, the cause of Christian unity has remained very precious to the Christian and Disciples' movement. They have sought to restore the "ancient order of things," rejecting doctrinal formulations as "tests of fellowship," to reclaim this unity.

The reader may be helped to understand these ecclesial communities by noting the richness of the Christological claims that are implied. An ability to transcend time and culture, to gather a human community, and to maintain unity and orthodoxy without verbally articulated norms are ascribed directly to the Lordship of Jesus Christ.

The Disciples' movement, with its message of freedom, diversity, simplicity of worship, and a reasonable faith, moved swiftly from the American frontier to many parts of the English-speaking world, and in the missionary expansion of the late 1800s and early part of this century, found its way to Africa and Asia, where it formed part of newly created Church unions, for example, Church of North India, the Kyodan in Japan, and the Church of Christ in Zaire. At present, the Disciples participate in the Consultation on Church Union, and have a special ecumenical partnership with the United Church of Christ. Three international dialogues—with the Roman Catholic Church, the Russian Orthodox Church, and the World Alliance of Reformed Churches—are sponsored through the international Disciples Ecumenical Consultative Council.

The dialogue between the Disciples of Christ and the Catholic Church began in the U.S. with the National Conference of Catholic Bishops, but eventually became an international bilateral. It has produced a memorandum on sharing the Eucharist (1968), *An Adventure in Understanding* (1973), *A Report* (1981), *Apostolicity and Catholicity* (1982), and *The Church as Communion in Christ* (1993). Its present work on conciliar authority and the structures of *koinonia* promises to produce similar fruitful results.

The 1993 report acknowledges that at first sight it seems as if the two communions have very little in common, "Indeed

Roman Catholics and Disciples appear so different and live in such different ways that for many of their members the proposal that their differences could be overcome is nearly incredible" (17). However, the dialogue claims that in regard to ecclesiology the churches, "converge on some notable points," (18) "share the same understanding of the basic nature of the Church," (20) and have come "to a very important agreement concerning the nature and mission of the Church" (47).

Discussions of divergences and common ground in regard to the continuity of the tradition, Eucharistic theology and practice, and even ministry and episcopacy, where the contrasts appear most divergent, have provided the framework for more developed levels of agreement as the dialogue progresses. The ethos of nineteenth-century Protestantism as it developed within American frontier culture and the global stance of Catholicism offer a challenging exercise in ecumenical reconciliation. Yet, the ecclesiology of *hoinonia*, which is in the process of reception in both of the churches, has provided an inestimable resource in bringing these two churches closer in the common Trinitarian faith, grounded in common celebration of Christ in worship, pointing toward a common future by the power of the Holy Spirit.

Conclusion

The historic American Protestant churches—Reformed, Methodist, Baptist, and Disciples, have given a constant Christian witness to the faith and have contributed greatly to American culture. The Reformed churches have contributed the separation of powers, representative democracy, and the court system that have become the secular polity in the United States. The strong Methodist social concern has paralleled the development of Catholic social teaching in this country. The ecumenical urgency of the Disciples of Christ has acted as a catalyst and example for Christians of all traditions to emulate in their enthusiasm to realize Christ's will for the Church.

As Pope John Paul reminds the churches, "At the stage which we have now reached, this process of mutual enrichment must be taken seriously into account" (UUS 87). Theologians and church leaders from the ecumenical Protestant churches have begun the ecumenical movement in its modern form, and have initiated Catholics into the movement. It is essential that Catholics find a way of understanding these churches as they understand themselves while embarking upon a study of these important dialogues and their results.

On the first Sunday of Advent of the year 2000 several of these churches may celebrate a ceremony of recognition and reconciliation at the Church of Christ Uniting, crowning years of careful dialogue, prayer, and theological work. The Presbyterian Church, the International Council of Community Churches, the United Church of Christ, the Episcopal Church, the African Methodist Episcopal Church, the United Methodist Church, the African Methodist Episcopal Zion Church, the Christian Church/Disciples of Christ, and the Christian Methodist Episcopal Church have before them proposals of a covenant based on common principles of *koinonia* ecclesiology which, if agreed upon, would lead to full communion in faith, sacramental life, witness, and decision making. Sufficient numbers of these churches who have participated for over thirty years in the Consultation on Church Union have agreed with the proposal before them that the reconciliation could be celebrated, whether or not all of the nine churches are yet able to agree. This process itself is a sign of the Holy Spirit's reconciling will alive among the churches in their pilgrimage toward unity for which all Christians pray.

What the Reformed-Catholic dialogue affirms of these two traditions can be confessed by all of the churches discussed in this chapter:

> We wish to voice our conviction that what unites us as Christians is more important, more essential, than that which separates us as Roman Catholics and Reformed. Even if full communion is not yet granted us, we cannot define our relations to each other simply in terms of separation and division. (*Towards a Common Understanding of the Church*, 65 in IS no. 74 [1990], 102)

Study Questions

1. What types and varieties of churches are most involved in the ecumenical movement? What characteristics of these churches might lead them to the search for unity together?

2. Identify and review the characteristic features, including the ecclesial order, of the Reformed churches in dialogue with the Catholic Church. How has the history of these churches shaped the American ecumenical context?

3. Enumerate the subjects of discussion and the major areas of contribution of Presbyterian/Reformed-Catholic dialogue.

4. Review the key historical and theological developments, including ecclesial structure and Eucharistic theology, in the rise and unfolding of the Methodist movement.

5. How has the Methodist-Roman Catholic dialogue been distinctive? Why have the issues explored, such as spiritual experience, been chosen and what outcomes have been achieved?

6. Explain the theological bases of *restorationist* ecclesiology and the Disciples' "No creed but Christ" doctrine.

7. What have been the results, particularly in regard to *koinonia* ecclesiology, of the Disciples-Catholic dialogue?

8. How might the results of the Roman Catholic dialogues with the Presbyterian and Reformed Churches, the United Methodist Church, and the Disciples of Christ serve local parish or diocesan ecumenism? What challenges might one anticipate?

Selected Readings

Burgess, Joseph, and Jeffrey Gros, eds. *Building Unity: Ecumenical Dialogues with Roman Catholic Participation. Ecumenical Documents IV.* New York/Mahwah: Paulist Press, 1989, pp. 35–82, 291–322, 371–483.

——. *Growing Consensus: Church Dialogues in the United States, 1962–1991. Ecumenical Documents V.* New York/Mahwah: Paulist Press, 1995, pp. 9–172, 529–42, 614–28, 649–58.

Disciples of Christ-Roman Catholic International Commission for Dialogue, 1995–96, "Agreed Account." *Mid-Stream* 35 (October 1996): 477–89.

———."1995 Theme: The Gospel and the Church." *Mid-Stream* 35 (October 1996): 363–416.

———."1996 Theme: The Content and the Authority of the Early Councils." *Mid-Stream* 35 (October 1996): 417–75.

Ganoczy, Alexander. *The Young Calvin*. David Foxgrover and Wade Provo, trans. Louisville: Westminster/John Knox, 1987.

Gros, Jeffrey, and William G. Rusch, eds. *Deepening Communion*. Washington D.C.: U.S. Catholic Conference, 1998, Parts II, III.

Gunneman, Louis H. *United and Uniting: The Meaning of an Ecclesial Journey*. Cleveland: United Church Press, 1987.

Heitzenrater, Richard P. *Wesley and the People Called Methodists*. Nashville: Abingdon Press, 1995.

McDonnell, Killian. *John Calvin, the Church, and the Eucharist*. Princeton: Princeton University Press, 1967.

Meyer, Harding, and Lukas Vischer, eds. *Growth in Agreement: Reports and Agreed Statements of Ecumenical Conversations on a World Level. Ecumenical Documents II*. New York/Mahwah: Paulist Press, 1984, pp. 153–66, 277–388, 433–64.

Reformed-Roman Catholic International Dialogue. *Towards a Common Understanding of the Church*. Pontifical Council for Promoting Christian Unity, *Information Service*, no. 74 (1990): 91–118.

Rouse, Ruth. "Voluntary Movements and the Changing Ecumenical Climate." In Ruth Rouse and Stephen Neill, eds. *A History of the Ecumenical Movement 1517–1948*. Philadelphia: Westminster Press, 1967, pp. 307–49.

Sell, Alan P. F. *A Reformed, Evangelical, Catholic Theology: The Contribution of the World Alliance of Reformed Churches, 1875–1982*. Grand Rapids: Eerdmans, 1991.

Shriver, Peggy L. *Having Gifts That Differ: Profiles of Ecumenical Churches*. New York: Friendship Press, 1990.

Thompson, David M. "Faith: The Individual and the Church." *Mid-Stream* 34 (January, 1995): 61–73.

Tillard, O.P., Jean-Marie R. "Faith: The Believer and the Church," *Mid-Stream* 34 (January, 1995): 45–60.

Wainwright, Geoffrey. *Methodists in Dialogue*. Nashville: Kingswood Books, 1995.

Wilmore, Gayraud S. *Black Religion and Black Radicalism: An Interpretation of the Religious History of Afro-American People*. Maryknoll, NY: Orbis Books, 1983.

11

Evangelical and Pentecostal Communities

Amazing Grace! How sweet the sound that saved a wretch like me!
I once was lost, but now am found;
Was blind, but now I see.
'Twas grace that taught my heart to fear, and grace my fears relieved;
How precious did that grace appear
The hour I first believed!
Through many dangers, toils, and snares, I have already come;
'Tis grace hath brought me safe thus far,
And grace will lead me home.

John Newton

Not all Christians view the unity of the Church in the same way. For a variety of theological, cultural, historical, and ideological reasons some Christians are reluctant or even hostile to collaboration with some other Christian communities. Dialogue that seeks to cross this imposing chasm must begin with dialogue of charity and mutual understanding, but can sometimes, as a result of new mutual trust gained, advance to the deeper levels of the dialogue of truth. This chapter will outline the relationships that have developed between the Catholic Church and some of those churches and movements that are most distant from and suspicious of it, and suggest ways of proceeding to improve these relationships.

In *Ut Unum Sint* Pope John Paul reiterates a theme from the Decree on Ecumenism and draws attention to the fact that although doctrinal dialogues are of high importance, dialogue engages the whole person and the whole of Christian witness:

> "It is right and salutary to recognize the riches of Christ and virtuous works in the lives of others who are bearing witness

to Christ, sometimes even to the shedding of their blood.
For God is always wonderful in his works and worthy of
admiration." (UUS 47)

There are many forms of witness in which Christians who are
at a distance from one another in terms of history or theology can
rejoice together. This field for ecumenical exploration has just
begun to be utilized by some Christian groups. Many forms of witness in interpersonal relationships and community life are ripe for
ecumenical engagement and ecumenical learning among Catholic
and the Pentecostal, Evangelical, and Fundamentalist Protestant
communities with which relationships have been difficult.

Some Christians who are not sympathetic to the ecumenical movement in its ecclesiological dimension will collaborate in
spiritual, evangelistic, and a variety of social witness elements,
and enter into a conversation of mutual understanding. Other
Christians who are aggressive in evangelism, evaluating others as
less Christian than themselves, are nonetheless recognizable
from the Catholic perspective as fellow Christians. These groups
are to be distinguished from semi-Christian groups, such as the
Mormons and Jehovah's Witnesses, and from aggressive non-
Christian groups.

There is some unfortunate confusion about these distinc-
tions, particularly among those who come from secluded
Catholic cultures or isolated Catholic communities, and have not
had personal experience of the pluralism characteristic of the
contemporary world. In Catholic self-understanding, all persons, of whatever religious views, are the possessors of the dignity with which God has endowed human nature (Declaration on
Religious Liberty). Non-Christian religions of great antiquity,
which possess rich traditions of lived experience, doctrinal elaboration, and profound moral authority, are accorded a special
place of respect (The Declaration on the Church's Relations with
non-Christian Religions). Groups which from the Catholic perspective cannot be identified as definitively Christian are
nonetheless potential bearers of God's truth and grace for their
participants. The reader is urged to learn only to use language
about other groups that they use of themselves. Terms such as
sect and *fundamentalist* ought to be used by Christians of others

only when they are used by the partner in question. This is equally true of both Christian and other communities.

As with the previous chapter, it will be important to review here what has been discussed in chapters one and five, and to explore in more depth the Christian situations in other parts of the world. The Christian groups discussed in the present chapter are smaller than most of the churches previously discussed, but are also the fastest growing groups, with particular significance in Africa and Latin America. For Latin American and Southern European Catholicism some of these groups present a particular challenge, as there has been a presumed cultural hegemony and a tradition of a special relationship between the Church and culture, if not between the Church and the state. In Eastern Europe and the Middle East the Orthodox also find it difficult to deal with pluralism, and frequently see the action of both these groups and of the Catholic Church as *proselytizing*.

Evangelical/Roman Catholic Dialogue

The term "evangelical" has been variously employed since the time of the Reformation. It was used rather sparingly before that time. It was utilized by Erasmus and others, in a pejorative sense, to refer to Luther's alleged narrowness and fanaticism. Luther used the term to refer to all who accepted the doctrine of justification by grace alone. In the eighteenth century the title "evangelical" was identified with portions of the Great Awakening in the Church of England that did not break off into the emergent Methodist or into other renewal movements.

At the present time one can identify at least four common usages of the term "evangelical": (1) Bible-believing Gospel Christians, which would include active Catholics who are animated by a serious biblical piety; (2) Lutherans as contrasted with Reformed and other Protestants, such as the Evangelical Lutheran Church in America; (3) Protestants who stress personal conversion, salvation by faith in the atoning death of Christ, inerrancy of Scripture, and evangelistic zeal; and (4) a subculture of conservative Christians, primarily but not exclusively Protestant, who may not share complete doctrinal agreement with each other, but who recognize one another as partners in a broad political and cultural assimilation and application of the Gospel. Christian fundamentalists may consider themselves Evangelical, but "Evangelicals" is a larger category, both theologically (3) and sociologically (4) than fundamentalist.

During the nineteenth century many of the populous, culturally prominent, and centrist Protestant groups began to recognize a need for joint action to meet the missionary and social concerns of the day. Abolition, prostitution, inadequate educational opportunities, alarming excesses in the use of alcohol, the needs of the urban poor, the desire to send out Protestant missionaries on a worldwide scale and to evangelize the largely unchurched western frontier drew Methodists, Congregationalists, Presbyterians, and Baptists into common efforts. These collaborative groups, such as the American Board of Foreign Missions, the Evangelical Alliance, the Women's Christian Temperance Union, and the World Student Christian Federation, were able to mobilize considerable common Christian witness and began to build a sense of greater commonality than division across doctrinal differences. There was, however, an antipathy to Roman Catholicism in this early ecumenical development, which has continued to influence Evangelical ecumenical activity.

In the late nineteenth century and early twentieth century this broad transconfessional group began to experience the same kinds of interior pressures from the world of modernity and reactions to it, some favorable and some resistant, as did the other churches.

The classical Protestantism of today, which crosses most Protestant doctrinal boundaries, is the heir to that portion of the Evangelical Protestant mainstream that embraced modernity a century ago. It has continued to emphasize the social justice activities that had been prominent in the nineteenth century. In the mid-twentieth century a branch of this classical stream, concerned that key theological elements of the faith might be eroded or oversimplified by the closeness of the churches to secular modernity, made a self-conscious turn toward orthodoxy in the Neo-orthodox movement, and sought to reappropriate the classical Western Christian tradition in a renewed interpretation.

The more conservative stream emerging from the Evangelical alliances of the nineteenth century produced a cluster of movements and trends. The various groups discussed in the present chapter—Evangelicals, Fundamentalists, Pentecostals, and Holiness communities—are heirs of this second stream.

The Christian fundamentalist movement, an important minority among Evangelicals, has its roots in U.S. Presbyterianism, with a basis in Princeton theology. The term is most closely connected with a group of theological tracts published between 1910 and 1915 under the title *The Fundamentals. The Fundamentals* is a series of twelve paperback volumes affirming the divinity of Jesus; the virgin birth; the substitutionary atonement; the bodily resurrection of Christ; an immediacy of Christ's second coming; and the primacy, verbal inspiration, and inerrancy of the Scriptures.

Fundamentalism should be distinguished from the broader movement of Evangelicalism. In the mid-1940s, an antifundamentalist "new evangelicalism" emerged in the ministry of such prominent forces for leadership as evangelist Billy Graham, theologian Carl F. Henry, Fuller Seminary, and the periodical *Christianity Today*. The establishment of the National Association of Evangelicals gave this new movement a forum for ecumenical activity among the participant churches. The NAE Statement of Faith gives a good insight into the doctrinal concerns of the new Evangelicals and their spiritual ecumenism.

The member churches of the NAE represent a variety of communities from the Reformed, Lutheran, Radical Reformation, and later Protestant traditions.

The American Evangelical movement experienced another surge of renewal in the 1970s with a deeper theological interest, ecumenical openness, and social activism. The journal *Sojourners* and the ministry and theology of Ronald Sider, Donald Dayton, Mark Bronson, John Stott, and Richard Mouw are characteristic of this attempt to recapture the nineteenth-century alliance of conservative and centrist Protestantism with active social concern.

NATIONAL ASSOCIATION OF EVANGELICALS STATEMENT OF FAITH

1. We believe the Bible to be the inspired, the only infallible, authoritative Word of God.
2. We believe that there is one God, eternally existent in three persons: Father, Son and Holy Spirit.
3. We believe in the deity of our Lord Jesus Christ, in His virgin birth, in His sinless life, in His miracles, in His vicarious and atoning death through His shed blood, in His bodily resurrection, in His ascension to the right hand of the Father, and in His personal return in power and glory.
4. We believe that for the salvation of lost and sinful people, regeneration by the Holy Spirit is absolutely essential.
5. We believe in the present ministry of the Holy Spirit by whose indwelling the Christian is enabled to live a godly life.
6. We believe in the resurrection of both the saved and the lost; they that are saved unto the resurrection of life and they that are lost unto the resurrection of damnation.
7. We believe in the spiritual unity of believers in our Lord Jesus Christ.

NATIONAL ASSOCIATION OF EVANGELICALS MEMBER CHURCHES

Pentecostal Tradition
    Assemblies of God
    Christian Church of North America
    Church of God (Cleveland, TN)
    Church of God, Mountain Assembly, Inc.
    Congregational Holiness Church
    Evangelistic Missionary Fellowship
    Elim Fellowship
    Fire Baptized Holiness Church of God of the Americas
    International Church of the Foursquare Gospel
    International Pentecostal Church of Christ

International Pentecostal Holiness Church
Open Bible Standard Churches
Pentecostal Church of God
Pentecostal Free Will Baptist Church, Inc.

Holiness Tradition
Christian & Missionary Alliance
The Church of the Nazarene
Church of the United Brethren in Christ
Churches of Christ in Christian Union
Evangelical Church of North America
Evangelical Congregational Church
Evangelical Methodist Church
Free Methodist Church of North America
Missionary Church, Inc.
Primitive Methodist Church, USA
The Salvation Army
The Wesleyan Church

Free Church Tradition
Baptist General Conference
Brethren in Christ Church
Conservative Baptist Association
Evangelical Free Church of America
Fellowship of Evangelical Bible Churches
General Association of General Baptists

Peace Church Traditions
The Brethren Church (Ashland, OH)
Evangelical Friends International of North America
Evangelical Mennonite Church
Mennonite Brethren Churches, USA

Reformed Tradition
Christian Reformed Church in North America
Conservative Congregational Christian Conference
Evangelical Presbyterian Church
Midwest Congregational Christian Fellowship
Presbyterian Church in America
Synod of Mid-America (Reformed Church in America)
Reformed Episcopal Church
Reformed Presbyterian Church of North America

Other Traditions
  Advent Christian General Conference
  Christian Catholic Church (Evangelical Protestant)
  Christian Union
  Conservative Lutheran Association
  Worldwide Church of God

Evangelical/Roman Catholic
Dialogue on Mission (1977–1984)

The Evangelical movement contains a variety of parachurch groupings, such as the World Evangelical Fellowship. These relationships are more personal than ecclesiastical. Because Evangelical ecclesiology and soteriology are so different from that of the Catholic Church, it is an ecumenical challenge to identify an appropriate partner for institutional and public dialogue. An initial conversation took place with representatives of the Pontifical Council for Promoting Christian Unity and a group of individuals, leaders in the international evangelical community. It covered a variety of topics, as can be noted in the outline of the text produced, *Evangelical-Roman Catholic Dialogue on Mission:*

INTRODUCTION
1. REVELATION AND AUTHORITY
    1. Revelation, the Bible and the Formulation of Truth
    2. Principles of Biblical Interpretation
    3. The Church's Teaching Authority
    4. Can the Church Be Reformed?
2. THE NATURE OF MISSION
    1. The Basis of Mission
    2. Authority and Initiative in Mission
    3. Evangelization and Sociopolitical Responsibility
    4. God's Work Outside the Christian Community
3. THE GOSPEL OF SALVATION
    1. Human Need
    2. The Person of Jesus Christ
    3. The Work of Jesus Christ
    4. The Uniqueness and Universality of Jesus Christ

The report is in no sense an "agreed statement" or an exhaustive commentary upon all theological questions, but contains a record of some shared insights and a host of areas where agreement does not yet exist. Nonetheless the dialogue has produced a considerable amount of consensus in regard to Christology, Scripture, Church, and culture which will permit Evangelicals and Catholics to offer common witness.

On the other hand, disagreements in reference to authority, church structures, Mariology, and salvation demonstrate the depths of the divisions and the challenge which the two communities face in remaining faithful to their traditions while seeking to engage together in the Christian commission to evangelize the world.

The contrasting positions on ecclesiology and soteriology are succinctly stated:

> In the one case, the gospel reconciles us to God through
> Christ and thus makes us a party of his people; in the other,
> the gospel is found within the life of his people, and thus we
> find reconciliation with God. (3.3)

Having addressed the issues that divide Evangelicals and
Catholics, the report enumerates a number of areas where they
can offer common witness: Bible translation and publishing; use
of media; community service; social thought and action; dialogue; worship; evangelism. Such common witness should be
clearly related to the Gospel and should express the religious
motivation which animates it.

At the present time there are plans for a continuation of this
dialogue. The World Evangelical Fellowship will be the partner
with the Pontifical Council rather than an informal group of Evangelical scholars. In many parts of the Evangelical world ignorance
of Catholicism, stereotypes of the church and of the ecumenical
movement, and a history of tensions make these conversations
and wider knowledge of them an important priority. It may be
hoped that the great desire for common witness which pervades
the report will lead to further dialogue, reflection, decision,
action, and prayer that will draw Christians ever closer to each
other in discipleship to the Lord Jesus.

Dialogue has already demonstrated an improvement in
concrete relations among Evangelicals and Catholics. An Evangelical relief agency, World Vision International, has developed
an ecumenical policy of collaboration with Catholics and Orthodox and has formulated a set of nonproselytizing directives for
its employees. In the United States, an ongoing conversation
between the National Council of Churches, Evangelical mission
agencies and the U.S. Catholic Mission Association has important international implications.

Relations with the National Association of Evangelicals, local
Evangelical associations, and parachurch groups can benefit from
the resources provided by dialogue. Collaboration on social issues
has taken a different form than with some other Protestant
churches. Evangelicals have shared an urgency about abortion,
pornography, and euthanasia in common with Catholics, but have
been less energetically committed to racial justice, world peace,

and economic and immigrant concerns that Catholics have shared with some other Christian groups. Inevitably, partisan politics, even when common witness brings Christians together in common public policy concerns, has the potential for pitting one part of the Christian community against another in the secular political arena.

Southern Baptist/Catholic Conversation

The Baptist churches trace their origin to seventeenth-century England, where Separatists, unable to "purify" the Church of England, separated from the Puritans and advocated separation from the state Church. In 1607 a group of these separatists left England and sailed to Amsterdam, where freedom of religion prevailed. During their stay in Holland, these early Baptists had contact with the Mennonites, who had become convinced of the scriptural basis of believers' baptism. From the middle of the seventeenth century, there were Baptist churches in the American colonies. The settlement of Roger Williams at Providence, Rhode Island, and the Church formed there in 1639 on Baptist principles, is generally regarded as the beginning of the Baptist Church in this country. There is a "Landmark" Baptist tradition, still alive in some of the Southern and African American Baptist congregations, that seeks to trace an apostolic succession of congregations back to John the Baptist and declines to recognize even other Baptist congregations which do not claim such a lineage.

Baptists are congregational in governance, consider baptism and the Lord's Supper ordinances rather than sacraments, baptize only believing adults by immersion, and affirm religious liberty and the separation of church and state. Baptists, wary of institutional integration, are eager to cooperate in mission and evangelization, but are much less comfortable with designs of doctrinal or structural unity. In 1905, the Baptist World Alliance was formed in London to promote unity and fellowship among the Baptists of the world, to secure and defend religious freedom, and to proclaim Baptist principles.

On the international level, Baptists and Roman Catholics engaged in dialogue from 1984–1988, sponsored by the Commission on Baptist Doctrine and Interchurch Cooperation of the

Baptist World Alliance and the Vatican Secretariat for Promoting Christian Unity, under the overall theme, "Christian Witness in Today's World." The common statement, issued in Atlanta in 1988, gives a synthesis of the major themes discussed during the five years of the dialogue.

The purpose of the dialogue was articulated as "mutual understanding of certain convergences and divergences" and to "establish relations and maintain a channel of communication... to identify new possibilities...to address existing prejudices between our two world confessional families." It was hoped that the conversation would encourage "similar efforts at various levels in church life." In this it differs from those dialogues oriented toward full communion.

The central theme of "Christian Witness in Today's World" was developed through subthemes including "the call to conversion" and discipleship (13–18); a community of disciples with a mission (17); the Church as the "Koinonia of the Spirit" (19); the Church as the locus where the Spirit continues God's redemptive work begun in the Son (22); and the freedom to respond to God's offer of grace (41).

Areas requiring further exploration included theological authority and method (45–47); the shape of the Church as "koinonia in the Spirit," particularly in local congregations (48); the relationship between faith, baptism, and Christian witness (49–51); the different forms of evangelism/evangelization (54); and the place of Mary in faith and practice (56–57).

The positive developments and contributions of this dialogue include new mutual insights into the role of the laity, the role of devotions and the Bible, the clarification of differences in regard to adult and infant baptism, and into the understandings of the role of Mary in salvation history. Concerns of proselytism, common witness, and respect for religious liberty were able to be considered together. Areas of collaboration, witness, local mission, and neighborhood outreach, and the need for further study on a number of issues between the traditions were also expressed. The Catholic Church remains open to further dialogue, but reluctance among some Baptist churches in majority Catholic lands such as Brazil have made it impossible for the time being.

In the U.S., Baptists are organized into numerous conventions, the largest of which are the Southern, the American, and the three National conventions. The Southern Baptist Convention, the largest U.S. Protestant community, now considers itself Evangelical, although it is not a member of the National Association of Evangelicals. It is an international church body with extensive missions around the world. Unlike other Baptist conventions, the Southern Baptists do not belong to the World Council, but they are members of the Baptist World Alliance.

The Southern Baptist relationship with the U.S. Bishops' Conference extends over thirty years. Recent tensions within this Convention, and a transfer of leadership from a moderate to a conservative orientation have caused the Conversation with Catholics to evolve as well. Between 1971 and 1993 there were a wide range of dialogues on regional and national levels, which produced published reports on authority, abortion, church and state, marriage, worship, conversion, life in the Spirit, grace, and the Church. Three important national reports were published in 1982, 1984, and 1989. A series of pamphlets for congregational use were published together between 1991 and 1994 on *Environment, Poverty, Racism, Life,* and *Sickness, Disability and Healing.*

In 1994, under the new conservative leadership, the Southern Baptist Convention authorized an ongoing conversation. In the conversation such issues as Scripture, soteriology, church, mission, and religious liberty will be taken up.

In many local rural communities across the American south, close collaboration between Catholics and Southern Baptists occurs. The Glenmary Home Missioners have been important leaders in fostering the pastoral dimension of this relationship and in encouraging the theological dialogue. While there is still much anti-Catholicism in this community, the common Biblical ground, seriousness about faith and church, primacy of family values, and deep community involvement, challenge these two largest Christian communities in the U.S. to find ways of proclaiming Jesus Christ together wherever they live side by side.

The Pentecostal/Catholic Relationship

The twentieth-century Pentecostal movement celebrates a gift of the Holy Spirit in postconversion spirituality, which is termed baptism in the Spirit. This gift is oriented to mission and ministry, and is associated with the restoration of the New Testament charisms, of which the gift of tongues possesses a particular significance as the initial evidence of the baptism in the Spirit. The Pentecostal pioneers of this century perceived this outpouring of the Holy Spirit in terms of a revival with distinctive features—a spiritual inundation comparable to the initiation of the Gospel and demonstrating the nearness of the Parousia.

This fresh spiritual impulse acts as a complement to and a restoration of the Gospel, which was rediscovered in the Reformation and exemplified further in Wesleyan sanctification. It is manifested anew in the "foursquare gospel" of Jesus as Savior, Healer, Baptizer in the Holy Spirit and the coming King. Here, it is believed, is true restoration of the lived apostolic faith of the early Christians.

Most Pentecostals attribute the genesis of the movement to the work and ministry of Holiness evangelist Charles Parham in the first years of the twentieth century at Bethel Bible College in Topeka, Kansas, where Agnes N. Ozman received the gift of the Spirit on 1 January 1901. The movement received a further impetus from the multiracial Azuza Street revival in Los Angeles in 1906-1909 under Pastor William J. Seymour, which quickly propelled a local revival movement to the ends of the earth. Pentecostalism had spread to other parts of the U.S., Europe, India, China, and South Africa within the span of two years. Mexican converts in the Azuza Street revival brought the movement into Latin America where it has been highly successful and is now the dominant Protestant movement in many countries. In the U.S. Hispanic/Latino community there has been significant Pentecostal presence throughout the century.

The largest Pentecostal church is the Church of God in Christ, a historically African American church. The revival at Azuza Street in Los Angeles was fully integrated. Eventually Black and White denominations emerged separately as the movement settled into denominations. In 1994 the Black and

White Pentecostal churches came together to form an ecumenical organization among themselves, the Charismatic and Pentecostal Fellowship of North America. The leadership of the Pentecostal churches has been reluctant about institutional relationships with other Christian churches beyond those that are members of the National Association of Evangelicals. However, there is a significant history of Pentecostal ecumenical involvement of other kinds. The Society for Pentecostal Studies, which has had Catholic and Protestant membership from its beginning, provides a context for personal ecumenical encounter with those from the classical Pentecostal churches.

Given the reserve, if not animosity, toward the ecumenical movement among the leadership of the Pentecostal denominations, the development of the international Pentecostal-Roman Catholic dialogue over the last three decades has been astonishing. Much of this accomplishment is due to the initiative of South African Pentecostal Dr. David DuPlessis and to the emergence in the late 1960s of an active Catholic charismatic movement, with all of the elements attributed to the classical Pentecostal experience, but in communion with the Catholic Church and with full respect for its sacramental theology and hierarchical structure.

Three rounds of international dialogues have produced reports: (1972–1976, 1977–1982, and 1985–1989). A fourth round will publish a report on proselytism. The 1989 report "Perspectives on *Koinonia*" is outlined here:

INTRODUCTION (1–12)
   I. *KOINONIA* AND THE WORD OF GOD (13–28)
       a. Jesus Christ the Perfect Word of God (14–16)
       b. The Written Word of God (17–28)
   II. THE HOLY SPIRIT AND THE NEW TESTAMENT
       VISION OF *KOINONIA* (29–38)
       a. *Koinonia* with the Triune God (29–33)
       b. Oneness of the Church (34–36)
       c. *Koinonia* and Gospel Witness (37–38)
   III. *KOINONIA* AND BAPTISM (39–69)
       a. The Meaning of Baptism (39–42)
       b. Faith and Baptism (43–51)
       c. Baptism and the Church (52–55)

The authors of the document trust "that this dialogue might inspire dialogue on national and local levels between Roman Catholics and classical Pentecostals,...and recommend to their parent bodies that the dialogue continue" (109). As the development of *koinonia* in this dialogue indicates, very different Christian groups have found in *koinonia* an entry into the ecumenical discussion.

The three rounds of dialogues, and particularly the last, deserve study because they address a number of areas not studied in other dialogues: the communion of saints, the relationship of pneumatology to sacraments and ecclesiology, and a theological basis in *koinonia* for churches with what would seem to be insuperable ecclesiological differences.

The dialogue affirms that *koinonia* is a dynamic and dialogical category which requires "mutuality in its many dimensions" (73). Catholic partners in the dialogue admit "to a lack of mutuality at the local and universal levels...surrounding lay participation in decision-making processes, and the lack of sufficient involvement of women in leadership" (74). The Pentecostal participants, on the other hand, acknowledge that sometimes "they forget that the Spirit is given not only to individual Christians, but also to the whole community" (76).

Yet the considerable differences between the two communities are not avoided. Pentecostals marvel, without disavowing the Johannine admonition in regard to one's own sinfulness, that "it seems possible for some Roman Catholics to live continuously in a state of sin, and yet be considered members of the Church" (78). Catholics wonder if Pentecostals "have an adequate tradition of bringing those who have fallen into sin into a process of repentance and a sense of God's forgiveness?" (79).

The points of difference in regard to Scripture, authority, ecclesiology, baptism, and sacraments discussed in the dialogue will be important in moving beyond stereotypes, and assisting pastorally those working with Pentecostal and Catholic congregations, couples, families, and students.

Conclusion

One may be surprised at how much relationships between Catholics and Evangelicals have developed, especially in local situations, through the important leadership of individual priests and other church workers, and the experience of Evangelical/ Catholic marriages. Drawing on the work of Father Avery Dulles, S.J. in "Ecumenism Without Illusions: A Catholic Perspective," one may suggest elements for an *interim strategy* for developing informal ecumenical relationships:

1. Correct misleading stereotypes, in the interests of truth, justice and Christian charity.
2. Be open to surprise in the authenticity of the Christian faith and practice of others.
3. Reach toward recognition of the holiness and resources for spirituality in all ecumenical partners.
4. Find ways of removing suspicion, fear, and resentment, and to support one another spiritually by prayer, advice, and mutuality.
5. Develop respect for others' religious freedom and integrity.
6. Pursue an ecumenism of mutual enrichment, learning to give and receive truth and conviction from one another without compromise.
7. Rejoice in the common Scripture, common prayer, and the common hope of eternal life that already unites us.
8. Engage in joint witness and social action in areas where joint convictions are shared.
9. While we remain in separation, be open to growth in

peace and patience. Only grace transcends the seem-
ingly insuperable Christian divisions.

10. Continue to pray to Christ that we may all be one, a
prayer that can only be realized by the power of the
Holy Spirit.

Mission, the common proclamation of God's saving word
in Jesus Christ, is at the very heart of the ecumenical movement.
The Evangelical, Pentecostal, and Holiness churches affirm the
priority of a particular understanding of mission over the visible
unity of the Church which has been central to Catholic ecumenical life. Yet the glimmers of common spiritual aspirations, contacts in charity, zeal for renewal, and commitment to biblical
truth bind together all who confess Jesus Christ. Rich resources
have emerged to stimulate relationship in the Catholic dialogues
with Evangelicals, Baptists, and Pentecostals.

Study Questions

1. Review the variety of ways that the terms *sect, Evangelical,* and
fundamentalist might be correctly used in speaking of Christian groups
and theological positions.

2. Review the development, the statements of faith, and varieties
of churches involved in the Holiness, Pentecostal, and Evangelical
Christian communities.

3. What are the key theological concerns that the Evangelical-
Roman Catholic Dialogue on Mission addressed? How might these be
approached to further understanding and reconciliation between the
Catholic Church and Evangelical Christians in local situations?

4. Review the history and beliefs giving rise to the Southern Baptist Convention.

5. What areas of new mutual understanding have emerged in the
Southern Baptist/Roman Catholic conversation?

6. What is distinctive about the history and theology of the Pentecostal movement?

7. What have been the key areas of theological concern and the contribution of the Pentecostal/Roman Catholic dialogue?

8. Pentecostals, Southern Baptists, and other Evangelicals are a vibrant and expanding portion of the Christian world. How might relationships with these groups, which are sometimes difficult for Roman Catholics, Orthodox, and classical Protestants, be developed on the local level to support deepening ecumenical overtures?

Selected Readings

Blumhofer, Edith L., and Joel A. Carpenter, eds. *Twentieth-Century Evangelicalism: A Guide to the Sources.* New York: Garland, 1990.

Burgess, Joseph, and Jeffrey Gros, eds. *Building Unity*: *Ecumenical Dialogues with Roman Catholic Participation. Ecumenical Documents IV.* New York/Mahwah: Paulist Press, 1989, pp. 484–90.

———. *Growing Consensus: Church Dialogues in the United States, 1962–1991. Ecumenical Documents V.* New York/Mahwah: Paulist Press, 1995, pp. 457–580, 659–73.

Cleary, Edward L., and Hannah W. Stewart-Gambino, eds. *Power, Politics and Pentecostals in Latin America.* Boulder: Westview, 1997.

Dayton, Donald W. *Theological Roots of Pentecostalism.* Grand Rapids: Francis Asbury Press, 1987.

Dulles, Avery, S.J. "Ecumenism Without Illusions: A Catholic Perspective." *First Things* 8 (1990): 20–25.

"Evangelical-Roman Catholic Dialogue on Mission, 1977–1984." Pontifical Council for Promoting Christian Unity, *Information Service*, no. 60 (1986): 71–97.

George, Timothy, and Richard Land. *Baptists: Why and Why Not, Revisited.* Nashville: Broadman & Holman, 1997.

Gros, Jeffrey. "Southern Baptists Affirm the Future of Dialogue with the Roman Catholic Church." *Ecumenical Trends* Vol. 24, no. 2 (1995): 3–6.

Gros, Jeffrey, and William G. Rusch, eds. *Deepening Communion.* Washington D.C.: U.S. Catholic Conference, 1998, Parts V, VI, VII.

Hocken, Peter. *The Glory and the Shame: Reflections on the 20th Century Outpouring of the Holy Spirit.* Wheaton: Harold Shaw Publishers, 1994.

Howard, David. *The Dream That Would Not Die: The Birth and Growth of the World Evangelical Fellowship, 1846–1986.* Grand Rapids: Baker Books, 1986.

Kinnamon, Michael, and Brian E. Cope, eds. *The Ecumenical Movement: An Anthology of Basic Texts and Voices.* Grand Rapids: Eerdmans, 1997, 358–63, 383, 237–38.

Marsden, George M. *Fundamentalism and American Culture: The Shaping of Twentieth-Century Evangelicalism, 1870–1925.* New York: Oxford University Press, 1980.

——, ed. *Evangelicalism and Modern America.* Grand Rapids: Eerdmans, 1984.

Matthews, Arthur. *Standing Up, Standing Together: The Emergence of the National Association of Evangelicals.* Carol Stream: The National Association of Evangelicals, 1992.

McDonnell, Kilian, ed. *Presence, Power Praise: Documents on the Charismatic Renewal.* Collegeville: Liturgical Press, 1980.

Meeking, Basil, and John Stott, eds. *Evangelical-Roman Catholic Dialogue on Mission, 1977–1984: A Report.* Grand Rapids: Eerdmans, 1986.

Meyer, Harding, and Lukas Vischer, eds. *Growth in Agreement: Reports and Agreed Statements of Ecumenical Conversations on a World Level. Ecumenical Documents II.* New York/Mahwah: Paulist Press, 1984, pp. 421–32.

New Vatican Working Group on New Religious Movements. *Sects and New Religious Movements.* Washington D.C.: U.S. Catholic Conference, 1995.

Saliba, John A. *Understanding New Religious Movements.* Grand Rapids: Eerdmans, 1995.

Secretariat for Promoting Christian Unity, Secretariat for Non-Christians, Secretariat for NonBelievers, and Pontifical Council for Culture. "Vatican Report on Sects, Cults and New Religious Movements." *Origins* 16:1 (May 22, 1986): 1–10.

Conclusion:
The Future of Ecumenism:
Implications for Ecclesial and
Pastoral Proclamation

O God of unchangeable power and eternal light,
look favorably upon thy whole Church,
that wonderful and sacred mystery;
and by the tranquil operation of thy perpetual providence
carry out the work of human salvation;
and let the whole world feel and see
that things which were cast down are being raised up;
that those which had grown old are being made new;
and that all things are returning into unity
through him by whom all things were made,
even thy Son Jesus Christ our Lord.

Gelasian Sacramentary

Cardinal Joseph Ratzinger has spoken of the Church as "a company in constant renewal." The ecumenical movement is a common pilgrimage of Christians in spiritual renewal who aspire to attain a more intimate relationship to Christ in the Trinitarian life, and hence draw closer to one another. In this final chapter we will address the future of ecumenism and its implications for Catholic ecclesial and pastoral proclamation. Three themes will chart its progression: (1) the present ecumencial agenda of the Church, (2) the ecclesiology of *koinonia*, and (3) the importance of a spirituality of ecumenism.

The ecumenical pilgrimage, so central to Christian identity and the pastoral priorities of the Catholic Church, is rooted in faith in Jesus Christ and zeal for the Church and its unity. This faith and zeal have a specific history, content, and set of spiritual

234

resources which nourish the Christian along the way and enrich the Christian life, even before the goal of full communion is achieved. At this moment in the journey the challenge of education is a major priority. The publication of the *Catechism of the Catholic Church*, the encyclical *Ut Unum Sint*, and *The Directory for the Application of Principles and Norms on Ecumenism* should challenge educators, catechists, and preachers at every level of church life to work with their ecumenical colleagues to integrate the results of the decades of dialogues, and the hopes of an ecumenical future, into the consciousness and experience of Christian life.

All the churches are faced with a variety of pastoral challenges which require them to take account of their own internal struggles. Yet these are shared challenges even when they appear with more urgency in another church than our own. For example, if we are searching for a common ground on an ethical issue, such as sexuality or concern for the poor, the debates are common even when they are articulated in only one church. When it is a question of catechetical or sacramental renewal, our ecumenical urgency toward the common faith and our quest for full Eucharistic communion should lead us toward common and complementary educational and liturgical approaches.

Three Stages in the Ecumenical Movement

In preparation for the celebration of the 2,000th anniversary of the birth of Christ in the great Jubilee, the churches pray that they come closer to the prayer of Christ for full communion. As we survey the situation of the churches during these last thirty years we can note a development from the initial contacts of collaboration and tolerance to a serious engagement in dialogue of charity and truth, progressing in our own day into decisions for deeper bonds of communion among the churches. While the pilgrimage moves forward, these stages overlap, and participation varies from one culture and church to another. The work of one stage continues as the others develop.

Moving from the Chicago-Lambeth Quadrilateral in 1888, through the Edinburgh Conference of 1910, the founding of the World Council in 1948, and the emergence of the Catholic

Church into the ecumenical movement in 1961, foundations were laid for the ecumenical movement as we understand it today, as was outlined in chapters one, four, and seven. We have noted in chapter eleven that such contact exists among evangelicals and is emerging with other Christian communities. Earlier models of the restoration of the New Testament Church, of a nondenominational Christianity, or of return to a static Orthodoxy or Roman Catholicism, have been replaced by a more sophisticated vision.

A second major stage, as noted in chapters six and seven, was initiated by the intensive dialogue that engaged the churches to move beyond comparison of their differences and merely collaborative relationship in mission. The Christological methodology of the Faith and Order movement, its success after the Montreal 1963 World Conference, including *Scripture, Tradition and the Traditions,* as well as the massive bilateral and church union developments noted in chapters eight, nine, and ten introduced an immensely productive stage of the ecumenical movement which is continuing at present.

This stage has had a significant impact and has changed the way in which Scripture studies and theology are now carried out. The Catholic Church has been an ardent supporter of these World Council, bilateral, and multilateral dialogues. Most dramatically in the 1980s, the ARCIC *Final Report,* the World Council's *Baptism, Eucharist and Ministry,* and the Lutheran-Catholic work *Justification by Faith* stimulated the Church to begin to reevaluate the theological basis for unity for the first time since the Council of Florence (1439).

A third stage has begun, with a series of concrete proposals which bring the churches to authoritative decision. Common Declarations with the Eastern churches, some of which enable Eucharistic sharing; unions of churches, of which there have been five major examples in the last forty years in the United States alone; and a variety of proposals before the churches in these years on the threshold of the great jubilee 2000 illustrate the vibrant tenor of this stage of development.

The concept of a united Church as an institutional merger bringing together the corporate structures of the various bodies has largely been put aside in recent decades. The perspective of this third stage envisions unity by stages, with phases of shared life over a reasonable space of time. An early sketch of this vision of Conciliar Fellowship was articulated in 1975 by the World Council. A more descriptive statement was the Lutheran-Catholic *Facing Unity* of 1980, discussed in chapter nine. It proposes multiple phases. Two are particularly important: the reevaluation and resolution of mutual condemnations and a transition from the collaborative exercise of *episcopé* to collegial exercise of episcopacy, with joint ordinations and community participation in the selection and affirmation of episcopal leadership. This vision of conciliar union by mutuality and by stages seeks to honor and receive the gifts of each community while advancing toward full communion.

The proposal for *Churches in Covenant Communion: The Church of Christ Uniting*, under consideration by the Episcopal, Presbyterian, Disciples of Christ, African Methodist Episcopal, Christian Methodist Episcopal, United Methodist, and African Methodist Episcopal Zion Churches, the United Church of Christ, and the International Council of Community Churches, envisions a phased union which will entail a service of recognition and reconciliation to be celebrated the first Sunday in Advent 2000 for those churches which have taken positive action by that time. The Catholic Church, though not a member of this essentially American union proposal, has been represented by canon lawyers, liturgists, and theologians working with these churches on their pilgrimage toward full communion.

In 1997 the Episcopal and Evangelical Lutheran churches considered a *Concordat*, which would enable not only common work in mission, but also common episcopal ordinations in the future and full interchangeability of ordained ministers. This phased unity, while somewhat different from the *Facing Unity* and *Covenant Communion* proposals, is designed in light of the ecclesiology developed in these and articulated in *Toward Full Communion* (1991). The *Concordat* proposes that the Lutherans would suspend the requirement of subscription to the Augsburg Confession by Episcopal priests acting in their churches, while the Episcopalians would suspend the requirement in the preface to the Anglican *Ordinal*, which stipulates that all pastors be ordained by bishops in the apostolic succession. Eventually, all ordinations would entail bishops in the apostolic succession. This proposal for Anglican-Lutheran reconciliation, as noted in chapter nine, is somewhat different from, but is complementary to, that approved by the Baltic, British, and Scandinavian churches.

On the basis of *A Common Calling: The Witness of Our Reformation Churches in North America Today* (1993), Evangelical Lutheran, Presbyterian, Reformed, and United Church of Christ Churches have approved a *Formula of Agreement* overcoming the mutual condemnations on Eucharist, Christology, and predestination of the Reformation period and initiating full communion among them. Since there were never differences over the ordained ministry among these churches, this was not an issue that needed to be resolved among them, as it will be with Anglican, Catholic, or Orthodox partners. The proposal discussed in chapter nine, Joint Declaration on Doctrine of Justification, will provide a first stage of putting aside mutual condemnations between Lutherans and Catholics.

Whether any or all of these proposals will have institutional success at this time is merely a footnote to the bigger issue in this third stage of ecumenical development. All of the churches will have been transformed by the dialogue and approach to decision making. Undoubtedly the unsuccessful proposals will lead us to discern how, in the Lord's good time, more adequate formulations can be designed to serve that goal. All these considerations, however, evidence the quality of education and spiritual formation that is so urgently needed at this stage in the ecumenical movement to afford all of us the patience and zeal to continue the pilgrimage to which we are called and upon which we are embarked.

The Canberra Assembly encouraged the movement from dialogue to decision when it articulated these concrete challenges for the churches:

> The challenge at this moment in the ecumenical movement as a reconciling and renewing movement towards full visible unity is for the seventh assembly of the WCC to call all churches:
> • to recognize each other's baptism on the basis of the BEM document;
> • to move towards the recognition of the apostolic faith as

expressed through the Nicene-Constantinopolitan Creed
in the life and witness of one another;
- on the basis of convergence in faith in baptism, eucharist
  and ministry to consider, wherever appropriate, forms of
  eucharistic hospitality; we gladly acknowledge that some
  who do not observe these rites share in the spiritual experience of life in Christ;
- to move towards a mutual recognition of ministries;
- to endeavor in word and deed to give common witness to
  the gospel as a whole;
- to recommit themselves to work for justice, peace and the
  integrity of creation, linking more closely the search for
  the sacramental communion of the church with the struggles for justice and peace;
- to help parishes and communities express in appropriate
  ways locally the degree of communion that already exists.
  (3.2)

This third period has also been characterized by the expansion and deepening of the universality of the churches in the
ecumenical movement. The postcolonial period and the subsidiarity and collegiality articulated in the Second Vatican Council have begun to decrease the Eurocentric character of both the
theology and the vision of the unity of the Church. New diversi-
ties have been introduced with the inculturation of the Gospel in
Asia and Africa and appreciation of the five-hundred-year contributions of Latin American Christian experience. Likewise, the
voices of women, and an appreciation of the Church's responsibility in the world and for creation have both enhanced and
deepened the complexity of the ecumenical journey. The three
stages of the ecumenical movement chart an ecumenical future
that is both challenging and promising.

Koinonia and the Ecumenical Future

Perhaps one of the most unexpected fruits of the founding
of the World Council and the meeting of the Second Vatican
Council was the manner in which the ecclesiology of *koinonia*
took root not only in World Council relations, but also in the
Catholic Church. In 1948 the World Council used the category

in its constitution, "a fellowship of churches," and it became a key ecclesiological theme in Vatican II, was reaffirmed in the Extraordinary Roman Synod in 1985, and matured in a variety of ecumenical dialogues emerging from the second stage of ecumenical discussion. We have sketched the outline of *koinonia* ecclesiology in chapter three.

Several international Catholic dialogues with Eastern Orthodox, Oriental Orthodox, Anglican, Lutheran, and Methodist partners have articulated explicitly the vision of the communion we seek and have resolved some of the most intractable obstacles to full *koinonia*. Other international dialogues between the Catholic Church and the Disciples and Reformed are aimed toward the same full communion, but have moved toward it with more measured steps. Even dialogues between the Catholic Church and Pentecostal and Baptist groups, which have not formulated a goal of fully visible unity, have founded their work of promoting mutual understanding in communion ecclesiology.

The Catholic Church has come to see the importance of the local church or diocese as an important dimension of *koinonia*, where the bishop is its sacramental representative and expression, in union with the college of bishops and its center, the bishop of Rome. The dual focus of the bishop as center of unity in the local church and in *koinonia* with the worldwide communion of churches is further witness to the unity modeled on the divine Trinity.

The Catholic understanding of *koinonia* is exemplified by the active participation of the laity as the people of God, which contrasts with a merely secular democratic understanding of the Church. Communion is grounded in the common mission of all Christians, received in baptism and preceding the differentiations of functions, charisms, or ministries. While there are tensions among members of the Church as there are between divided Christians, the theology of *koinonia* provides a solid basis for securing unity in Christ. The understanding of the Church as a *koinonia* and of the real, if imperfect, *koinonia* that exists among the still divided churches, will require the spiritual and ascetic qualities such as a deep sense of caring and openness, a commitment to dialogue, and a total reliance upon God. As Theresa of Jesus reminds us:

Let nothing trouble you
Let nothing frighten you
Everything passes
God never changes
Patience obtains all.

All of this development of the theology of communion, vertical and horizontal, with the triune God and with the communion of Christian believers, occurs within the shared context of the World Council vision of the Faith and Order Commission and the Joint Working Group between the WCC and the Vatican. The 1991 World Council enumeration of elements necessary for full communion is helpful in delineating where the issues that still divide the churches are under discussion toward resolution:

ELEMENTS OF FULL COMMUNION FOLLOWING THE OUTLINES OF THE CANBERRA TEXT 2.1

1. The common confession of the apostolic faith:

Confessional Character of the Church
Creedal and noncreedal churches
Christology
Chalcedonian and non-Chalcedonian churches
Assyrian Church of the East and Churches
which accept Ephesus (431)
Lutheran and Reformed churches
Pneumatology
Eastern and Oriental Orthodox and Western churches
Trinity
Oneness Pentecostals and Trinitarian churches
Justification
Roman Catholic Church and Reformation churches
Peace Witness
Anabaptist, Quaker and Just War churches
Racial Witness
African American and churches that tolerated
slavery and racism

---

2. A common sacramental life entered by the one baptism and celebrated together in one eucharistic fellowship:

Lutheran and Reformed churches
Episcopally-ordered and nonepiscopal churches
Roman Catholic, Orthodox churches and
Reformation churches
Believers' baptist and paedobaptist churches

3. A common life in which members and ministries are mutually recognized and reconciled:

Episcopally-ordered and nonepiscopal churches

4. And a common mission witnessing to the gospel of God's grace to all people and serving the whole of creation. The goal of the search for full communion is realized when all the churches are able to recognize in one another the one, holy, catholic and apostolic church in its fullness:

Denominational and "churchly" ecclesiological
understandings of the Gospel
Spiritual ecumenism and visible unity as a goal

5. This full communion will be expressed on the local level and the universal levels through conciliar forms of life and action:

Congregational and catholic ecclesiologies
Episcopal and nonepiscopal churches

6. In such communion churches are bound in all aspects of life together at all levels in confessing the one faith and engaging in worship and witness, deliberation and action:

Congregational churches and conciliar churches
Global and national churches
The Catholic Church (and its papal claims)
and other churches

The vision of the Church as communion has not as yet developed to full fruition in the comprehension of the nature of grace and of the bonds of communion between Christ and believers in the Incarnation and Redemption. It has, however, reversed the complete identification of the Church and Christ, the subsequent equation of the Church as the prolongation of the Incarnation, and a triumphalistic ecclesiology in Orthodox and Catholic theology. It accentuates the Trinitarian and sacramental character of the *koinonia* of Christ to Church and believers, thus recapturing many elements of the more ancient Mystical Body ecclesiology and maintaining the identification of the Church as the Body of Christ while preserving its differentiation.

The understanding the doctrine of *koinonia* in terms of "divinization" from the Eastern tradition and of grace rather than a mere "participation" or "sharing" in Trinitarian life, should lead the Christian churches to the Trinitarian center of the Christian faith, recognizing the Holy Spirit as the source of our baptismal and Eucharistic life in Christ and as uniting the community mystically in Christ. Such a vision should situate all the Christian churches on an authentic ecumenical course.

The development of the implications of this communion with the Trinity in Christ will entail serious horizontal developments as well, if the third stage of ecumenism is to bear its full fruit in the life of the Church. This includes common affirmation of the apostolic faith; deepening a common sense of tradition; renewing the relationship between Scripture, tradition, and the teaching office of the churches; developing a hermeneutic that sees the faith in the light of the *hierarchy of truths;* being nourished by the spiritual traditions of other churches as well as sharing one's own; bringing alive the conscious faith implicit in the baptism of all; internalizing the central role of the Bible in all areas of life; recognizing the convergences that have already occurred in liturgical life; and developing structures of accountability within the Church that hold all of us to our ecumenical commitment.

The future will call forth deepened work on the role of Mary. The U.S. Lutheran-Catholic Dialogue VIII, *The One Mediator, The Saints, and Mary* (1983–1990), has been pioneering in this field. Because dialogues proceed from the most firm common ground to the more difficult issues, other dialogues have only begun discussion of the place of Mary in the Church's life that this more developed dialogue has been able to engage. Much work will be needed to develop an ecumenical interpretation of one's own and one another's approaches to popular devotion and piety.

The renewal of Marian theology and practice in the Catholic Church has been encouraged by *Lumen Gentium* (chapter eight) and *Marialis Cultus* of Pope Paul VI, in particular. These offer hermeneutical guidelines to prevent abuses and to contribute to a genuine Mariology. Devotion to Mary derives from the understanding of Christ and his saving role. Renewal in Marian theology and practice is a parallel to the ecumenical contact and biblical devotion that have developed since the Council. There has been a significant contribution from the international Ecumenical Society for the Blessed Virgin Mary.

Spiritual Ecumenism

Finally, pilgrimage toward unity and living in the tension between the divine imperative toward unity and the human experience of separation is nourished and sustained by the Holy Spirit with the help of concrete spiritual resources. This book began with the presupposition that the pursuit of ecumenism is fundamentally an exercise in spiritual theology, and that "Spiritual Ecumenism" remains the raison d'être of its development. As a consequence, in this last part of the work, it is well to concentrate upon this question in reference to ecclesial and pastoral proclamation.

There are several elements to emphasize. The necessity of Christian conversion emanates from the Gospel injunction, "The kingdom of God is at hand. Repent, and believe in the gospel" (Mark 1:15). Conversion takes different forms: some occur very suddenly, while others are more gradual. Ecclesial conversion entails understanding and affirming Christ's essential call to his community in history. Conversion to one's own particular confessional tradition consists in a deeper attachment to the Triune God, to the overcoming of the sinfulness which impedes an enduring fidelity to the Gospel, and to an effort to seek "full communion" among the churches. Conversion on the part of churches requires them to acknowledge the sin of division and to renew themselves in their ecumenical commitment. It includes a willingness to reform their own structures in the light of the Gospel.

A collective identity of any kind, and especially among churches, is always a paradoxical phenomenon that involves a tension among the forces of unification, integration, harmonization, and social interaction. As a living reality, conversion alone can provide simultaneously for reception of new insights and fidelity to the tradition. Living in the tension of a pilgrimage in fidelity to both our call to an uncharted future and continuity with the apostolic heritage demands prayer, openness, and continual conversion of spirit. In the ecclesiastical sphere conversion alone can provide the essential ingredients needed for the church to remain vital and true to itself.

Christian identity, founded as it is on Scripture and living tradition, upon the confession of the faith, and articulated in postapostolic witnesses, in liturgy, and in the creeds, is a dynamic and radical process. It includes a secure grounding in one's own community and an openness to the eschatological "beyond" which constantly summons it forward. The Church as a "mystery" is required to strive to become more "catholic" and "reformed" in the sense of always moving to reclaim its spiritual reality, and to overcome any contradictory attitude to the Christian Gospel.

Symbolic gestures are an integral part of the process of turning to conversion, particularly on the part of separated Churches. In this regard, one must admire the abilities of the recent popes to employ symbolic gestures in the service of ecumenical rapprochement (UUS 71–73).

Movement into the third stage of ecumenism requires conversion, not only of theological formulations, but also of the hearts and minds of believers and of the institutional structures by which the Church lives. The decisions which authorities have already taken evidence a spirit of forgiveness and humility which is a necessary element of the Christian conversion process. The spiritual disciplines which serve an ecumenical spiritual life include, in addition to prayer for ecumenism, prayer with other Christians, participation in and appreciation of the variety of worship styles and spiritual traditions, reading the biographies and spiritual resources of other traditions, developing friends in other traditions, cultivating a style of personal and ecclesial hospitality, and finding experiences of dialogue to nourish one's own ecumenical zeal and to expand one's ecclesial horizons.

Finally, an ecumenical spirituality entails attention and prayerful assessment of the classical marks of the Church to deepen our commitment together to unity; to recognize the holiness at work in separated fellow Christians; to expand our understanding of catholicity in order to incorporate the variety of cultures, races, and traditions that Christ has given the churches; and to deepen and expand the understanding of apostolicity to encompass the modes of continuity testified to in the ecumenical results.

The ecumenical documents should not be seen as only theological resources for church leaders and academics. Rather, they should be read in a spirit of prayer and wonder at the *magnalia Dei* occurring in our midst and as written testimonies to the movement of the Spirit among us. They should call the Church to conversion and become occasions to deepen faith and renew worship and church life. The New Evangelization articulated by Pope John Paul, with its new ardor, methods and vision, is inherently ecumenical, as he noted in Germany, 1996:

> The new evangelization is therefore the order of the day. This does not mean the "restoration" of a past age. Rather it is necessary to risk taking new steps. Together we must again proclaim the joyful and liberating message of the Gospel to the people of Europe....The task of evangelization involves moving toward each other and moving together as Christians, and it must begin from within; evangelization and unity, evangelization and ecumenism are indissolubly linked with each other....Because the question of the new evangelization is very close to my heart, as bishop of Rome I consider overcoming the divisions of Christianity "one of the pastoral priorities." (*L'Osservatore Romano*, English ed., 27/5 [3 July 1996) nos. 3, 5)

Conclusion

The ecumenical task takes place in a variety of cultures, in a variety of churches, and with the various gifts the baptized bring to their pilgrimage. However, the faith of the Church and of the churches together in this pilgrimage finally sustains them in this work of the Holy Spirit. As the stages of the ecumenical movement move forward, as the elements of communion between the churches deepen, the spirituality of all is enriched by fidelity to God's call and the eschatological hope of the reconciliation for which we pray.

In addressing the June 1994 extraordinary consistory of cardinals, Pope John Paul entrusted the care of ecumenism to the intercession of the Blessed Virgin and expressed his own hopes for the future of the Church thus:

> In view of the year 2000, this is perhaps the greatest task. *We cannot come before Christ, the Lord of history, as divided as we have unfortunately been during the second millennium.* These divisions must give way to *rapprochement* and harmony; the wounds on the path of Christian unity must be healed. As she faces this Great Jubilee, the Church needs *"metanoia," that is, the discernment of her children's historical shortcomings and negligence* with regard to the demands of the Gospel. Only the courageous acknowledgment of faults and omissions for which Christians have in some way been responsible, as well as the generous intention to remedy them with the help of God, can give an effective impetus to the new evangelization and make the path to unity easier. Here indeed is the essential core of our mission according to the explicit words of the divine Master, as he was about to face the dramatic events of his Passion: "That they all may be one, even as you, Father, are in me, and I in you, that they may also be one in us, so that the world may believe that you have sent me." (Jn 17:21) (IS no. 87 [1994], 218)

Study Questions

1. Describe the three stages of the Ecumenical Movement. Where do you see the local congregation in which you participate?

2. What are the concrete challenges to the churches which were issued by the Canberra Assembly? Where do they touch your Church?

3. How has the ecclesiology of *koinonia* developed since Vatican II and the founding of the World Council?

4. Enumerate the elements of full communion in the 1991 Canberra text and where they are under discussion in the dialogues reviewed in this volume.

5. What is the significance of the role of Mary in the ecumenical dialogues?

6. In the final analysis, the ecumenical movement is an exercise in spiritual and ascetical theology which aims to call the Church to holiness and conversion. Explain. What personal program of spiritual formation and nurture can support your own ecumenical commitment? That of your community?

7. What challenges does *koinonia* ecclesiology place on the ministry and apostolic tasks of your own life? How are you personally most able to participate in the ecumenical development of the Church?

8. What challenges do you see for the immediate ecumenical future? What resources do you see as most likely to empower the Church's successful meeting of these challenges?

Selected Readings

Bria, Ion, and Dagmar Heller, eds. *Ecumenical Pilgrims: Profiles of Pioneers in Christian Reconciliation*. Geneva: World Council of Churches, 1995.

Evans, Gillian, Lorelei Fuchs and Dianne Kessler. *Encounters For Unity: Sharing Faith, Prayer and Life*. Norwich: Canterbury Press, 1995.

Groupe des Dombes. *For the Conversion of the Churches*. James Greig, trans. Geneva: World Council of Churches, 1993.

Hinson, E. Glenn, ed. *Spirituality in Ecumenical Perspective*. Louisville: Westminster/John Knox Press, 1993.

Hotchkin, John. "The Ecumenical Movement's Third Stage." *Origins* 25:21 (November 9, 1995): 353–61.

John Paul II. "Linking Evangelization and Ecumenism." *Origins* 26:9 (August 1, 1996): 139–141.

——. "Toward the Year 2000." Pontifical Council for Promoting Christian Unity, *Information Service*, no. 87 (1994): 217–18.

Kinnamon, Michael, and Brian E. Cope, eds. *The Ecumenical Movement: An Anthology of Basic Texts and Voices*. Grand Rapids: Eerdmans, 1997, pp. 497–525.

Newbigin, Leslie. *Unfinished Agenda: An Autobiography*. Geneva: World Council of Churches, 1985.

Puls, Joan, O.S.F., *Every Bush Is Burning: A Spirituality for Our Times*. Geneva: World Council of Churches, 1985.

Ratzinger, Joseph. *Called To Communion: Understanding the Church Today*. Adrian Walker, trans. San Francisco: Ignatius Press, 1996.

Root, Michael. "A Striking Convergence in American Ecumenism." *Origins* 26:4 (June 13, 1996): 60–64.

Ryan, Thomas. *A Survival Guide for Ecumenically-Minded Christians*. Collegeville: Liturgical Press, 1989.

Schmidt, Stjepan. *Augustin Bea: The Cardinal of Unity*. Leslie Wearne, trans. New Rochelle: New City Press, 1992.

Index